HIT ME!

HIT ME!

Fighting the Las Vegas Mob
by the Numbers

DANIELLE GOMES
AND JAY BONANSINGA

LYONS PRESS
Guilford, Connecticut
An imprint of Globe Pequot Press

Copyright © 2013 by Danielle Gomes and Jay Bonansinga

Lyons Press is an imprint of Globe Pequot Press.

Project editor: Meredith Dias
Layout: Sue Murray

Library of Congress Cataloging-in-Publication Data is available on file.

ISBN 978-0-7627-8072-3

Printed in the United States of America

10 9 8 7 6 5 4 3 2 1

For my hero, my dad, who taught me to see the world in black and white, then paint it with my own color. In loving memory of Dennis Gomes, Doug Gomes, and Ronald Gomes.

—*Danielle Gomes*

To Dennis Gomes, a good man in every sense of the word.

—*Jay Bonansinga*

Contents

Prologue
Don't Look Away

Let justice roll down like waters, and righteousness like an ever-flowing stream.

—Amos 5:24

In late 2004, Dennis Gomes had just returned from one of his regular lunchtime workouts to his muted, earth-toned office at the Tropicana Hotel in Atlantic City. His longtime secretary, an efficient and loyal woman named Jean Price, had been waiting for him.

"Dennis, you got a call from an FBI agent while you were out."

"What does he want?"

"He didn't say. Just said he wanted to talk to you. He was calling from Chicago."

Gomes shrugged. "Okay, Jean, thanks. I'll follow up on it."

Price left the call slip on the circular table in the center of the office, and then vanished back into the labyrinth of corridors and the myriad tasks facing the administrative assistant to the general manager of one of the nation's busiest casino chains.

Gomes settled down behind the table to clear his head. The office—designed with Gomes's management style in mind—had no hard corners, no imposing desk, none of the typical accoutrements of the alpha executive. The soft pastels, calming abstract art, family pictures, and welcoming flow gave off the air of a Japanese garden—more place of meditation than high-level corporate battleground—a space in keeping with Gomes's Taoist philosophies.

Compact, well-groomed, still fit at sixty-one, Gomes sat back in his chair, pondering the purpose of a call from the Bureau. *Probably purely routine . . . just checking up on some applicant.* Still dressed in the white, loose-fitting pants and jacket of a trained martial artist, Gomes knew his *gi* would faze no one at the office. His coworkers were accustomed to seeing the head honcho—a fifth-degree black belt at Tang Soo Do, and a second-degree black belt at Hapkido—haunting the hallways in dojo attire. On some level, the uniform of Korean self-defense seemed apt clothing for the rough-and-tumble world of casino management.

Gomes called the FBI's Windy City field office. A moment later, a steady, businesslike baritone crackled over the line: "Mr. Gomes?" The agent even managed to pronounce his name right on the first try. This rarely happened. Properly pronounced, "Gomes" rhymes with "homes"; however, most pronounce it like its double-syllable counterpart, "Gomez."

"Yeah?"

"I'm a special agent with the FBI, and I'm working on an organized-crime case in Chicago. The prosecutors asked me to call you to see if you might be able to help us out with the case."

This was not at all what Gomes had expected, yet he replied, "Sure . . . whatever I can do to help."

There was a sudden gravity in Gomes's voice. The brief back-and-forth had rattled the cage of unfinished business and old battles that Gomes had locked away decades ago. Meanwhile, this agent spoke with the flat, uninflected deadpan of an archetypal government man, even as he delivered historic news, calmly stating, "Well, basically we're putting together what will probably turn out to be the biggest organized-crime case in the history of the United States. And with your background, sir—your history in Nevada—you would be invaluable to us. As a matter of fact, we've always been impressed by how forward-thinking you were back then. Your investigations were really ahead of their time."

"I appreciate that," Gomes said, and then paused. "But I thought this stuff was all tried at one point by the federal government."

Gomes was referring to the 1986 trial of Joseph Aiuppa, John Cerone, Angelo LaPietra, Joseph Lombardo, and Milton Rockman, in which the defendants had allegedly skimmed $2 million through their hidden interest in the Stardust Casino. This trial was the culmination of an eight-year-long FBI investigation. The jury had found the defendants innocent because the government failed to link the defendants to the conspiracy to conceal ownership of the Stardust, and to skim funds.

"Yeah . . . but they didn't really accomplish what we're going to accomplish."

Gomes remembered the first time the feds had gone after the criminal power structure in the gaming industry. He remembered what a mess it had been—the hubris of the federal prosecutors, their refusal to tap the treasure trove of data that Gomes had collected over the years, the clash of egos, the missed opportunities.

"We have a Mob guy who's flipped," the agent said then, "and he's admitted to several murders, one of them tied to the Outfit's activities in Vegas."

"Okay."

"We'd like your help with some of the facts . . . and most importantly, we want to ask if you'd be willing to testify in Chicago when the case finally comes to trial. Basically you'd be a key witness, providing the motive for one of the murders that this guy committed."

"May I ask the name of the victim?"

"Jay Vandermark."

In the real world, second chances don't come along very often. Opportunities to set the record straight are rare. Ordinarily the work of well-intentioned people—even that of extraordinary individuals on death-defying crusades—drifts away into the currents of history unresolved, forgotten, relegated to footnotes. So, on that winter day, toward the end of 2004, when Dennis Gomes heard the name Jay Vandermark, and all the memories of Gomes's years as chief of the Audit Division of the Nevada Gaming Control Board came flooding back, he did not hesitate.

In the early 1970s Gomes had been one of the principal architects of then Nevada governor Michael O'Callaghan's plan to eradicate organized crime from the casinos. Driven by a relentless determination and an almost preternatural sense of justice, Gomes had spearheaded numerous high-profile raids on skimming operations and back-door larceny.

He personally supervised the infamous Argent Corporation case—a topic explored in the Nicholas Pileggi book and 1995 Martin Scorsese movie, *Casino,* starring Robert De Niro, Joe Pesci, and Sharon Stone. Gomes revolutionized the way casinos are operated, installing guidelines that are still on the books today. But when it came to beating the Mob in an escalating, deadly game of chess, Gomes had narrowly escaped with his sanity—not to mention his life—running up against a stalemate of systematic corruption.

It had all been a stone in his shoe for more than three decades.

Which was why, on that gray morning in 2004, when confronted with the opportunity to tell the sordid tale of George Jay Vandermark and the rogues' gallery populating the back rooms of Sin City, he did not give one thought to the dangers of testifying in front of a star chamber of wiseguys. Without a single twinge of reluctance, he responded to the special agent's request in the affirmative. Of course he would help.

Once and for all, after more than thirty years, in front of God and man, he would set the record straight.

———

The Gomes family, at the time of the FBI agent's initial call, lived in a stately three-story Colonial in the piney woods north of Atlantic City.

That night, Dennis Gomes came home and broke the news to his wife, Barbara, as carefully and gently as possible. Gomes was not sure how she would feel about the prospects of opening these old wounds. But Barbara Gomes—a willowy former dancer, and the spitting image of Audrey Hepburn—reacted with the kind of steely spine that can only come from being married to a former lawman for thirty-plus years: She thought it was pretty terrific.

Barbara Gomes knew how exciting it was to finally put all the lost pieces of the puzzle together. She remembered well the time when they were young, and Dennis was fighting the good fight. Barbara remembered the frustration, the agonizing close calls, and maybe, most of all, the implacable sense of justice that made her fall for this upright, bare-fisted truth-seeker in the first place. She knew that this was important, this was *just*—and maybe even inevitable.

All of which was good . . . because there would be plenty of waiting.

A case this far-reaching and historic took months and months to prepare. Sometimes years. In the back of his mind, Dennis Gomes was vaguely aware of the hurry-up-and-wait nature of such endeavors. Still, he did not fully comprehend the scope of this case until the days and months passed, from 2004 to 2005, into 2006, and several additional telephone conversations, followed by a visit to his home by key prosecutors, revealed the epochal nature of these proceedings.

The case would come to be known as the "Family Secrets" trial—one of the largest indictments of organized crime in US history. Under the auspices of the Racketeer Influenced and Corrupt Organizations Act (RICO), the feds were putting a "hit"—as one wag on the prosecution team put it—on the Mob. The case featured fourteen defendants, eighteen murders, and nearly forty years of various and sundry activities, such as bookmaking, loan-sharking, extortion, torture, intimidation, and—there is no better phrase for it—domestic terrorism.

In addition to its scale, this case was different because of the prosecutors' point of attack. In the past, the government would begin with instances of "thuggery," and then would ask jurors to connect the acts with orders handed down from on high. The Family Secrets approach would be to start with the bosses—to prove first that the organizational hierarchy existed, and then to show that the crimes were committed in service of these bosses.

Among the fourteen defendants indicted, several were top bosses who figured prominently in Dennis Gomes's personal history in Las Vegas. One of these bosses had allegedly signed off on the murder of George Jay Vandermark—the Mob's slot-machine man at the Stardust Casino—a man whom Gomes, in the mid-1970s, had worked diligently to flip. Vandermark had been on the verge of cooperating with Gomes right before he vanished on a so-called Mexican vacation. Although the crime was never solved, authorities pieced together foul play by talking to other informants, many of whom also ended up taking sudden and long-lasting "vacations."

But the thorn in Dennis Gomes's side all these years was that Vandermark had held the key to the skimming going on at four major casinos on Gomes's investigative docket.

Now these long-buried memories were being dredged up by a team of crew-cut, straight-arrow investigators, who showed up on Gomes's doorstep in mid-2005 to seal the deal in person. Also present was the lead prosecutor in the case, Mitchell Mars of the US Attorney's Office, who impressed Gomes with his no-nonsense, friendly manner. There was none of the pomposity that Gomes had encountered over the years with other federal prosecutors.

This feels like a fraternity, Gomes thought as he sat down with the feds in his spacious living room for coffee and Q & A. They asked Gomes a slew of questions about his investigations in the seventies, and explained that Gomes's role in the trial would be as a sort of historian, providing the whys and wherefores for certain assassinations and disappearances.

"What you did in Las Vegas was a major accomplishment," Mars said to Gomes at one point, referring to all the years Gomes had spent turning over rugs in casinos and revealing the corruption slithering underneath.

Sadly, back in the 1970s, very few of Gomes's masters—from the governor's office to the upper echelons of Nevada's gaming regulators— had seemed particularly grateful to Gomes for his revolutionary investigative work.

"I would think this trial would be a golden opportunity for you to finally make things right," Mars summed up. "It'll make all that good work you did mean something."

Gomes appreciated the sentiment, and also appreciated the fact that the government was prepared to subpoena him. He thought that was a good idea, especially since he was not a cop anymore. Gomes did not want anybody, especially the wiseguys, to think he was simply *volunteering* to testify—doing it because it felt good. The appearance of a court order— not that it would change anything for Gomes—was more of a practical matter, a veneer of protection for his family.

The peace of mind was helpful, especially after the feds said their good-byes and returned to Chicago . . . and the waiting began.

As his court date drew near, Dennis Gomes started getting nervous. But not for the reasons one might guess. Not because of fears of Mob reprisals, no matter how appropriate those fears might be in such a high-level case. And not because of the exposure of residing in an isolated grove of pines that creaked and whispered late at night, providing shadowy egress for all manner of potential stalkers. On the contrary; Gomes got nervous for a far more prosaic reason. He hated public speaking.

In Catholic grammar school Gomes had suffered from reading problems. He had struggled with class recitations and detested the moments he had to read aloud from that thick doorstop of a book known as *The Early Reader.* In second grade, one particularly mean-spirited nun would scream at the eight-year-old Gomes as he slogged through his stammering recitals. *Sister Mary Vincenzo.* Gomes would remember that dreaded name for the rest of his life. When the yelling proved too much for little Dennis, on an otherwise forgettable day, he started to cry. Sister Mary Vincenzo was relentless, yelling even louder and making him complete the task regardless of his tears.

Humiliations like those stick with a person. Dennis Gomes would grow up to be a force of nature in law enforcement, but he never much liked to talk in front of people. And now he realized the biggest organized-crime trial of this new century would bring him before not only the lidded gaze of gangsters, but also the glare of the klieg lights.

As July 30, 2007, loomed on the calendar, Gomes began to make arrangements for the trip to the Windy City.

Normally, whenever he traveled, he liked to have his family in tow. But this time, he didn't feel right bringing his wife and daughters along to the trial. He didn't want them hearing or seeing the things that would be exhumed on the witness stand. The Gomes girls, however, insisted on coming along, and being there for their dad. The truth of the matter was, despite his reticence, Gomes felt relieved that they were coming. He was happy to have the moral support.

So he and Barbara decided to turn the journey into a quasi-vacation, culminating with a trip to their daughter Mary's home in Iowa. They'd just be taking a quick detour through a courtroom in Chicago.

———

From its days as a gaslit abattoir of stockyards and reaper works, Chicago has always been a city that works hard. On the swampy threshold of the Great Lakes, this teeming, bustling city is a place of blue-collar legend—from the Haymarket Riot to the rough-and-tumble days of the Daley political machine. Its history was written by the blistered hands of stevedores, train-yard workers, meatpackers, and foundry men.

But the invisible grease beneath the city's industry always came from crime.

No single icon of Chicago looms larger than Al Capone. For most of the twentieth century, Capone represented the Roaring Twenties and the *rat-a-tat-tat* of tommy guns (which foreigners still mime today as an international symbol of the town). But Capone's legacy goes deeper than posters in pizza parlors and punch lines for bad burlesque.

Al Capone consolidated organized crime in Chicago. Unlike the warring factions of *La Cosa Nostra* on the East Coast, the Chicago version of the Mob flourished throughout the second half of the twentieth century as a monolithic criminal enterprise. Known as the Outfit, the organization reached its zenith in the 1970s, with its tentacles reaching into everything from high-interest "juice" loans to pornography, from gambling parlors to vending machines. The Outfit owned cops, politicians, and vast amounts of real estate. It was only logical that it would spread its influence across the country into Glitter Gulch.

The Chicago in which Dennis Gomes and family arrived on a hot, blustery afternoon in July 2007 no longer thrummed with submachine guns or sputtered with gaslights. This Chicago was a gleaming cathedral of glass spires, the skyline reflecting off the opal reaches of Lake Michigan. The old speakeasies and bootleg temples west of town were now patchworks of tree-lined suburbs, corporate parks, and endless corridors of strip malls. But the influence of the Outfit still clung to the place like ghosts. On this very day—as the Gomes crew were gathering their luggage at O'Hare and hunting down their rental car—federal prosecutors were preparing to perform an exorcism.

The Gomeses drove into the city and found their hotel—The "W" City Center—just two blocks from the Dirksen Federal Building. They checked in, and while Barbara and daughters Danielle and Gabrielle explored the neighborhood, Dennis Gomes walked the two blocks over to the courthouse for a meeting with Assistant US Attorney Mars.

After methodically going over each and every question they were going to ask, Mars went on to add one last piece of assurance: "We're really going to emphasize your law enforcement training here, Dennis, mostly to impress upon these wiseguys that you were a *real cop*, not just some regulator. To these guys, once you're a cop, you're always a cop. They're not going to question your expertise."

Gomes gave him a nod and took a deep breath. "I appreciate that, Mitch."

On his way back to the hotel, walking through the lakeshore breezes, Gomes felt almost giddy with confidence. He felt protected. He felt the trial was under the control of steady hands. In fact, he felt comfortable enough to go out to dinner that night for a pleasant evening with Barbara and Danielle and a couple of old friends. They drank wine and talked about the old days, and all the good cheer took Gomes's mind off his pending performance.

That night, before bed, the Gomeses gazed out their window at a Hollywood film crew shooting a scene from *Batman Begins*—a make-believe gang perpetrating make-believe evil—and then Gomes finally turned in. He slept soundly, at peace with his destiny, and his Taoist mind-set: going with the flow.

The next morning, after breakfast, Dennis and family walked to the courthouse together. The Dirksen Federal Building is a thirty-story black edifice of steel and glass facing the lake—as sedate and innocuous as it is imposing—like a monastic tower planted amid a futuristic landscape. A special agent for the FBI met the family at the entrance, and ushered them up to the twenty-fifth floor.

After well wishes from the family, Gomes was taken to the witness room.

The spartan, institutional waiting area could have easily been a side room at the Department of Motor Vehicles: no burnished wainscoting or American flags, just chairs and tension. Two other hearty souls already occupied the waiting room—somebody's former girlfriend and an ex-cop—but Gomes kept his thoughts and his eyes mostly to himself. He didn't know these people—they could be anybody—and besides, Gomes was too keyed up and excited to chat about the 90-degree weather or the latest Cubs game.

Gomes had experienced similar moments in kickboxing tournaments: that buzz of adrenaline right before a match. He just wanted to get in there and start fighting, get it done.

But the clock seemed to be slowing down.

———

While Dennis Gomes waited in the witness room, his wife Barbara, and daughters Danielle and Gabrielle, all sat in the courtroom gallery, within clear view of the Mob royalty lined up at the defense table, only a few feet away, looking like deposed dictators: Anthony "Twan" Doyle, Paul "The Indian" Schiro, James "Jimmy Light" Marcello, Frank "The Breeze" Calabrese, and Joey "The Clown" Lombardo.

In the awkward silence following a listing of horrifying charges, including everything from throat-slitting to dumping bodies in lime pits, Barbara Gomes heard a voice in her ear.

"You see that gentleman over there?" the voice whispered. An FBI agent was standing next to Barbara, discreetly pointing out one of the mobsters. "At one point, he had people waiting for your husband in Mexico . . . and if Dennis had crossed the border, chances are he never would have come back."

Then the agent turned and whispered to Danielle Gomes, "You have no idea how close your dad came to dying."

All at once Barbara Gomes felt the fear pressing down on her, constricting her throat. Right then she decided that maybe being here was not such a terrific idea after all; maybe staying home would have been more prudent.

At that moment, in a side chamber adjacent to the courtroom, Barbara's husband was reaching a different conclusion: It was time to face the crowd.

Earlier that morning, back at the hotel, after sprucing himself up and getting into his dignified black suit, Gomes had looked at himself in the mirror. The reflection of a cop stared back at him.

Once a cop, always a cop.

"Mr. Gomes?" the voice of the bailiff came from across the waiting room at precisely 10:19 a.m. Central Standard Time.

Gomes stood, brushed himself off, and followed the court official through the inner door.

The first impression Gomes got as he entered the courtroom was a vague sense of light and dark—dark suits, bright diffused light from high ceiling fixtures, dark burnished wood, and the bright mosaic of the crowd, all the faces, all shapes and ages, turning toward *him*. Even a sketch artist, seated near the front, paused and studied the new subject entering the courtroom. No cameras were allowed in the room, which only added to the tense, almost funereal atmosphere.

Then Gomes saw, in the front row of the spectator section, sitting side by side as though waiting in a pew for a church service to begin, the smiling faces of his family: the Gomes girls.

This reassuring vision gave Gomes a shot of encouragement and strength ... and maybe even pride. But then, as he followed the bailiff past the gallery to the witness stand, Gomes turned and looked straight ahead.

And his stomach clenched. As he walked past the jury box, past the judge's dais and the watchful gaze of the Honorable James B. Zagel, and then past the crowded prosecution table, Gomes's gaze fixed on the row of tables dead ahead of him, against the far wall.

There are moments in life when the passage of time slows down. Car accidents. Marriage proposals. Battlefield action. These are the rare flashpoint moments from which everything that comes after will be measured, and every prior event will be marked as BEFORE.

This moment—in the hushed, crowded room in the Everett M. Dirksen US Courthouse—was one of those moments for Dennis Gomes.

As he approached the witness chair, he found himself staring directly—at eye level—into the baleful gazes of Chicago's underworld kingpins.

Lombardo, Marcello, Calabrese—positioned behind the witness box—each watched Dennis Gomes approach with the inscrutable, languid, impassive stare of a rattlesnake. No barriers. No Italian-style enclosures separating the accused. Only about twenty feet of air between the death-dealers and the truth-teller.

I'm not looking away, Gomes found himself thinking before taking his seat. *I'm not going to look away ... not until I make that turn.*

It only took a few more seconds for Gomes to reach the witness chair and turn to settle in, facing judge and jury.

Although it was a minuscule blip of time—maybe two or three seconds—that brief instant when his gaze met and held the stares of hard-core killers would turn out to be a defining moment for Gomes.

Then, on that muggy July day, in that hushed courtroom, for the next forty-five minutes or so, Gomes laid out a foundation of history, motive, and opportunity that would become one of the linchpins of the government's case against the Outfit. His testimony would give onlookers a teasing glimpse into an amazing story . . .

. . . the story of Dennis Gomes and his systematic attack on corruption in Las Vegas.

Part I

Bullets and Pencils

And they came to Jerusalem. And he entered the temple and began to drive out those who sold and those who bought in the temple, and he overturned the tables of the moneychangers and the seats of those who sold pigeons; and he would not allow anyone to carry anything through the temple.

—Mark 11:15

Double-Down

LOOK HIM RIGHT IN THE EYE.

Thirteen-year-old Dennis Gomes stood on the edge of the playground adjacent to old St. Clare's school, clenching his fists. The other kids, who had been playing a game of marbles, now backed off into the shade of the eucalyptus trees to watch from a safe distance.

Ten feet away from Dennis on the cracked cement, an eighth-grade bully had just knocked down a weaker boy. Mild-mannered seventh-grader Robert Hays struggled to keep the waterworks from flowing, but it was a losing battle. He choked back a sob, his face already smudged and livid. Sadly, since the Hays boy had grown accustomed over the years to being called cruel names, this was just another day at the office.

But then the bully, a big portly kid with ham-hock arms and almost no neck, paused mid-assault at the sound of a sharp cry from across the playground.

"I said leave him alone!" Dennis Gomes shouted a second time, fists clenching harder. Physically, Dennis was not exactly an imposing figure. He was gangly, baby-faced except for the out-of-place, masculine cleft chin of his father—a chin seemingly waiting for the rest of Dennis's body to catch up. But there was something *substantial* about the kid. Something approaching *gravitas* . . . even at this age.

The massive boy turned, put his hands on his hips, and shot a baleful glance at Dennis Gomes. "Who's gonna make me?" the big kid wanted to know.

Dennis's throat was dry, but he spoke as clearly as possible, almost calmly. "*I'm* gonna make you."

Fight or flight was the term, as Dennis Gomes would find out later. For now, he had no words for this feeling of hair bristling on the nape of his neck and muscles contracting around his midsection. In some distant compartment of his mind, however, were the words *Always look a bully right in the eye.*

The bully chortled, shook his head with amusement. Then he went back to where poor little Robert Hays was struggling to his feet, wiping the snot off his face. The bully shoved the weaker kid back to the ground, almost as if demonstrating his dismissive attitude toward big talkers like the Gomes boy.

"I told you to leave him alone!" Dennis Gomes was approaching, his fingernails digging into his palms, his gaze unnaturally locked on the eyes of the overweight kid. "Now get lost!"

Nose to nose, the boys stared at each other.

"What are you gonna do about it?" the big kid finally inquired.

"I'm going to beat the shit out of you if you touch him again."

"Oh?"

The burly boy turned and gave the Hays kid one more push for good measure.

Dennis jumped on the bully.

Like all schoolyard tussles, the fight was sudden, sloppy, and melo-dramatic. Dennis Gomes landed very few punches, but he must have caused *some* damage, because the big kid started sputtering and stumbling backward. The fight seemed to go on forever. The bully was so huge he wouldn't go down. But finally, in a flurry of blows, the smaller boy drove the freckled Goliath to the ground.

And that was when Dennis Gomes learned his first hard lesson in group dynamics.

Now on top of the bully, still pummeling wildly like an engine that was revving out of control, Dennis started sensing the strangest change in the air: Onlookers were now rushing past the battling boys, as though the fight had become some kind of group activity or schoolyard game, like Red Rover or kickball. But stranger still was the fact that they were throwing things at *Dennis.* Throwing things at the *rescuer*—not at the bad guy. They were turning on the good guy!

They were putting wads of gum in Dennis's hair and tossing candy wrappers at him, just generally expressing their disapproval, as though they resented his brazen disregard for the balance of power.

It took Dennis a long time to figure out why they were mad at him. He didn't know it then, but fate had already begun to steer his destiny.

During the course of his life, he would learn, again and again, the cost of justice.

—◆—

Born in 1944, in San Jose, California, one of the middle siblings in a family of four boys, Dennis Gomes had a twin brother who died shortly after birth. Though he never knew his twin, Gomes thought about his lost brother every day of his life. He often wondered how everything might have turned out differently if his brother had lived.

Gomes spent his early childhood in the small bedroom community of Sunnyvale, California—just west of Santa Clara—in the wooded area that would one day become known as Silicon Valley. When he was four, Dennis and his family moved a few miles to Santa Clara, occupying a cozy little cottage smack-dab in the middle of an orchard.

Gomes's father, Stephen, was a second-generation Portuguese construction laborer, and an avid boxer, whose parents had settled in Hawaii years earlier to work in the sugarcane fields. A tall, lanky man with a strong jaw and receding hairline, Steve Gomes had seen action in the Pacific as a sailor in World War II. But despite his tough exterior, he was a gentle man who instilled a rock-solid sense of right and wrong in his boys.

Gomes's mother, Mildred, was a petite, olive-skinned woman with a quick smile and a love of books and knowledge. Although she made the most of her husband's scant salary, she struggled to make ends meet each month.

Like most children, Gomes inherited traits from each of his parents. Young Dennis would grow up to be a two-fisted thinking man with an iron-strong love of justice and a deep compassion for those who needed it most.

In spite of this modest blue-collar environment, Gomes never thought of his family as poor. A pair of corduroy pants for school, maybe some Levis and a couple pairs of shoes, and Gomes felt rich. When the pants inevitably wore out, Gomes saw the patches as a fashion statement.

When those patches wore out, there would be little patches on the big patches—a natty look for the boy.

Shoes would get resoled again and again, until each step the boy took would make a clapping noise as he sauntered down the sidewalk. At one point, the neighbor kids were so impressed by Dennis Gomes's *so-what* attitude—and his trademark *whap-whap-whap* sound as he strutted down the street—that they started cutting the front soles of their own expensive shoes so they, too, would clap.

As young as age six, Gomes had an uncanny sense of social justice. On one occasion he overheard a neighbor lady mumbling under her breath, after glaring at a Portuguese family puttering around in their front yard, "Look at that. These Portuguese are ruining the neighborhood." Gomes didn't say anything to the lady, but he did think to himself, *That lady doesn't know what she's talking about.*

At St. Clare's, one of California's oldest Catholic grammar schools, Gomes wasn't a natural student, perhaps suffering from a touch of dyslexia. He got into more than his fair share of mischief, but he also got along well with most of the nuns. He enjoyed the spirited talks that many of the Sisters would encourage in class.

As little Dennis grew, he explored the miles and miles of fruit orchards with his pals—a wonderland of hills and switchbacks and train tracks—which instilled a sense of freedom in the boy. He would jump trains and interact with hobos and started dreaming of travel and adventures beyond the patchwork quilt of trees circling his world.

One time, the young Gomes led his friends on a wild goose chase along a dry creek bed that snaked through the wilderness. They biked for hours, until Dennis spotted a paved road. They took the macadam for a while, until, out of nowhere, a small single-engine plane swooped down toward them, close enough for the pilot to wave.

The kids thought this was pretty swell, waving back at the aviator and pretending to return imaginary gunfire, when all at once a squadron of airport vehicles and trucks came out of nowhere, lights spinning. The boys were immediately surrounded. It turned out they had inadvertently ridden onto one of the main runways of the San Jose Airport, preventing the approach of scores of planes.

The cops came, loaded the bikes onto paddy wagons, and hauled the kids home. Dennis got his hide tanned that day . . . but maybe it was worth it. The experience was his first up-close encounter with lawmen. They made an impression on the young boy, with their spit-shined uniforms and lead-loaded confidence.

Dennis Gomes the teenager earned the reputation of being one of the toughest kids at Bellarmine College Preparatory School in San Jose, and his 130 IQ helped put him in the top tier academically. Juggling late-night extracurricular activities at the neighboring all-girls school, while ripping through religious studies and science classes, Gomes found himself starting to think about his future.

By this point, Gomes's father had worked his way up from laborer to carpenter to superintendent in the construction field, and now was working for a builder, making inroads into the exploding real estate market in Nevada. In 1960, the Gomes family moved to Las Vegas.

Established as a desert outpost in the early twentieth century, Las Vegas did not leave the launchpad as a city until Bugsy Siegel and Meyer Lansky showed up in the mid-1940s with a boatload of dirty money and a neon-lit dream. Over the next decade and a half, this oasis town blasted off into the gambling stratosphere.

By the time the Gomes family arrived, in early 1960, the place had reached a heyday. The Rat Pack had just set up housekeeping at the Sands, and Elvis had just started shaking his pelvis with Ann-Margret in *Viva Las Vegas*. The big casinos such as the Sahara, the Riviera, the Dunes, the Stardust, and the Tropicana were hitting their strides. But like all single-industry towns—Detroit and Los Angeles among them—Las Vegas was a lot more than just its core business.

The lifeblood of the town was its population of honest working people, from croupiers to caterers, from cab drivers to construction workers. Nellis Air Force Base employed thousands of civilians, as did the growing mining industry. Homes and apartment complexes were sprouting faster than prickly pears.

As Stephen Gomes settled into his new role as a developer for these burgeoning communities, churning out dream homes for a city specializing in dreams, seventeen-year-old Dennis transferred to Bishop

Gorman High School, a Catholic institution on the east side of town, in the shadows of the red-tinged Spring Mountains. Gomes loved the new school—especially the girls, who commanded a little too much of his attention—and his grades slipped a little.

One day, shortly after he enrolled at Bishop Gorman, Gomes was strolling down the noisy central corridor with a friend, when he noticed an attractive girl coming in the opposite direction. "Who in the world's that?" Gomes marveled under his breath. She was a stunner—a flaxen-haired beauty, a shoe-in for that year's homecoming queen honors.

"Oh, that's Linda Layman," the friend informed him.

"Wow."

"Don't get too excited, Tiger; everybody wants to date her, and she won't go out with anyone."

The rest of the world—the noisy hallway, his friends' voices—faded away as Gomes watched the girl make a turn down a side corridor and vanish into a classroom.

"Everybody on the football team has taken a crack, and she's been a no-go," the other boy added. "So you might as well forget it . . . because if *they* can't get anywhere with her, *you're* not going to be able to get anywhere with her, either."

But what Gomes's young friend did *not* know was that Dennis Gomes was a young man who gravitated toward lost causes and impossible dreams. "Don't ever dare Denny to do something," Gomes's mother, Mildred, once said to his best friend, Bobby Schmidt. "Because no matter how stupid it is, and no matter how dangerous it is, he'll do it. So never challenge him!"

Things started happening quickly for Gomes. Within weeks of starting at Bishop Gorman, the lovely Linda Layman and Gomes were going steady. A few years later, he and Linda were engaged, then married, and Gomes found himself staring down the barrel of college. He started thinking seriously about careers.

Early on, as a kid in Santa Clara, he had dreamed of being a fighter pilot. But as he grew, Gomes started imagining himself as something else—something that had probably colored his boyhood dreams from the moment he'd stopped that bully from beating up poor little Robert Hays—a righteous, incorruptible, ice-water-in-his-veins, professional lawman.

The notion had been brewing for some time, stirred by the hardships of his blue-collar background. There had been other moments and events in Gomes's young life that would drive him toward a life devoted to justice. Gomes would never forget the time his father tried to start a private firm. Here was a man who had worked his whole life—backbreaking manual labor, mostly—to build a nest egg. After a long, difficult, and often humbling search, Steve Gomes finally found a moneyman willing to finance a small company that would supply doors to builders. Sadly, the money guy turned out to be a con man who absconded with all the revenue.

The IRS hounded Steve and Mildred for years afterward, and Dennis Gomes remembered being incensed that this "piece of shit" grifter had gotten away with such a crime. The urge to track down scum like that—to see justice done, to right the wrongs visited upon innocent people—began to smolder like an ember inside young Dennis Gomes.

Meanwhile, pop culture was filled with images of a profession that operated on an almost mythological plane in the America of the 1950s and '60s. These were the days before J. Edgar Hoover was outed as a ruthless, reactionary cross-dresser . . . the days before Nixonian enemy lists and Jim Crow conflicts in the South . . . before all the counterculture stereotypes of FBI agents as tools of the fascist state.

This was a time when the myths of the Untouchables, Eliot Ness, and Melvin Purvis were still burning in the collective unconscious. The image of the FBI agent as a dapper, gallant, educated paladin of truth and justice reflected the new white-collar society.

Dennis Gomes had read somewhere that there are two basic paths to becoming a G-man: law or accounting. He simply could not see himself as a lawyer. After weighing the options that his C-plus grade point average had left him, Gomes ended up at the University of Nevada at Las Vegas. It wasn't the nation's most prestigious home of higher learning, but it had a liberal admissions policy, and Gomes couldn't afford to be choosy.

His new wife, now pregnant with Gomes's first child, was adamantly opposed to being married to a college boy. She fought hard against

Gomes's master plan of becoming an accountant, before ultimately becoming a fed. She saw starvation in their future—foreclosure, bankruptcy, homelessness, and poverty, straight out of Charles Dickens. She threatened to divorce Gomes. She begged him, she cajoled.

"What is wrong with you?" Gomes asked her flat out one evening over a simple dinner in their modest little one-bedroom apartment near the campus.

"You're never going to be able to pull this off," she said, sobbing.

"I don't care what you say, I'm doing this," Gomes retorted. "I'm going to work forty hours a week, and you don't have to work at all."

"But how many classes will you be taking?" she asked.

"I'm going to take a full load. I want to graduate in four years."

"That's impossible!" She sobbed harder. "Don't you realize that's *impossible?!*"

But where Linda saw certain failure, a man named Reuben Newman sensed potential. Newman, a tough little bald guy, former paratrooper, and an accounting professor at University of Nevada–Las Vegas, saw a diamond in the rough in Gomes.

"You're one of the best accounting students I ever had," Newman said to Gomes at one point. "I'm gonna keep my eye on you, and if you ever— *ever*—get a grade below a B, I'm going to kick your ass."

Gomes wasn't sure he was as brilliant as Newman claimed, but he did not want to let him down. He soon learned that the professor actually was tracking every one of Gomes's grades. Newman would make little comments about each grade, just to make sure Gomes knew he was keeping an eye on him. Little by little, Gomes started believing he might be just as smart as the rest of the students. And by the time he was nearing graduation, now at the top of his class, he realized that perhaps Reuben Newman was right—even though none of it had come easy.

With a grueling work schedule to maintain, and a baby to support, Gomes would study at night, sacrificing sleep and sanity for grades. Times weren't just hard, they were desperate. On more than one occasion, Linda would storm into Gomes's workspace, overcome by rage and frustration, and dramatically tear the pages out of his textbooks, wadding them up and throwing them away. Not willing to indulge his wife's anger, Gomes would merely retrieve the crumpled pages, calmly smooth them back out, tape them back into his textbook, and go back to work without comment.

Right after graduation, Gomes landed a job—with Professor Newman's help—at one of the largest international accounting firms in the world: Peat, Marwick, Mitchell and Company. He was one step closer to realizing his dream of becoming a federal agent. The FBI has employed agents with accounting backgrounds since its inception. These agents specialize in approaching the investigation of a crime through the money trail. Forensic accounting is used to investigate everything from corporate fraud to terrorism. FBI agents who come from the accounting world are required to be certified public accountants (CPAs) or possess a comparable certification, a licensure attainable only after two years of work experience. Gomes still had big-time dues to pay, but for the first time in his life, the lofty goal of becoming a member of the top law enforcement agency in the nation was clearly visible on the horizon.

Peat, Marwick, Mitchell sent Gomes to Hawaii. By then, Linda had given birth to their second child, but the marriage was crumbling. Crying herself to sleep at night, Linda felt lost in Honolulu. Gomes struggled to help her, yearned to make her happy. But deep down he feared he was fighting a losing battle.

At the same time that he was engaged in a seemingly endless conflict at home, Dennis Gomes was proving himself a natural at the accounting game on the island. With his Portuguese roots and his Hawaiian family background, Gomes was trusted by the locals, considered more than just another mainland *haole* (Hawaiian slang for foreigner).

During this period, Dennis and Linda had their second child, a baby girl named Mary Lee. Linda, Doug, and Mary were settling into a routine. Things were looking up.

In time, Gomes's success began to extend beyond the high-level accounting he'd been hired to do. With his bosses' blessing, Gomes started ferreting out fraud—getting practice at the investigative side of the business. Initially, he viewed his effort as a natural extension of his standard numbers-and-figures work, but it was actually much more. Gomes was preparing himself for law enforcement work.

By the fall of 1969, Gomes was ready for his CPA exam—a requirement for the FBI—which he passed with flying colors. Meanwhile, he had risen at Peat, Marwick, Mitchell to the position of supervising senior accountant in the Audit Division. He decided to parlay his achievements by going to graduate school for an MBA in finance. While his supervisors at Peat, Marwick, Mitchell would be pleased, Gomes was doing it out of a drive to become the best FBI agent the Bureau had ever seen.

At the University of Washington, Gomes worked as a professor's assistant while he completed the MBA program. Moving back to the college lifestyle in the ever-cloudy Seattle was a decision that did not sit well with Linda; but Dennis had a goal in mind and no amount of crying and fighting would deter him.

Master's degree in hand, Gomes left Peat, Marwick, Mitchell; joined Coopers and Lybrand as a management consultant in Seattle, Washington; and started visiting FBI field offices, making certain the right people knew his name, and of his interest in someday joining the Bureau. By early 1971, he was raising eyebrows among federal recruiters. In no time, offers were being put on tables.

Then came the call. Gomes was bound for Quantico—the elite FBI training academy in the wooded wetlands of Virginia. But it wasn't that easy. A nearly simultaneous opportunity arrived with a call from Gomes's father.

Taking a break from filling out the last of the application materials for the FBI, Gomes listened as his father explained there was a job opening, working for Michael O'Callaghan, the new governor of Nevada.

Gomes knew the broad strokes of story. Nevada's government had always been controlled by the gambling industry, but the 1970 election had been a game-changer. The dark-horse candidate O'Callaghan—a war hero and crony of LBJ's, with no ties to gambling—had taken office amid a restless fervor for change. And now the new guy wanted to clean house. He wanted to get back all the lost tax revenue that was hemorrhaging out of the casinos due to the sticky fingers of the Mob.

"That's the guy," Steve Gomes replied. "I understand he's really hot to beef up the Gaming Control Board."

Another thing Dennis Gomes knew was that his dad worked for a good friend of Michael O'Callaghan's; whatever inside information Steve Gomes had, it was probably reliable.

"They have this division, Audit, and I guess they're looking for somebody to run the thing, to whip it into shape."

"That's a law enforcement agency, isn't it?" Gomes asked his dad.

"Yeah, I guess it is."

"There's just one problem, Dad. I'm an accountant. I don't have any law enforcement experience."

Gomes could almost hear his dad smiling. "No experience, huh? That never stopped you before."

Dennis Gomes was impressed by the sixty-year-old home on Mountain Street that served as the Nevada governor's mansion. *Must make it a hell of a lot easier to get what you want out of a meeting at home when you live in a place like this,* he thought. His older brother, Steve Jr., who was being considered for a job in the welfare sector, also attended the meeting.

The Gomes brothers were introduced to Phil Hannifin, chairman of the Gaming Control Board, and George Miller, head of the Nevada welfare system, the two men who could soon be their bosses. Dennis came into the meeting determined to keep an open mind and make a good impression, not just for himself, but also for his father, who had set this all up. But the meeting took an unexpected turn early on when Steve, a left-leaning intellectual who by this time had earned a PhD, launched into an angry diatribe about systemic abuse in the Nevada welfare system—specifically a series of sex scandals at a local all-girls reformatory. Whether Dennis agreed with his brother or not, he knew this was neither the time nor the place to go on the attack. Thankfully, the discussion turned to crime prevention and law enforcement. For several minutes Dennis Gomes talked about law enforcement and the tools in his arsenal as an accountant. He was lucid, focused, and articulate. The other gentlemen listened closely to what he had to say.

At last, the governor—a balding, barrel-chested man in his early forties—told Dennis he wanted "to clean out organized crime in Las Vegas."

Gomes nodded, remaining silent.

"They basically control everything in Vegas," O'Callaghan went on. "But I didn't take one penny of campaign money from these people. Most of that money went to the other guy. I got in on a fluke. The people elected me. So I'm going to go after these Mob guys."

Gomes liked what he was hearing, but still remained silent. He just kept listening as the governor explained the job of running the department that detects organized-crime infiltration into the casinos and investigates alleged skimming, the exploitation of hidden interests in these gaming establishments.

"If you were to accept this position, Dennis," O'Callaghan explained, "you would carry a gun. You would officially become a peace officer. And you would go to peace officer training school, which is a lot like a police academy." O'Callaghan leaned toward Dennis and looked deep into his eyes. "Understand?"

"Yes, sir."

"Well, Dennis?" The governor looked at him. "You interested?"

—◦—

It took less than a month for the governor's office to finalize its decision. Dennis Gomes, at twenty-six, would become one of the youngest people ever to head up a department of this magnitude—a law enforcement agency charged with the daunting mission of eradicating the Mob from Las Vegas. Gomes was so young, in fact, that government press releases at the time conveniently added a few years to his age.

It did not take long for Gomes to move the family back to Las Vegas from Seattle. Linda was happy to be home, and this took some pressure off of Dennis.

In the weeks leading up to his first day on the job, Gomes found it hard to focus on anything else. He lay awake at night visualizing the dream coming true. He envisioned walking into the Department of Audit for the first time so clearly that he could almost hear the heels of his freshly polished shoes clicking against the tile floor—a far cry from the clapping sound his resoled shoes used to make on the sidewalk. He thought about the crack staff he'd be working with. The best of the best. And he couldn't wait to lead them down the rugged road of crime fighting. A modern-day Eliot Ness greeting his hard-bitten minions.

In his imagination Gomes saw the bustling office in which he would be working like something straight out of *Dragnet, Naked City, The Untouchables, Manhunt, The Defenders*. In his mind's eye, he would walk into that high-stakes, high-adrenaline world on his first day to find a room full of Untouchables—fearless, lantern-jawed, eagle-eyed accountant cops—as adept with their handguns as they were with their adding machines. He pictured a supermodern facility crackling with activity, hundreds of individuals poring over evidence of skimming and Mob influence, and yet, all of it choreographed and organized with military precision.

When the inaugural morning arrived, Gomes spent an inordinate amount of time at the mirror. He wanted to look sharp, slick, and professional for his colleagues. Announcements had gone out that week that the new division chief was arriving today, and Gomes didn't want to come off as some earnest, wet-behind-the-ears youngster playing cops and robbers.

He drove to the government building in downtown Las Vegas. The place was a nondescript office building just off Fremont Street that could have housed anything from the county dogcatcher to a bunch of self-storage lockers. He took a deep breath before pushing open the heavy glass-and-oak door and walking in. There was just a hint of anxiety in his voice when Gomes told the receptionist who he was and why he was there. An attractive woman in her twenties, with auburn hair and long lashes, she smiled and directed him to the elevator, which brought him to his floor.

As he entered the department's door, he thought, *Do I have the wrong room?* The place was a large, austere office scattered with boxes and empty desks and unidentified stacks of paper. Stranger still, there was a grand total of six warm bodies in the room, most of whom looked as though they were approaching retirement age and would be better off on a shuffleboard court.

In one corner, an old geezer was sitting in his cubicle, alternating between doing tax returns and reading the newspaper. Gomes would later find out that this guy was moonlighting, doing tax work on the side and spending much of his workday clipping coupons from *The Sun.*

The man looked up and noticed Gomes staring with disbelief. "Hey, kid. What do you want?"

"What do I *want?*" Gomes shook his head. "I'm Dennis Gomes, the new division chief."

The old man pursed his lips, slipping his newspaper back into his drawer. "No kiddin'. . . Well, welcome aboard."

At that point another so-called "agent"—whose desk was not far from where Gomes stood—sprang to his feet to greet the new boss. Gomes met him halfway to say hello, and the younger man, who looked as though a strong breeze would knock him over, started trembling as though afflicted with palsy. A cross between Barney Fife and a scared rabbit, the man could barely get out the words, "Welcome to the division, sir. I'm Lindsey Jacobson."

Gomes looked around and found a third guy who appeared to be in charge . . . sort of. A grouchy, curmudgeonly old gent named Sam Rosenberg, Gomes found out later that this guy had been an investigator in New York during the 1960s era of US Attorney Robert Morris Morgenthau, working with the crusading prosecutor on corruption cases against politicians and organized crime.

After a few minutes of awkward small talk, Gomes asked Rosenberg to pull all the "investigation files" so that Gomes could get the lay of the land.

"What investigations?" Rosenberg asked, as though Gomes had just asked to see their drawer full of leprechauns.

With a sigh Gomes said, "Let me see your investigative work papers."

Rosenberg stared blankly. "We don't do investigations."

"Well . . . what do you do here, exactly?"

"We do audits."

"Audits of what?"

Rosenberg shrugged. "Casinos, basically. We make sure they're paying their taxes."

"All right, then, let me see your audit work papers."

"Work papers?"

"For God's sake, show me the paperwork from the last audit you did."

It took nearly half an hour.

The old man reluctantly rifled through pile after pile of papers, finally producing a handful of loose pages.

Dennis Gomes—a man trained at the top accounting firms in the world, a man who was, even at the tender age of twenty-six, accustomed to orderly binders, fully indexed and cross-referenced, with glossaries and tables of contents and footnotes—held the loose pages as though holding a dead cat.

Gomes let out a pained sigh and set the stack of garbage down on the desk.

CHAPTER 2

Gunsmoke

THE BLACK DESERT SKY ABOVE LAS VEGAS PULSED WITH NEON GHOSTS that night. Elvis was on his second encore at the Hilton, and the late-night shift was just kicking into gear along the Strip. But downtown, behind a shaded window, a single high-intensity desk lamp—lost in all of Sin City's flash—burned well past midnight. Sleeves rolled up, his face buried in files, the new division chief of the Gaming Commission's Department of Audit was devouring every shred of intel he could find.

Mug shots, cold-case files, police reports, old court transcripts . . . they all passed before Gomes's bleary, sleep-deprived eyes that night. If David was going to take on Goliath, he would do it systematically. And it all began with study. Gomes was cramming. Before a single pistol would be drawn on a shooting range, before a single raid would be conducted, Gomes would arm himself with knowledge.

Being the trained accountant that he was, Gomes decided that the best way to address his Mob problem would be a two-phase approach. In phase one he would diagnose the problem, and in phase two he would create a division to address the problem. His more venturesome side would get its chance, but before all the high action, he needed the backstory.

———

It all began with Bugsy Siegel's vision of a playground in the desert. The Flamingo Hotel and Casino would be an enormous success. Once people found out about this oasis in the middle of the desert, they would flock to it like greedy sheep. The Flamingo first opened on December 26, 1946, to a dismal turnout. It closed and reopened March 1, 1947, with a debt close to $4 million. In the first couple of months the Flamingo managed to make a meager profit. Unfortunately, it wasn't enough, and Bugsy was laid off gangland style, June 20, 1947. However, within a year the Flamingo's profits skyrocketed to $4 million.

The ultimate success of the Flamingo prompted the Mafia to build more casinos during the late 1940s and '50s on the Las Vegas "Strip," including the Dunes, the Thunderbird, the Sahara, the Riviera, the Tropicana, the Desert Inn, the Stardust, the Sands, the Aladdin, and other large casinos. At this time, the regulation of gaming was extremely lax. Folks in power were more focused on seeing their young city grow than on monitoring what was fueling that growth. As a result, the Mob was able to earn money criminally and transfer that tainted money fairly openly. This early involvement of the Mafia in Vegas was well documented in Nevada's public records, and was considered to be basic common knowledge by many of the city's residents.

Gomes learned that an enormous portion of organized crime—known variously as the Mafia, the Syndicate, *La Cosa Nostra,* or the Mob—was composed of fifteen associated families throughout the major cities in the United States. The principalities were: New York (five families, including New Jersey), Buffalo, Boston (or the entire New England area), Philadelphia, Chicago, St. Louis, Cleveland, Miami (though much of Florida was also controlled by the New York families), New Orleans, and San Francisco / Los Angeles.

Each family had control over the various criminal activities within their respective geographical areas. Additionally, each family was allowed to extend its activities into areas that were not geographically designated as the territory of any particular family. The Mafia considered these locations "open cities." Las Vegas from its birth through the 1970s was the archetypal "open city." At one time or another all of the Mafia families had been engaged in illegal activity in Las Vegas. Much of the criminal action in Vegas was not necessarily individual family operations, but joint ventures sponsored by two or more families. Generally, cash would be "skimmed"— profits underreported, and the unreported excess moved elsewhere—from the casino winnings and then distributed to each respective Mob family in accordance with the number of points it owned in the joint venture.

Gomes had expected the Mob to be involved in Nevada's gaming. During his interview with O'Callaghan, the governor was adamant about hiring a straight arrow to clean out organized crime from the casinos. But Gomes did not expect the Mob to have control over gaming to the degree his probing suggested. The picture that was emerging of Nevada's corrupt foundation was startling. And to make matters worse, the state's law enforcement and regulatory agencies at best seemed to be in a state of denial, and at worst, possibly in on it.

———

"It's not as bad as it looks, Dennis," said Gary Reese, deputy chief of Intelligence and Investigations for the Nevada Gaming Control Board, behind closed doors.

Reese, once a square-jawed deputy for the Clark County Sheriff and now an overweight paper-pusher, betrayed nothing in his level gaze. His office was two hundred square feet of gray—gray carpet, gray cinder block, gray cork ceiling tiles. Even the overhead fluorescent lights looked gray.

"Sure, everybody knows that the Mob is a part of Nevada's history— it's almost quaint, like the Hoover Dam, and cowboys and Indians—but that's ancient history. It's all been cleaned up." Reese was referring to the public story that the creation of a gaming regulatory agency (the Nevada Tax Commission) in the 1950s, and later, the passage of the Gaming Control Act, which replaced the Tax Commission with the Nevada Gaming Commission, had swept the Mafia out of town.

Gomes fidgeted in his chair, which was positioned in front of Reese's desk.

"Look, I know you want to get off on the right foot, Dennis. I respect that. But you've got to keep in mind—we've worked hard to make sure anybody that gets a casino license is a legitimate businessman. Gaming licenses are a privilege, not a right."

Gomes sighed. "It just doesn't add up, Gary."

Reese smiled, and looked as though he was about to end the meeting and send Gomes off with a pat on the back. "Look on the bright side, Dennis; you're going to be tucked away in a comfortable air-conditioned office doing audits. And you're never going to have to get your hands dirty with organized crime."

At this point, Reese rose and came around his desk and ushered Gomes to the door. The two men shook hands. But Gomes paused. "Let me ask you something, Gary."

"Anything."

Gomes looked into the man's eyes. "Would you have a problem if I looked through your intelligence files?"

Reese's smile faltered slightly, his reply coming out in a monotone. "I'm afraid that won't be possible at this time."

"May I ask why?"

"You're not a member of the LEIU." Reese was referring to the Law Enforcement Intelligence Unit. "I'm sorry, Dennis."

"But what if I got—"

"My hands are tied, Dennis." Reese gave him a cold smile. The meeting was over.

On his way out of the building, and all the way back to his office, Dennis Gomes had a gnawing sensation in his gut that things were not as they appeared. Gomes simply wasn't buying what Reese was selling.

⸻

A few days later, in early February 1971, Gomes found himself in a secret meeting with the proverbial "anonymous source"—in this case, a man much older than Gomes, who would confirm all of his suspicions. The two men spoke at a back table in an innocuous diner. The source was a gaming insider who had seen it all.

"Don't let them kid you—the Mob is as much a part of Las Vegas as it ever was."

Gomes looked at the well-traveled face on the other side of the table and wondered what motivation the old man had for arranging this meeting. But he wasn't about to ask. The guy might get spooked.

"I was told that the Gaming Control Board cleaned them out," Gomes countered.

"That's what they want you to think. The state sanctifying the Nevada Gaming Commission only swept everything under the rug."

"Go on."

The man sighed. "The Mob uses 'front men' who appear clean on paper but are nothing more than puppets for the Family."

"I had a feeling." Now it was Gomes's turn to sigh.

"It looks clean to their surface investigations," the man went on, "and that's all that matters to them."

Gomes now had some corroboration that he was sitting on a powder keg. He finished his coffee, thanked the old-timer, and the meeting broke up.

Not only was the Mob problem worse than anticipated, but Dennis Gomes was already starting to rattle people's cages. Simply his appointment as chief of the Audit Division had created turbulence within the other divisions of the Gaming Control Board.

There were whispers that the Enforcement and Investigations divisions had been complaining about his division. Many believed that Gomes's team was only going to get in the way of their license-applicant and criminal investigations. Gomes decided that the best course of action was to assume the worst and mold his division into the solid crime-fighting crew he'd envisioned when he took the job.

—◦—

The Gaming Control Board (GCB) was then—and still is—composed of three divisions: the Audit Division, the Investigations Division, and the Enforcement Division. If the Mob was secretly controlling Nevada's gaming industry, then the Investigations and the Enforcement divisions were not accomplishing their designated duties. Consequently, Gomes needed to learn a whole lot more about his brother divisions within the Gaming Control Board. In this way he could figure out where his division fit in, and how it could be most effective.

As he had done so many times before in his life, Gomes went about the business of educating himself. He learned that the Enforcement Division's sole function was to detect cheating by casinos, and the Investigations Division's only area of concern was the investigation of the backgrounds of applicants for gaming licenses. Gomes also learned that these two divisions of the GCB were almost entirely composed of ex–police officers who had no professional experience in finances or accounting.

During this initial period of building his unit, Gomes also made it his mission to get to know his four agents better. Sam Rosenberg had been an investigator/accountant for the famous New York Mob-busting US Attorney, Robert Morris Morgenthau. A short, crusty, tough, no-nonsense man, Rosenberg was glad to have Gomes leading the team; he was bored doing basic surface audits, and wanted to get into deeper investigations. In fact, Rosenberg was instrumental in the formulation of the division's new investigative procedures.

On the opposite end of the spectrum was Lindsey Jacobson, a practicing Mormon who wanted little to do with anything relating to law enforcement. At the sheer mention of the Mob, one could see the man shake. He was, however, a great auditor. Gomes knew that his thoroughness would be an asset to the division.

Soon, Gomes had figured out how his division would have to operate to be successful and remain viable. His task would be to uncover and prevent the Mafia from holding any "hidden" interests in Nevada's casinos, and the only way to accomplish this would be to follow a menacingly guarded paper trail. Consequently, he would need a group of highly trained hybrid agents who paired extensive accounting or financial knowledge with an equally developed law enforcement ability.

Gomes eventually went to chairman of the GCB, Phil Hannifin, with a report of his findings, along with a formal request for the authorization to hire more agents. Despite the protests from the Enforcement and Investigations divisions, Hannifin was in full support of the direction Gomes was taking—a new species of investigator for the Gaming Control Board, the accountant cop—an homage to the Treasury Department agents that brought down Al Capone in 1931.

—◆—

"Are you comfortable carrying and using a gun?" Gomes asked the fifty-seventh applicant, a milquetoast type with thick spectacles, sitting across the desk from him.

The man blanched. He looked like he'd just been told he needed to parachute out of a plane. "Well, to be honest . . . a gun? No. No, sir. I had assumed . . . I mean, well, I had hoped that I'd just be doing audits."

Gomes smiled politely, thanked the man for coming in, and crossed his name off the list.

Another applicant, a stocky, athletic individual with long sideburns: "Oh, yeah, you bet your ass I'll pack heat for you."

"Okay, hold on—"

"I'm a big gun guy," the man continued. "Pretty deadly with the iron, to tell you the truth."

"Okay, calm down—"

"What kind of piece are we talking? Three fifty-seven? Forty-four magnum? Something smaller? I can get you a great deal on—"

"Thanks," Gomes interrupted. "We'll give you a call if we need you. I appreciate you coming in."

Another name scratched off the list.

———

Gomes had to come to grips with the reality that in many cases, the stereotypes of the accountant and the cop were apt. Accountants were apples and lawmen were oranges. He kept at the hiring process, though, over the course of several weeks. In short, if the applicant was comfortable with a gun but not excited about it, Gomes would continue with the interview. A finance or accounting background was a requirement, and any law or law enforcement experience was a major boon. This was how Gomes found Dick Law.

A certified public accountant and a lawyer, Law was a levelheaded gentleman with a stable family life. When Gomes asked him if he would be comfortable carrying a gun, he replied, "If that's what is required, sure—I have no problem with carrying a gun. It doesn't really matter one way or another to me."

If applicants made it this far, Gomes would finish the interview by setting them up in an empty office with a pencil and paper, then ask them to write a justification for their moral values.

Gomes did this for a number of reasons. First, it allowed him to gauge how well an applicant organized his or her ideas—how logical he or she would be in conducting investigations. It was also a way for him to learn about their core values. Gomes didn't hire anyone who was superficial in his or her response. If an applicant wrote, "My ethics are based on the Ten Commandments," Gomes read, "I only do what I am told and I don't think for myself"—and they were out.

Gomes threw out a lot of applicants, but he was also beginning to hire some impressive agents, like Duane Noyes. Noyes was a former FBI agent with a specialization in intelligence gathering. He was a buttoned-down, well-groomed, handsome, sophisticated sort. Above all, Noyes filled an important position that Gomes was looking for. Based on his brief experience with the head of "Intelligence," Gary Reese, Gomes predicted that it would be difficult to gain access to the Investigations Division's intelligence files. Reese had essentially shut the door. Accordingly, Gomes had hoped to find someone who would be capable of helping him establish an intelligence unit within his own division. Noyes fit the bill perfectly, and assured Gomes that he would be able to create an intelligence unit that would eclipse the Investigations Division.

Gomes was going to need this kind of man.

—————

As the days passed, this unprecedented team of hard-nosed, iron-nerved number-crunchers was starting to coalesce. And others were taking notice, but not all were responding with praise. The Investigations and Enforcement divisions didn't believe that Gomes's unit needed any law enforcement expertise; they felt that the role of Gomes's division should be limited to conducting audits. A much harsher criticism came from Gomes's own household.

"Dennis, what's wrong with being a CPA?" Linda asked through her tears one night after Gomes had dragged himself in at 11:00 p.m. after working another brutal day. "You could make so much more money. Why are you doing this to me?"

"I don't want to be an accountant. I hate accounting, and I'm miserable when I have to do anything related to it."

"You're being selfish. You have a family to take care of."

"You're not working. I'm still supporting you."

Linda looked at him for a moment, then let out a shriek and reached for a glass pitcher, hurling it at Gomes.

Gomes ducked. The pitcher shattered against the wall.

Gomes straightened back up and just stared at his wife. He was accustomed to these outbursts—even somewhat sympathetic. Linda's mother had abandoned her and her sister at a very young age. Linda was raised in an orphanage and really didn't have anyone but him, which made Gomes cut her a lot of slack in arguments.

On this night, he just walked away, shaking his head.

It didn't take long for Gomes and his men to impress Gaming Control Board chairman Phil Hannifin. Based on the preliminary investigative work of the Audit Division, Hannifin ordered the Investigations Division to hand over the financial aspects of all gaming licensing applicant investigations to Gomes's unit. This meant that Gomes and his team would take over the tasks previously handled by the Investigations Division: conducting background checks on all applicants, and tracking the source of the funding, the applicant's business relationships, business dealings, and asset holdings. Gomes realized that the Investigations Division was fighting a losing battle against the onslaught of hidden interests—a bunch of bureaucrats fighting a plague of locusts with fly swatters.

In fact, Gomes learned that the Investigations Division's idea of tracing the source of potential investment funds in any casino was to send a request to the potential investor's bank in order to find out whether or not the money was there. If the money was there, the Investigations Division would approve the applicant and confirm that they had checked out the source of funds. Gomes knew that this method was a charade. In order to truly check the legitimacy of the source of the investment, the real origins of the funds had to be tracked and identified.

Within weeks of taking control of the financial aspects of applicant investigations, Gomes's team began identifying corrupt funds and denying applicants that would have been easily approved under the former procedures of the Investigations Division. One such instance is the Audit Division's investigation of Alvin Malnik, and the subsequent ban on business dealings they instituted between Malnik and Caesars World, Inc.

This did not sit well with the higher-ups at the Investigations Division. But, how could it? The "bean counters" were making these cops look incompetent. So, when word came down from above that all divisions of the GCB, including Gomes's, would be going to POST school (Peace Officer Standards and Training) in order to become licensed to carry a weapon and make arrests, the Investigations Division erupted in protest.

"How could you let a bunch of snot-nosed fucking accountants run around with guns?" the chief of the Investigations Division complained to Hannifin. "They'll shoot off their own goddamn feet, and maybe ours, too."

But Hannifin, who had already seen results from the Audit Division that greatly outpaced his expectations, stood his ground; all three divisions were to attend POST school. The taunts continued, and moved from behind Gomes's back to straight to his face: "The only lead you should be shooting is out of a pencil."

—◦—

Gomes would spend half of his day working on building up the Audit Division and the other half at POST training. The three divisions of the Gaming Control Board learned the rules of evidence gathering and crime-scene processing, criminal law (including Mirandizing), surveillance techniques, personal safety / self-defense, traffic stops, automobile accident investigation, how to process an arrest, conducting raids, ambush strategy, and finally, weapons training. The instructors were from the sheriff's department and the FBI.

Gomes and his agents impressed the instructors right away by acing the written exams. However, the bean counters were still forced to deal with the continued, unrelenting slew of taunts from the other two divisions.

—◦—

"Raise your weapons! Ready!" the firing range instructor ordered.

Gomes was indeed ready, his finger poised on the trigger of his "snubby"—the Chief's Special—a five-shot, J-frame .38 caliber Smith & Wesson. Gomes had unusually large hands for his five-foot-ten-inch frame, and had to have a special grip adapter installed. Now his gun was perfection. It was light and accurate for a two-inch barrel, with all the power of something bigger, especially with the hollow-point magnum loads he used. This meant that he could easily conceal it, but not lose any power.

The weather was beautiful that day out at the desert firing range. The sun was high and bright, and the wind was light. Cathedrals of hillocks and buttes scraped the distant horizon, and the scent of juniper carried on the breeze. Visibility was excellent.

Gomes, his agents, and the other divisions were all lined up in a big row on the scabrous vacant lot that had been converted into an outdoor range. There were close to thirty agents facing the black silhouettes on white paper. Gomes and his crew weren't used to these official settings—they felt awkward in their Gaming Control Board hats, sunglasses, and noise-canceling headphones.

That day, in line with all of those agents, Gomes was nervous. *What if my guys lose their accuracy in this setting?* he thought.

"Raise your weapons!" the instructor boomed. "Ready ... aim ..."

"Stop—stop! I can't shoot!" yelled an agent down the line.

"Lower your weapons. Stand down," the instructor ordered. Everyone lowered their weapons. The instructor walked over to the complaining agent.

"What the fuck is wrong?" the instructor asked the complainer, James Chaney, a handsome young black agent from the Enforcement Division. Gomes knew Chaney casually and liked him. Chaney was the only regular agent who had no objection to accountants packing heat. He was also a joker.

"All the targets are black. I can't shoot," Chaney said.

He has a point, Gomes thought, chuckling to himself.

"Come with me," said the instructor.

Chaney was taken into a white shed behind them. Gomes could hear the men rummaging around. He glanced down at his hands and noticed that his knuckles had turned completely white. Stretching his fingers, then hands, he felt that unwelcome knot in his gut followed by the familiar rumbling. *This is the last thing I need right now*, he thought. Gomes did not exactly have a stomach of steel, and stressful situations usually required a visit to the porcelain throne. He looked around; the only bathrooms were a fifteen-minute walk back to the main building. His stomach rumbled again. *What is taking them so long? Shit!*

Finally, Gomes heard the voices echoing from the shed: "Will this work? Can you shoot this fucking thing?"

"Yeah, that's perfect."

The instructor, a short, round, grumpy old guy, emerged from the shed, trudged across the line of fire, hung up the new target, a white silhouette against a black background, and returned to his outpost.

Gomes tightened his grip and closed his eyes; he focused his mind on the target and imagined his bullets striking in a tight cluster.

"Raise your weapons!"

Gomes opened his eyes.

"Ready! Fire!"

The guns went off in unison. The firing lasted for about twenty seconds, leaving the range covered in a veil of smoke.

The smell of gunpowder clouding his senses, Gomes narrowed his eyes and anxiously tried to get a look at the targets. A moment later a light breeze danced across the firing line, revealing the targets. There was silence . . . then the range erupted in laughter, only this time it was Gomes and the Audit Division agents who were laughing.

Their targets had compact, perfect hits. From what Gomes could tell, the other divisions' agents had barely hit their marks, if they'd hit them at all. Once the scores were official, the Enforcement and Investigations divisions' accuracy rate was farcical compared to the elite scores of the "bean counters." And everyone knew it.

As it turned out, even the criminals would soon know it.

CHAPTER 3

Whispers

"SCREW THAT ASSHOLE—I'M GOING TO GET MY HANDS ON THE intelligence one way or another," Gomes told Agent Duane Noyes on a cold March afternoon in 1971.

Noyes, a former FBI intelligence officer, and one of Gomes's right-hand men, was having lunch with Gomes at a diner away from the Strip, frequented by off-duty cops and legal types from downtown. The place was an old-school Naugahyde dive, with banquettes and pictures of poker-playing bulldogs.

"Why don't you just join the LEIU?" Noyes suggested, referring to the Law Enforcement Intelligence Unit that Gary Reese repeatedly cited as the reason he was keeping files away from Gomes's "prying" eyes. "There's a convention coming up in Oakland. I'll take care of the application; then you can go to the convention and become an official member."

"I don't know."

"Look, I'm already a member of the organization of Former FBI Special Agents," Noyes proffered. "With those two associations we'll have access to any intelligence you could possibly need. I'll be able to put together an intelligence unit that will make Gary's files look like nothing more than the Clark County phone book."

Gomes liked this idea.

The next day, he easily sold Gaming Control Board chairman Phil Hannifin on it. But Gomes was taken aback when his boss decided to send both Gomes *and* Gary Reese to the convention. *I can put up with this asshole for a week or so,* Gomes assured himself.

The convention wasn't until April 1971, so Gomes had time to tie up some loose ends.

———

One of the major functions of the Audit Division was to conduct standard audits of each casino. Gomes knew that the routine financial examinations typically turned up very little. Criminal involvement had been taken "off the books" in the 1950s and early '60s, and there was now no written record of hidden interests and skimming. Nevertheless, there was a statutory requirement that Gomes's team had to perform at least *some* audits.

While Gomes was waiting for the LEIU convention, he turned his focus to surveillance. He devised three main components to his surveillance program: surprise raids, undercover observations, and the development of a network of informants. During surprise raids the Audit Division agents would spontaneously show up to monitor the procedures in the various casino count rooms, to make sure that all money was being accounted for, and that the proper conduct was being followed. There was danger and volatility in these raids, and Gomes and his men knew it.

In a coordinated undercover observation, the agents would disguise themselves as low-level gamblers or tourists in a casino, anything to blend in, and they would watch the action, taking mental snapshots of anyone or anything that seemed suspicious or out of place. Gomes became obsessed with this activity, and although he would sometimes engage in it with other agents, he felt more comfortable by himself. Personal surveillance could begin at night and continue until dawn, with Gomes roaming the casinos where organized criminal activity was suspected, surreptitiously listening to the conversations of executives and others, secretly observing procedures designed to prevent skimming.

In an effort to conceal his identity, Gomes regularly changed his appearance. At first, he dressed like the typical tourist, wearing a pair of shorts and one of those cheap Las Vegas T-shirts they sold at the airport, or any five-and-dime. Later, as his public profile became more familiar to outsiders, he would become more extreme in his physical transformations. He sported a mustache and let his hair grow out. He became a chameleon, adapting to the tawdry dress codes of the back rooms into which he would soon insinuate himself.

— ⁓ —

"Gomes, take out your pad and listen up. I have an assignment for you," Hannifin announced one morning after calling the young section chief down to the corner office.

"The SEC wants to go after Dell Webb for slipping cash and comps to hookers in exchange for cozy encounters with their casino customers. You follow me so far?" Dell Webb was a publicly traded casino company, and the US Securities and Exchange Commission had become quite suspicious of their activities as of late.

Gomes struggled to mask his excitement at getting his first official assignment. His Florsheims tapped under the table. "I'm with you so far."

"The Gaming Control Board wants us to nose around, see how widespread the activity is."

"Got it," he said, furiously scrawling notes.

"I want you to look into it."

"Got it."

Hannifin smiled at the twenty-seven-year-old eager beaver. "Now get to work."

— ⁓ —

The development of a network of informants was a long and complex process, but one at which Gomes would excel. In the beginning it simply consisted of talking to various casino employees, feeling them out, befriending the ones with potential, and then listening. An informant could be anyone from a low-level worker to a Mob associate, and everyone in between.

A gentleman we'll call Frank* was a legitimate, hardworking, sixty-something Italian American from New York. He had moved to Las Vegas in his twenties to pursue a musical career. He'd been luckier than most, finding work as a drummer in a successful lounge act that played

---

* Pseudonym

almost all of the casinos. But then middle age set in, bringing with it a shiny, bald head and a round belly. His band was pushed out by the slew of hungry young lounge acts that settled in the growing desert valley on a daily basis.

It was only a matter of time before Frank was forced to trade in his drumsticks for playing cards. He got his start at the blackjack tables, dealing cards to the drunk and the desperate. Eventually, Frank would work his way up to pit boss. He had been around town for a while, seen a lot, and he knew how things worked.

Frank liked Gomes and had no problem telling him what he knew. He didn't mind helping out—as long as no one would ever find out. No Italian from New York ever wanted the reputation as a snitch. Plus, he had friends back home that looked down on this sort of thing.

Early one morning, after Frank's graveyard shift, Gomes met him for coffee at a small Winchell's donut shop way off the Strip, nowhere near downtown. The place smelled of fresh pastries, cheap coffee, and last night's smokes. They took up a corner booth away from the windows.

"So, Frank . . . what do you know about casinos providing their big players with prostitutes?"

Frank took a deep pull on his Pall Mall. "Dennis, are you kidding me? A blind man could see what's going on. Every casino keeps a stock of hookers on hand."

"And the casinos pay them for their customers?"

"Yeah . . . absolutely."

"How do you know that? We've checked numerous cage records and haven't found any evidence of payment."

"The execs handle it."

Gomes nodded.

Frank added, "But I don't know where they pull the money from."

Gomes smiled. He had his first nugget of intel. He thanked Frank, paid for his donut and coffee, and left.

———

It was a brisk early March morning and Gomes was back in his office by 9:00 a.m. As soon as the rest of his agents filtered in, he called an impromptu team debriefing in the fluorescent-lit conference room. He wasted no time getting to the point.

"We need to get the prostitutes to tell us how they are getting paid," he told his troops.

"Have you ever dealt with a tramp?" scoffed Agent Rich Iannone. "C'mon, Dennis, hookers aren't going to give up this information."

Gomes had hired Rich Iannone because he was at least six and a half feet tall, and big all around. He had a full mustache and beard accompanied by a baritone voice. He didn't have any law enforcement experience, but his accounting background, master's degree, and sheer size was enough for Gomes to want him on his team. Gomes figured Iannone could easily be trained as a cop. The man also had a wicked sense of humor. When Gomes and Iannone were in meetings together, it was difficult to keep things serious.

"No, Rich, I have not dealt with hookers before," Gomes admitted. "And I hope you're not confessing your secret extracurricular activities to us. Are you?"

The room was overtaken by laughter.

"Ha ha, very funny. Touché, Gomes. No, I haven't personally dealt with any hookers, but I knew this guy in grad school who had a hooker pull a knife on him. Twice. They're not exactly a high-quality group of people."

Gomes and the Audit Division agents enjoyed their work; they had fun, they cracked jokes, but they all believed that their work was making a contribution to their community. Most importantly, when it was time to get serious, they did.

"Everyone will have a partner," Gomes explained. "Only one of you will have to deal with the prostitute. The other will be a witness and make sure that once you've flipped your hooker, she knows that the other agent is watching everything. Dick, you'll be my partner."

Dick Law was perhaps the only perfectly logical and pragmatic genius Gomes had ever met. One might consider Law a walking model of fidelity. He was very handsome, even with his bushy mustache, and could have had any girl he wanted. Yet, he was intensely dedicated to his lovely wife, who was legally blind and completely dependent on him. Gomes liked working with Law, because the man was so thorough, almost to the point of obsessiveness.

At length, the rest of the agents partnered up and they picked their casinos. Each pair would have two casinos to target over the next three days. Gomes wanted to have this investigation wrapped up before the end of March.

That night, Gomes and Law drove separate cars to the Aladdin, one of the gaudier, newer casinos near the south end of the Strip. Gomes walked into the casino bar a few minutes after 9:00 p.m., and Law arrived a little less than an hour later. Gomes immediately noticed four women whom he identified as prostitutes, and a fifth he suspected. He made small talk with the bartender, drank a Budweiser, and spread tip money around to attract some attention. A short while later, his eyes were drawn to a middle-aged man wearing a light blue suit and an ill-fitting toupee who was walking over to two of the suspected working girls. It appeared that the girls were arguing about something, and then one of them walked off just behind the suited man.

The other girl walked up to the bar by Gomes, sat down, and ordered a glass of rosé. Of all the girls Gomes could have landed, it had to be this one. She was an Amazon, probably standing close to six feet tall when barefoot, and true to hooker style, she was wearing six-inch heels. She was squeezed into a very tight, very short, purple dress, which left little to the imagination. She had exotic angular features. In another life she could have been a model, but years of hard living had taken a toll on her skin and her teeth. She was obviously past her prime, even for a hooker. She smelled of stale cigarettes and Shalimar—a perfume with which Gomes was all too familiar. It was his wife Linda's favorite.

Gomes was having second thoughts. The lady looked at him, he smiled, then looked down. *I can't do this. What was I thinking?*

"Hey, sweetie," she purred.

Oh God, what do I say . . . what do I say? He was panicking, and hoped it didn't show. "Hello," he replied.

"What brings you out tonight?" she asked.

"I just didn't want to go straight home after work."

"Oh, so a little partying?" She laughed and brushed his chest with her crimson-studded, tar-stained hand.

He looked up at her with one eyebrow slightly raised. "Yeah, I guess you could put it that way."

"You got something specific in mind, baby?" she asked.

"Maybe. What are my options?" Gomes managed a smile. *What are my options,* he thought. *How obvious can I be? She's going to make me.* The panic was returning. He grabbed his beer so that she wouldn't notice his sweat-dampened hands.

"Baby, for the right price I could make your wildest dreams come true." This was said with the wink of one sunken eye.

The bartender walked over. "Everything okay?" He looked directly at Gomes. He was probably worried that this kid needed saving. Gomes nodded his head and waited for him to leave. "All I have is fifty bucks," Gomes informed the woman.

"Well, I can certainly do a little something for that. Do you have someplace we can go?"

"I have my car; we can drive back onto Industrial." He figured she'd know what he was talking about. Industrial Road ran parallel to the west of the Strip, and was mainly occupied by gentlemen's clubs and dark bars.

She nodded in agreement and they walked out together. The woman towered over Gomes. He knew the sight of them would attract attention. He was twenty-seven years old, but looked four or five years younger. At five-foot-ten and 155 pounds, he was not exactly an imposing figure, especially next to a haggard six-foot-tall whore in a three-inch skirt. Gomes made sure to keep his head down in hopes that no one would notice him.

They walked out to his car; he opened the passenger-side door for her and then got into the driver's seat. He couldn't bear to keep up this act any longer, and immediately flashed his badge.

"Oh fuck . . . you piece a shit—you tricked me! What are you gonna do, asshole? I'm leaving. I didn't do nothin'."

She turned to leave but Agent Law was blocking her door with his badge out.

"Fuck you, kid!" she yelled. "You ain't got nothin' on me."

"Look, you can either cooperate, or we'll take you in and book you on prostitution charges," Gomes said calmly. By this time Agent Law had gotten into the backseat.

"Fuck. Cooperate? Cooperate with what? I told Mack I wasn't doin' any shit for free anymore."

Gomes was aghast. "What?! No! We just have a few questions. If you answer them, we'll let you go. We'll keep your identity completely confidential. No one will know that you talked to us."

"Fine, but my pimp better not find out 'bout this, so you gonna need to give me that money."

There was a part of Gomes that felt bad for her, so he gave her the fifty bucks. Gomes had obtained the money from an undercover fund that the State provided him for situations like this. It would turn out to be money well spent.

Once the prostitute got her money and knew she wasn't going to get arrested, she answered all of Gomes's questions with more detail and enthusiasm than he could have hoped for. She told Gomes exactly how the Aladdin paid the working girls for their services. She also gave him the names of the management that ran this operation, and the methods some of the other casinos were using to pay their "girls." She also provided Gomes with some information that he was not prepared for: The Las Vegas Metropolitan Police Department (known as Metro) was overrun by crooked cops.

——⌣——

Hannifin was ecstatic when Gomes turned in his report. The GCB immediately took official action on a very quiet, behind-the-scenes basis, with no publicity. Gomes also mentioned the claim the prostitute had made about Metro, to which Hannifin replied, "Gomes, it's a problem, but it's not our problem. Just keep your distance and let them clean up their own messes."

——⌣——

Gomes had been so busy that he had forgotten about the LEIU convention, and it snuck up on him. Linda was upset that he would be gone for a week, leaving her alone with their two children, and he didn't get much sleep the night before their departure.

During the past few months, Gomes had been out in the field, and loving it. He was not looking forward to spending the next week at a buttoned-up conference, sporting a little stick-on nametag. He really was not looking forward to spending all of this time with Gary Reese, the chief of the Investigations Division, and the self-appointed "supreme ruler" of the GCB's intelligence files.

When Gomes had first met Gary Reese, he remembered, the man seemed to be a jolly, fat old guy who wanted to "help [Gomes] out in any way possible." It hadn't taken Gomes long to see through this facade. Now the sight of Reese disgusted him—his triple chin, his thin, stringy, greasy, gray hair, and the dried-up wads of saliva in the corners of his mouth.

When Gomes arrived at the airport, he found Reese, who quickly said, "Dennis, I can't believe that Hannifin is making you go to this shit. It's such a waste of time for you. I only have to put up with it to maintain my LEIU status for the division. But that really doesn't mean anything for you. I don't see how this will help you with your audits."

"I'm actually looking forward to it," Gomes said. "Having access to these intelligence files will help me with my investigations."

"Look, kid, you're an accountant. You got brains. You should stick to the books and let us cops handle the dirty work. I care about you, Gomes. You're young, and you got a pretty little wifey at home. I would hate to see you get hurt, because you're caught up playing cops and robbers."

Gomes hated being called "kid," and he knew that the only thing Gary Reese was really worried about was that Gomes would expose him as a lazy and inept agent. During POST training, Gomes had learned that a common characteristic of the older ex-cops in the Investigations and Enforcement divisions was their innate jealousy of young up-and-comers. As a group they hated the idea of an energized rookie making them look bad, or forcing them to actually work. Reese sat at the top of this lowly bunch. Now Gomes not only had to spend the next five days with him, but due to budget constraints, they also had to share a hotel room.

The only comfort was the LEIU tag being waved like a carrot in front of him.

It was a supreme challenge for Gomes to maintain his composure around Reese for five days. They sat together in long, tedious classes about "link analysis," "deductive investigation techniques," and other topics while Reese snored in the back of the room. Gomes had to marshal every ounce of willpower he had to keep his disgust to himself.

On the last night of the conference, Gomes stayed out having drinks with a few of the detectives from Chicago. He wanted to make sure that Reese was asleep before he went back to the room he shared with the man. The detectives told Gomes all about Tony "The Ant" Spilotro, a violent enforcer for the Chicago crime family who had recently taken up residence in Vegas. They suspected Spilotro, along with mafiosi Mad Sam DeStefano, Mario DeStefano, and Chuckie Crimaldi, in the 1963 murder of Leo Foreman. The Chicago detectives used the Leo Foreman murder to paint a vivid picture of Spilotro for Gomes. This psychotic crew had beaten Foreman with a hammer, then tied him up and tortured him for days. They used an ice pick to repeatedly stab Foreman, then shot him in the buttocks with a .22, and finally finished the job with a rusty butcher knife that they used to carve large hunks of flesh out of his thighs.

This was just *one* of the torture-murders for which Spilotro was suspected.

Gomes returned to his room just after 11:00 p.m. with a notepad full of information. He was mentally exhausted, but more so repulsed by the thought of such a gruesome thug living in his town. Gomes had learned a lot during the convention—almost more than he'd wanted to—but at this moment, all he wanted to do was go to sleep, which would have been easy if Gary Reese hadn't been snoring like a chain saw.

As usual, Gomes gave a preemptory yell and Reese snorted and stopped. But it wouldn't take long for him to start snoring again within minutes. Gomes couldn't take it any longer; he was at his breaking point. So, he took his pillow and twisted the open end of the pillowcase until it became a long handle and the pillow was condensed down to a hard dense ball at the closed end of the pillowcase. As soon as Reese started snoring again, Gomes took his homemade flail and swung. He whacked Reese right in the face, hard. His months of frustrations triggered him to strike with much more force and enthusiasm than he should have, and Reese's head got pounded into the mattress. In the flash of an eye, Gomes covered his homemade hammer with his blanket, laid his head back down, and pretended to be asleep.

Reese sat right up, snorting and coughing and stammering, "Who's there? What's going on?!"

Through the slit of one eye, Gomes quietly watched Reese sputter and look around the room. Reese eventually lay back down and did not snore again for the rest of the night. Gomes got his first good night's sleep—maybe more from the satisfaction of long-overdue retribution than from lack of noise.

CHAPTER 4

The Cookie Jar

A COUPLE WEEKS AFTER GOMES RETURNED TO LAS VEGAS FROM THE LEIU conference, Gaming Control Board chairman Phil Hannifin presented him with his second assignment as division chief in May 1971.

The Enforcement Division had received information that a small casino operation in northern Nevada, Zimba's Casino, was involved in some illicit activity. Now it would be up to Gomes to run it down.

"Don't worry, we'll get the job done," Gomes assured his boss. "But can I ask you a question? If the Enforcement Division received the intel, why are you giving this to me?"

"We all agreed that this is going to require agents with a high degree of financial aptitude."

"And they don't mind?"

Hannifin then shot Gomes a sidelong glance. "Don't tell me you're questioning my decision."

"No, definitely not," Gomes backpedaled.

"Then go—and don't screw this up."

⊷

Zimba's was a small, inconsequential casino, but Gomes still considered this takedown his first truly meaningful sting. A first chance for him to use his abilities as an accountant and a cop at the same time, further validating the existence of his division. He suspected that his being assigned this duty had ruffled some feathers.

There was no specific information that could confirm Gomes's suspicions, but he instinctively knew that the Enforcement Division had been ordered to hand this case over to his division, and that they would never have done so of their own volition.

However the Zimba's assignment had reached the Audit Division, Gomes was happy to have it. He spent the rest of the week poring over the Zimba's case file. The Enforcement Division's intelligence basically boiled down to a discrepancy between the volume of business in the poker room and the reported revenue. It was interesting, but inconclusive intel. So Gomes would have to conduct his own surveillance prior to doing any sort of raid. This meant hours of waiting and watching.

As any cop knows, surveillance is both boring and intense. Gomes needed his best guys with him on this job, guys who could handle extreme stress. Staying sharp while waiting for something to happen requires unshakable nerves in order to remain inconspicuous while looking for the opportunity to strike.

This case was meaningful to Gomes outside the Gaming Control Board. Catching the owners skimming funds from a casino—which was a felony—would be the first time any state police or investigative agency had ever been able to make such a case against a Nevada licensee. Gomes was convinced that such an accomplishment would be a prelude to much bigger and more dangerous missions. With this in mind, he decided that Rich Iannone, Dick Law, and Sam Rosenberg would be the key guys to join him on this case. They would make the quick flight from Vegas to Reno on Tuesday; beyond that, there wasn't much planning Gomes could do.

Gomes waited until the Sunday night before his Tuesday flight to tell Linda that he had to go out of town again, and he planned accordingly. His parents had given him two tickets to see the Folies Bergere show at the Tropicana. Linda was looking forward to this evening together, so he hoped she wouldn't get too angry.

They had dinner at the Peppermill, a twenty-four-hour coffee shop located on Las Vegas Boulevard, right in the middle of the Strip. They sat at a table for two by one of the large windows. Neon lights in every shade of pink and blue darted across the ceiling, framing a series of massive fake cherry trees. Linda didn't say much during dinner that night.

After they finished eating, they had a drink in the Fireside Lounge, a back room of the Peppermill. As bright and festive as the dining room was, the Fireside Lounge was dark and mellow, but no less over the top. In the center of the room was a flaming pool, and there was always at least one couple brazenly kissing and fondling one another.

Gomes and Linda found two seats right by the fire-pit fountain. He tried to pull Linda close to him, but she complained, "Let go; I can't drink like that."

"What's wrong with you?" Gomes questioned her. "Did I do something to make you mad?"

"No, I'm fine."

"I have to go out of town again in a couple of days."

"Whatever . . . You're never here anyway."

The rest of that night Gomes tried to talk to her, tried to get back on track, but she remained cold and quiet.

By the time they got to the Tropicana, Gomes wasn't particularly looking forward to seeing the Folies Bergere. But he knew Linda wanted to see the show, and watching topless showgirls wasn't a bad way to spend a night. They arrived just as the show was starting. They had great seats, a booth, front and center. The music started, the showgirls glided out in their G-strings and massive headdresses.

He turned to Linda and whispered, "How do you think they walk with those hat contraptions on?"

She ignored him.

Gomes concentrated on the show. Some of the headdresses went up at least two feet in the air and then trailed all the way down to the floor. There were feathers, jewels, legs, and breasts everywhere. Gomes loved it.

Then, the number changed and the music became slow and soft. Gomes recognized the song—Ravel's *Boléro*. The most beautiful of all the dancers slinked out from stage left and met two male dancers at center stage. Every one of her movements was fluid, ethereal, and graceful. She would effortlessly lift her leg and it would almost hit her ear. A male dancer would pick her up and spin her with one arm, then throw her to the other male dancer. It didn't seem possible. Even more beautiful was how obvious it was that she loved what she was doing. Her passion was palpable.

As he watched in amazement, a wave of sadness washed over Gomes. He suddenly realized that he had been in an unhappy marriage with Linda since he was nineteen years old. Their passion, which had once burned hotter than the flame back at the Fireside Lounge, was now a thing of the past. His eyes still fixed on the dancer, he thought, *I will never be with a woman like that*. He looked at Linda and wondered what she was thinking.

The rest of the show seemed to last forever, almost as if it was taunting him. After the performance was over and they had each finished their drinks, Gomes and Linda headed straight home.

The ride was quiet.

"Did you like the show?" Gomes asked, finally.

"Yes," she replied.

That was the end of their conversation for the night.

—◆—

Gomes spent Monday preparing and packing everything he would need for the Zimba's trip. Shortly after dawn the following morning, Gomes, Iannone, Law, and Rosenberg left for the airport in an unmarked state car.

They had two rooms reserved at a small motel, walking distance to Zimba's Casino. Gomes, however, would stay with his best friend from college, Larry Clark, who had returned from Vietnam a few years earlier and was finishing his master's degree at the University of Nevada, Reno. Larry had a pullout couch that Gomes could sleep on. Although it wasn't fancy, or especially comfortable, the privacy made it ideal.

Gomes instructed the team to arrive at Zimba's Casino between 8:00 and 9:00 p.m., and to make sure to stagger their arrival times. Iannone was to focus on the slot operations; Law would concentrate on cage operations; Rosenberg's role was to check out the table games; and Gomes would keep an eye on the poker room and overall casino operations.

They parted ways, and Gomes drove to Larry's apartment.

"Larry, you look tired," was the first thing Gomes said to him.

"You know how grad school and exams are," Larry replied wearily.

"Yeah, but I had two kids and I was working to support them when I was getting my master's degree," Gomes teased him with a grin. "It's just you and your wife, and it looks like she's taking pretty good care of you."

"I definitely can't complain. Charlene is great."

"Then why do you look like shit?"

Larry told Gomes about his nightmares—how they brought him back to the war—especially a particular incident where a fellow soldier had panicked, run, and been gunned down.

"Have you talked to Charlene about this?"

"Sure, some; she tries to understand, but it's hard."

Charlene was working as a dealer at Harrah's to support Larry while he earned his degree. She was extremely attractive and quick to laugh at a joke, but also a tough, get-your-hands-dirty sort of woman who could mix it up with the guys.

"Have you talked to anyone else?" Gomes asked.

"Yeah ... I mean, pretty much anyone who was there has nightmares. I'm lucky. Some of the guys are barely able to function."

"Can you take anything?"

"No. There's no drug to stop dreams," Larry said with a sigh.

Not knowing how to respond, Gomes quickly changed the subject. "Do you have a lot of work tonight? Why don't you come with me to do surveillance at Zimba's? You'll help me blend in."

"All right, but if you want to blend in at Zimba's, you'll need to dress like a logger."

———

Dennis Gomes and Larry Clark donned their oldest blue jeans. Clark found a flannel shirt that he let Gomes borrow. While Clark was a few inches shorter than Gomes, they were built similarly, fit and trim. A Golden Gloves champion lightweight boxer in college, Clark had been a professional boxer as well; he'd held the North American championship belt, and had been ranked one of the top boxers in the world.

They walked into Zimba's just after 9:00 p.m. The casino consisted of about five hundred slot machines, a pit of fifteen tables, a center bar, a poker room with ten tables, and a coffee shop. Not exactly the gambling palaces that Gomes was accustomed to patrolling on the Strip. A haze of smoke hung just above the slot machines, turning the flashing lights into a dizzying array of melting colors. There was a slow, drawn-out country song playing on the sound system.

Gomes saw Iannone playing a slot machine close to the casino cage. He noticed Law at the center bar, nursing a beer, with a clear view of the cage. He soon caught a glimpse of Rosenberg at the blackjack table. Gomes and Clark decided to head to the coffee shop and grab a bite to eat. They chose a table with a good view of the poker room, and Gomes paid close attention to who was going in and out.

The clientele at Zimba's was just as Clark had described it. They all looked like lumberjacks, miners, or bikers, with the exception of a small group of men who kept moving between the poker room and the bar. These guys were dressed in leisure suits and butterfly-collared shirts. They weren't doing anything wrong; they just seemed out of place. Just enough to get Gomes's attention.

In Reno, Nevada, "The Biggest Little City in the World," there were many things that seemed out of place—just like the city itself. Gomes loved the way the crystal-clear alpine water of Lake Tahoe reflected the grand coniferous forest and jagged Sierra Mountains. To him, it all seemed like one of nature's most beautiful masterpieces. His parents used to take him and his three brothers here from California during the summers for camping trips. These had always been some of Gomes's fondest memories.

Seeing this beauty now, interrupted by the cold steel and electricity-gobbling neon city, it seemed to him like a crime against nature. At least Las Vegas was bordered by the emptiness of the desert. Zimba's was the ultimate blemish.

Gomes had a good view of the poker room and bar from where he was sitting, but he couldn't see the table games.

"Larry, keep your eye on the cage," Gomes said under his breath. "And tell me if they begin to collect the drop boxes."

The "drop box" is where the winnings from a particular table are collected and stored. Casinos usually collect the drop boxes late at night or early in the morning, so that the money from the busiest time in a casino—evening to early morning—can be accounted for promptly.

"What exactly are you looking for?" Clark asked.

"Nothing in particular." Gomes looked around casually. "Just anything that doesn't seem right."

"Have you seen anything that doesn't seem right?"

"Not really."

"If you're not looking for anything in particular, then why are we here?"

"Larry, stop talking."

"I'm just saying, I don't know what to look for."

"Use common sense. You've spent time in casinos."

After a tense moment, Clark asked, "How long are we going to be here?"

Gomes was starting to realize that bringing his friend along had been a mistake. Combining surveillance and socializing is just about impossible. But here they were, and he had to make the best of the situation. He had a job to do, one he could not afford to screw up.

"You don't have anything to do tomorrow," Gomes said, his voice calm. "Relax. Pick one thing, like one table or a particular person, and pay attention to every detail pertaining to that one thing."

The following day, Gomes met with Iannone, Law, and Rosenberg at the motel.

"Did anyone notice anything unusual last night?" Gomes asked in the lobby. The agents shook their heads.

Gomes sighed. "If there *is* something going on and we don't find it—but somebody else does, like the IRS—Hannifin is going to be really pissed off, and the other divisions will love it."

"But what if there isn't anything going on?" Law wanted to know.

"Tell me again," Iannone chimed in. "Why do we suspect something is going on at Zimba's?"

Another sigh from Gomes. "The Enforcement Division had information that indicated a discrepancy between the amount of play in the poker room and the actual reported earnings."

Rosenberg spoke up. "Seems like we won't know anything until we conduct the raid and check their numbers."

The truth of the matter was that at this point, there was really no telling what the raid would uncover. Iannone worried that they might not turn up anything, while Law was slightly more pessimistic in worrying that the Enforcement Division was setting them up to fail. Gomes had his own doubts, but as division chief, he couldn't let his men know this.

Gomes ended the conversation by explaining the new plan for that night: "We'll stagger our arrivals between ten and eleven tonight, then wait for the drop collection and the owner to show up at the cage for the count. That's when we'll identify ourselves."

Around 10:00 that night, after some rest at Larry Clark's and leaving his friend at home this time, Gomes returned to Zimba's. He hadn't planned on getting there until an hour or so later, but he was too antsy to sit still. He needed to get to work or he'd go nuts. He bought a beer, sat at the bar, and began his surveillance. Rosenberg walked in a few minutes later and took his place at a slot machine close to the cage, ordered a beer, and looked happily content pulling on the one-arm bandit.

Iannone didn't look quite as calm or content when he arrived at Zimba's around 10:20. In fact, he looked like he was going to kill someone. Gomes watched as some of Zimba's patrons dodged this mad grizzly as he walked in and took his place at the opposite side of the bar.

Finally, Law got there just before eleven, looking a little green. He walked across the casino floor and straight to the bathroom. A few minutes later he emerged and found a place at a slot machine close to the table-games pit. Gomes was glad he had been too nervous to eat. Otherwise, he would have landed in the stall next to Law. Gomes wondered how Rosenberg could remain so unaffected. He suspected that Rosenberg wasn't worried about his career; he was working for the fun of it, and maybe the money.

Gomes checked his watch; it was only 11:20. Time had never moved so slowly. Gomes watched a scrawny, wrinkled old man, his lips puckered against toothless gums, carefully lift a beer to take a long, slow gulp. Next to him was a woman—hard, unattractive, with stringy black hair and a leather jacket. He watched as she took a pull on her cigarette. Gomes felt like he was in some sort of alternate universe. He had just finished reading a book about quantum mechanics, and now, for a brief moment, Gomes wondered, *What if I somehow crossed into a different world, where time moves slower. Would I know if it happened? How do I know I'm not really dreaming? How does anyone truly know that what they are experiencing is a shared reality? What if it is completely individual, and no one really knows what anyone else knows?*

BANG!

Gomes jumped out of his seat. Snapped back to this reality, he noticed that a cocktail waitress had dropped a tray full of drinks, and broken glass was everywhere. *Focus, Dennis . . . focus,* he told himself. He checked his watch: 12:05 a.m. Less than an hour left to wait. Gomes got up from the bar and walked around the casino. More of the same; nothing unusual. The poker room was full for the second night in a row. Gomes didn't notice anyone in a leisure suit tonight.

He made his way back to the bar at around 12:40 a.m. and ordered another beer—not to drink, just to help him blend in. *Twenty more minutes, just twenty more minutes,* Gomes thought. Iannone was tapping his thumbs on the bar so loudly that Gomes wanted to yell *Stop!* Gomes checked his watch again: 12:59 a.m.

Then, 1:00 a.m. came and went.

1:10 a.m., 1:15, 1:17.

This is ridiculous, Gomes thought.

1:30 a.m. . . . 1:45. Still nothing. *They made us. No, someone tipped them off. The Enforcement Division, those fucking assholes. No, they wouldn't do that. It's probably just running late. Yeah, that's it. Keep your cool. Keep your cool.*

Gomes felt like he might pass out. The waiting was killing him. 2:00 a.m. and still nothing. 2:05 a.m. . . . . More waiting, watching.

Finally, at 2:07 in the morning, Security began the collection of the drop boxes.

Out of the corner of his eye, Gomes saw the little old man making his way over to the casino cage. In unison, Gomes, Iannone, Law, and Rosenberg converged on the man, hopefully their unsuspecting count-room officiator. They had their badges out. Gomes finally had a good view of this individual. He looked like he'd just rolled out of bed. His thinning white hair was sticking out in every direction. He was wearing khaki pants and a button-down shirt that he had obviously been sleeping in. His shirt had been buttoned incorrectly. He had a fuzz of white whiskers diffusing his facial features. He picked up the count-room keys.

Gomes got up and went over to the cage. "Please identify yourself and your position with Zimba's!"

"What do you want?" the old man growled.

"We're from the Nevada Gaming Control Board, and we are here to monitor your count procedures."

"I've never heard of the fucking Control Board checking on counts."

"Sir, please identify yourself and your position at Zimba's Casino."

"I'm Sam Sarlo. I'm the owner!"

"We'll follow you," Gomes said, tossing a nod to the members of his team.

Sam Sarlo walked with the speed of the decrepit old man that he appeared to be. Gomes wanted to pick him up and carry him through the maze of back hallways down a long flight of stairs to the count room, which in this casino turned out to be nothing more than a cubbyhole in the basement.

Sarlo and his assistant, a thick, middle-aged man who spoke only to his boss, began the count with the cash from the blackjack tables. After they had counted it, Gomes checked the logbook. Iannone and Law re-counted it, and Rosenberg double-checked the logbook. Everything was satisfactory.

Next, Sarlo and his assistant counted the cash from the craps winnings. Gomes and his team checked it, and once again, all was fine.

"Do you have any problems with my procedures?" Sarlo wanted to know.

"No, they're on the level," Gomes told him.

"Okay, well, great. The count is over."

"No . . . no, it's not. What about the poker winnings?"

The blood drained from Sarlo's face. "Oh, yeah, the cage must have forgotten to give them to me."

Gomes just waited.

"I'll go get them from the cage," Sarlo said. "I'll be right back."

Suddenly the old coot jumped up and ran out of the room. Gomes calmly trotted after him. Sarlo was running up the stairs two at a time. There was no remnant of the worn-out senior citizen that had hobbled down to the count room. He ran all the way to the cage at a sprinter's pace, weaving past gamblers and waitresses, unaware that Gomes was following him.

Quickly reaching behind the counter, Sarlo pulled up a full bank bag, unzipped it, and put his hand inside. But Gomes grabbed his arm just before he could pull anything out. Startled, Sarlo said, "Oh, Gomes . . . I found the bag. They must've forgot to give it to me."

"Then let's bring it down and finish this count," Gomes replied.

Now the speed and agility of the man Gomes had just followed was nowhere to be found. What remained was a breathless and pale old man who looked scared.

Once back in the count room, Sarlo reached into the bag, pulled out the money, placed it on the table, threw the bag on the floor, and quickly began counting.

"Wait!" Gomes interrupted. "We're going to need to restart the count."

"If you keep interrupting me," the casino boss grumbled, "this is going to take all night. I've done nothing wrong."

"Please pick up the bank bag and hold it upside down over the table," Gomes instructed.

"This is bullshit . . . never in all my years . . ." Sarlo mumbled something that sounded Italian to Gomes, then reached down to pick up the bag by the bottom seam. He held it over the table.

Nothing.

"Please hold the bag by the sides," Gomes ordered. Sweating profusely, Sarlo wiped his brow, held the bag by its sides, and turned it over. A small green ledger book tumbled out.

Gomes had to work hard to hold back a smile. He picked up the book, opened it. The ledger contained several years' worth of data listed in two columns—one under the heading REPORTED COUNT, and the other under the heading ACTUAL COUNT. The deception could not have been more obvious if it was lit up in Vegas Strip neon.

"Where did this come from?" Gomes asked.

"I don't know. I've never seen it before in my life!" Sarlo pursed his lips like a guilty little boy.

"It doesn't matter if you talk to us or not," Gomes said. "We have everything we need right here. I'm confiscating this ledger. Thank you for your help tonight."

Gomes gave a satisfied nod to his crew and walked out.

———

Gomes and his team returned to Vegas, where Gomes had a meeting scheduled with Phil Hannifin, on May 21, 1971. Gomes was surprised to see Tom Carrigan, chief of the Enforcement Division, at the powwow.

"We conducted undercover surveillance for roughly eight hours," Gomes began. "We didn't find anything out of the ordinary."

He could see Carrigan smirking. Gomes went on to explain that the count of the blackjack and craps winnings checked out. At this point, Carrigan had one hand over his mouth in order to cover his beaming satisfaction at Gomes's apparent lack of success.

"However," Gomes said, pausing for effect, and allowing himself the slightest grin when he saw Carrigan's brow crinkle, "the poker count did not check out, and we found this." Gomes showed the green ledger to Hannifin and Carrigan.

"Gomes, this is incredible!" Hannifin blurted.

Carrigan wasn't smirking anymore.

———

Zimba's was a classic skimming case. The poker winnings were under-counted and someone—possibly the Mafia—was pocketing the difference between the reported count and the actual count. Gaming authorities revoked Zimba's owner's gaming license for failure to report $70,818 in revenue. Sarlo escaped state incarceration due to his extremely poor health.

This investigation was Gomes's first real, albeit admittedly small, success. It was all he needed to give him the confidence to begin his assault on the major casinos. He was ready to fry the bigger and more deadly fish that had been stinking up the town since anyone had started to give a damn about what went on in Las Vegas.

CHAPTER 5

Hard Lessons

"WHERE ARE THE KIDS?"

"I asked your parents to watch them tonight," Linda Gomes replied, standing toe to toe with her husband in the living room of their apartment. "I need to talk to you."

"About what?" Gomes asked.

"I'm not quite sure how to say this." Linda's eyes welled with tears. "I'm not happy, Dennis."

In tears, Linda tried to explain to Dennis that it was time for her to find herself. She told Dennis that he had his life, he had his career, but she had not been able to be anything other than his wife and the mother of his children. Linda felt that because she had been his girlfriend since she was sixteen years old, now she needed time to find out who she was as a woman.

Linda wiped her tears. "I love Doug and Mary very much, but Mary is in preschool and Doug's already in the first grade. They will be fine. But I need to find myself."

She took a deep breath, tried to say the dreaded "D-word," but could not utter another sound.

June of 1971, Larry Clark was in Las Vegas, visiting family and applying for a position with Gomes as an Audit Division Gaming Control Board agent. Applying for the job was really just a formality; Gomes had planned on hiring Clark almost from the moment he'd taken the chief's position with the Audit Division.

Since Larry Clark was around, Gomes asked him to try and talk Linda out of her ridiculous divorce idea. Clark had assured Gomes that he would be able to convince her that they should stay together. However, after Clark talked to Linda, the man's attitude took a seismic shift.

"Dennis, you and Linda are miserable together," Clark said, sitting across from the couple at a secluded booth in an off-Strip diner. "And Linda, you basically went from an orphanage to Dennis. I see now that you truly need your chance to experience life on your own terms."

"What the fuck is wrong with you two?" Gomes said. He had a splitting headache. "This is not the right thing to do. And I swear to God, Linda, if you leave me, I will *never* take you back!"

"Dennis, calm down." Linda gave him a searching look. "This is something I have to do. Maybe we'll end up back together—I don't know."

"Didn't you hear me? If you leave me, I will never take you back!" Gomes wanted to say more, but he bit down on all the Catholic programming bubbling up within him, all the resentment, all the pain curdling into rage. "Do you understand what I'm saying?"

At last Linda muttered, "That's your decision, Dennis . . . whatever. All I know is that it's over."

Gomes threw himself into his work. Living at his parents' house, clinging to the temporary relief of daily visitations with his kids, he found little solace on the Strip. The empty laughter, liquid memories, and the narcotic abandon of high rollers did nothing to fill the well of dark emptiness growing inside him. Although his loneliness and sense of detachment allowed Gomes to blend more easily into the vice-laden, late-night scene of Las Vegas, in his darkest moments, it also led him to wonder whether he had become just another of the Strip's lost souls.

Gomes finally felt at home and one with his environment, and that scared the hell out of him.

It didn't take Gomes long to select his next target: the Circus Circus Casino. Intentionally or not, Gomes often found himself conducting most of his obsessive late-night surveillance at this casino. Circus Circus was a unique property—the first of its kind to cater to the family market. The casino did this through some unique gimmicks, such as trapeze acts over the gambling floor, carnival games, and sideshows surrounding the table games and slot machines. The circus acts were meant to entertain the children while the parents gambled away. The idea for this casino was conceived by Jay Sarno, a corpulent man who was known both for his creativity and his enormous appetites. He overindulged in just about everything, with a special focus on gambling, food, and sex.

Sarno, formerly a major stockholder in the original Mob-tainted Caesars Palace, had obtained financing for the construction of Circus Circus from the Teamsters' Pension Fund. Gomes was convinced that the pension fund was controlled by organized crime. He knew that historically the fund was the only major institutional lender willing to provide significant funding for Nevada's casinos.

Further adding to Gomes's suspicion of the Mafia's involvement was the information that Agent Duane Noyes was able to gather. It clearly linked to organized crime the backgrounds of various individuals employed as managers at Circus Circus. The icing on the cake was Gomes's late-night discovery of just exactly why Tony "The Ant" Spilotro had been given the liquor-store and gift-shop concession at the Circus Circus. This business was worth about $75,000 per month to the owner of the shop, and Gomes knew that the casino would never have given that away unless they needed to pay someone off. This piece of evidence led Gomes to suspect that the Chicago Outfit held a hidden interest in Circus Circus.

During Gomes's surveillance of Circus Circus, he had come across Rob,* a count-room clerk. If there was skimming taking place at Circus Circus, chances were that Rob knew how the money was getting skimmed. Gomes just needed to figure out how to approach the guy in order to obtain the information he needed.

A tall, lanky, worn-down, middle-aged man, Rob was nearly a ghost. His skin looked almost transparent. He had been used and thrown out

---

* Pseudonym

by basically everyone in his life, beginning with his single mother. He had learned how to survive in the streets, developing a core toughness thanks to this hard-knocks education. Surveillance had revealed Rob's angst about his "bitch of a mother," who had kicked him out of the house to make room for her "scumbag fuck friend."

At age forty, Rob prescribed himself a daily dose of stiff whiskey in order to cope with his abandonment issues. Every night, as soon as Rob's shift was over, he was always at the bar, knocking back more than a few. Gomes had casually talked to him at the Circus Circus bar a few times, learning that Rob had worked in casinos for close to a decade. The man's life might have been a mess, but he knew the ropes.

By the fall of 1971, Gomes had become a master at the art of blending in while conducting surveillance. He also had developed an ability to pick up on the smallest bits of seemingly useless information—information that only seemed useless until you combined it with Gomes's innate grasp of human nature and his long interest in psychology. He had a minor in psychology from the University of Nevada, and made the most of this background in the field. Gomes suspected that Rob felt underappreciated and used by his superiors, considering his backstory with his mother.

Though he felt sympathy for the guy, Gomes sensed that his rough background was something he could use to turn Rob into a very helpful informant.

———

"Rob, I'm going to be completely straight with you," Gomes began, speaking confidentially in the low light and soft din of the bar. "I'm going to trust you to keep what I tell you to yourself."

"Okay."

"You're a decent, hardworking guy, and I need your help. I'm a Gaming Control Board agent, and I'm investigating Circus Circus. I know that the Mob is skimming money."

"Why are you telling me this?" Rob asked.

"Because, you can make this case. I need your help. I swear that nothing you say will be used against you."

Rob nodded.

"You're a smart guy," Gomes pressed on. "You know Vegas. And, you know what's going on at Circus Circus. This is your chance to do something important, to make a difference. It's not right that these worthless gangsters get rich off other people's hard work."

This hit a nerve. Rob knew something was going on, and it bothered him that he may have been committing a crime simply by doing his job. Rob agreed to work with Gomes.

———

Gomes walked away from his first long conversation with Rob feeling so euphoric, he might have been on drugs. He had never done that sort of thing, but thought, *This is what it must feel like to be high.*

And there were no withdrawals to worry about; the only after-effects were a little twinge of guilt from faking his emotions and offering phony words in order to manipulate his informant. But at this moment in time, Gomes looked at it as part of the job, and was more worried about ever reaching a point where doing this kind of thing wouldn't bother him. Besides, Rob was getting something he needed—he was making a difference—and Gomes was doing what he believed was right.

From that point on, Rob acted like he finally felt important—even needed by someone. He loved talking to Gomes. He would get excited in anticipation of his secret meetings. In Rob's mind he was leading a second exciting life as a detective. Rob told Gomes that money was getting skimmed from the slot winnings of the Slots A Fun Casino, which was adjacent to and owned by Circus Circus. The coin was undercounted in the count room and then converted to cash and taken out by a man named Carl Thomas.

Thomas was the vice president of casino operations for both Circus Circus and its sister property, Slots A Fun. Gomes knew Thomas well and liked him a lot, because he treated his employees with respect. But Carl Thomas was also someone whom Gomes knew to be on the Mob's payroll. In addition to the information about the skim and how it was being handled, Rob also provided Gomes with other valuable facts about the casino. In fact, Rob began calling Gomes every time mobsters were hanging around the place.

In order to prepare for a major strike at Circus Circus, where he could catch the crooks red-handed during the skimming process, Gomes had his agents conduct multiple twenty-four-hour surveillances of Circus Circus and Slots A Fun. He felt that it would be reasonably easy to catch these guys in the skim with Rob on the inside, letting him know exactly when the moment was ripe to conduct his raid and catch everyone in the act. Then he would have Carl Thomas by the balls. Gomes felt that if he were able to nab Thomas on his home turf, Thomas would flip and rat out the wiseguys back in Chicago.

Carl Thomas had worked for organized crime during most of his long career. Gomes didn't know exactly how many mobsters Carl would be willing serve up on a silver platter, but he knew it could be a lot. And the tighter the noose around his neck, the more thugs he'd likely spit out. All the pieces were in place for a major success, everything lined up exactly as Gomes wanted it.

That's when Gomes got his first foul taste of bureaucratic poison.

— ⚊ ⚊

Shannon Bybee was the only Gaming Control Board member who was headquartered with Gomes in Las Vegas. The other two Board members, Phil Hannifin and Jack Stratton, were based out of the capital, Carson City.

One morning, Gomes got a call to meet Bybee in his nice corner office overlooking the downtown district. Bybee, a Mormon, and an honest lawyer whom Gomes respected and liked very much, was a big, well-groomed, very straitlaced corporate type. Importantly, Bybee was a straight shooter who had no issues with telling someone when there was a problem. He shook Gomes's hand firmly before the two men took their seats.

"Dennis, you have been doing exemplary work," Bybee began. Gomes was prepared for another shoe to drop, and was not surprised when Bybee said, "However, your investigations are crossing into the territory of the other divisions."

"No, Shannon, they're not," Gomes protested.

"Dennis, I'm not going to argue with you. You're doing a great job, but the other two divisions are getting pissed off because you are not keeping them informed or updated."

"That's because I don't trust them—and forgive me for saying this, but they're incompetent."

Bybee reclined in his chair, letting out a weary sigh. "Dennis, this is not a one-man show. The bottom line is that you have to keep the other divisions informed, and since you haven't been doing that, I want you to include one of the Enforcement Division agents with you and your guys when you are conducting surveillance, prior to your raid on the Circus Circus and Slots A Fun casinos."

"That's bullshit, Shannon," Gomes snapped. "They don't know what the fuck they're doing, and they will only get in the way!"

Bybee, a former cop prior to getting his law degree, tamped down his anger. "We can't have you running around creating problems within the divisions. You are going to include an Enforcement agent in order to keep interdepartmental peace. Understood?"

A long pause here. Finally Gomes relented. "Fine, but if they screw up one of my investigations, I will never include an outside agent again."

Will* was an ex-cop, forty-eight years old, short and stout, with a messy mop of brown hair, a thick, bushy mustache, and a blanket of body hair that he partially and proudly displayed with his low-buttoned shirts. In order to get acquainted with "Agent Will"—who came from the Enforcement Division, at Bybee's insistence—Gomes decided to bring him along on a surprise raid of the Churchill Downs Turf Club, a stand-alone legal race and sports book on the Strip.

During race- and sports-book raids, Gomes would make sure there was no siphoning off of book winnings taking place. He would do this by ensuring that all bets and all cash were being properly recorded. He'd also make sure that there was no organized-crime involvement, and that the licensed bookie wasn't "laying off" to organized crime or illegal bookies.

---

* Pseudonym

Laying off occurred when a particular book received too many wagers on one side of a game and passed some of the betting volume along to another book.

Finally, Gomes would make sure that no phone betting was taking place, and that the book was not using runners (individuals that would place bets for others). It was Nevada law that in order to place sports bets, it had to be done in person.

Churchill Downs Turf Club was a typical race and sports book. One side was devoted to horse races and the other side was devoted to sports. The games, races, and odds were written in chalk on the chalkboards that filled up the remaining wall space. Bob Martin was the handicapper for Churchill Downs, and was known around town as one of the best.

As with most of Vegas's freestanding sports books, the smell of cigar smoke assaulted the senses from the first moment you walked through the door. It was also populated by what looked like outcasts from a Brooklyn or Chicago senior citizens' home. This held true not just for the bookies and betting clerks who ran the place, but also for the cigar-smoking customers who frequented it.

It was a Sunday afternoon, during the start of football season. This specific time was chosen for a reason: There would be a lot of betting action. Gomes briefed his agents during the Churchill Downs pre-raid meeting, pointing out that Agent Will was joining them. Will seemed nervous and jumpy about the raid, and kept asking Gomes and his senior agents what he should do during the process. Gomes advised him to do nothing, say nothing, and touch nothing.

"Just stand there and observe," he told him.

Minutes before kicking off the raid, Gomes and the other agents met briefly in the Churchill Downs parking lot, just long enough to organize before tipping the book operators that they were coming in. Gomes noticed that Will was among the other agents who were climbing out of their vehicles.

The team moved in quickly. No one was happy to have them there. The agents got in the way of the clerks taking the bets and the customers laying the bets. Martin was pleasant and let Gomes and his agents go about their business, until one of the agents bumped a television and accidentally changed the game. Gomes thought the place might riot. He quickly grabbed the closest remote control to change the channel back, but it didn't work. One of his agents managed to get the channel back and quiet the crowd.

Suddenly, a uniformed man appeared in the doorway with a shotgun. Gomes and his agents immediately flashed their badges. Turned out Gomes had hit the panic button when he was trying to change the channel with the "remote." It took approximately five hours, but they finally managed to quietly wrap up the raid with satisfactory results.

Will never made it inside for the actual raid. He simply vanished. He later told Gomes that he had spotted a suspected Mob affiliate leaving the sports book and had followed him. Gomes never knew what actually happened to Agent Will during that first raid. Everyone felt certain that, at the last second, Will had panicked because he was so unfamiliar with the process and had no idea what to do with himself.

When Gomes later asked Will to provide the name of the Mob guy, or the license plate of the car that the reputed mobster had been driving, Will could not do so.

After Will's vanishing act during the raid of the Churchill Downs Turf Club, Gomes assigned him to busywork that would keep him out of the way but still appease Bybee.

Gomes wanted Will as far from the Circus Circus and the upcoming raid as possible. That's why he assigned Will to surveillance detail at the Riviera Casino—across the street from Circus Circus. Will was instructed to watch and take note of everyone that went in or came out of the Circus Circus or Slots A Fun in the hours leading up to the raid—and most importantly to be inconspicuous. No one was to know what he was doing there.

—◆—

The day of the next scheduled raid of Circus Circus approached. On that morning Gomes was at his office getting some last-minute details together when he received a frantic call.

"Gomes, they know! They know!" the panicky caller ranted. "Someone told them all about your plan. They know!"

"Rob, slow down. What are you talking about?" Gomes gazed wearily out the window of his office, bracing himself for his informant's news.

"We just got orders directly from Carl Thomas to stop the skimming," Rob explained. "They know!"

"How the fuck did this happen?"

"Somehow the cops found out. Carl Thomas walked in and told my boss, you know, my friend, that he needed two thousand dollars in cash from the coin room to pay off Metro, in exchange for the information about your raid."

Rob explained that he had no idea how or why Metro—short for the Las Vegas Metropolitan Police Department—had warned Carl Thomas of Gomes's impending raid. However, he did know that Carl Thomas had a dirty cop on the payroll.

Knowing that this raid would now be fruitless, Gomes canceled it. Then he went directly to Agent Will, who turned out to be very honest and forthcoming. Gomes did not want Will to know about Rob, because it would endanger his informant's life. In fact, none of Gomes's agents, except for Rich Iannone, knew about the man. However, as it turned out, Gomes did not have to be explicit to extract the necessary information from Will.

"Well, I parked in the Riviera valet, and the manager wanted to know what I was doing," Will explained to Gomes in a closed-door meeting later that day. "I told him that I was conducting surveillance on Circus Circus. He let me stay, but I guess he had called Metro before he talked to me. An old buddy of mine from Metro showed up, and I told him about our case."

"It's not *our* case," Gomes corrected him. "It was *my* case, but you fucking blew it! I specifically told you to park where no one would see you. I also told you not to tell anyone about this case, especially Metro."

Will replied, "He's my friend. He's a good guy!"

"Let me guess: Your old buddy is Sergeant Mack, right?"

"Yeah. How'd you know?"

"Did you know that your buddy went over to Circus Circus and told them everything?" Gomes seethed. "It's practically common knowledge that Mack is dirty."

Will was squirming, as though his clothes were suddenly too tight, or someone had cranked up the heat in the room.

"He's a disgusting piece of shit," Gomes continued. "You can go back to the fucking Enforcement Division; you won't be working with us anymore. Now get out of my sight!"

Gomes took a moment to collect himself as Will made a quick exit, then went straight to Bybee. Gomes knew he had a forceful argument on his side now, and the last thing he wanted to do was come off like a raging lunatic. So when he marched into his boss's office, he was determined to appear reasonable, even though he felt anything but.

As he laid out the blow-by-blow of how Will's incompetence had undercut extensive man-hours of good work, he sensed Bybee was getting it. When Gomes added that he would never work with another division again, Bybee agreed.

Gomes was holding out hope that the Circus Circus skim would start up again. However, shortly after this investigation, Gomes learned that the casino manager had died, and his informant Rob had been fired. Gomes realized that since Carl Thomas was aware that Gomes knew about the skimming at the Circus Circus and Slots A Fun casinos, he wouldn't dare reestablish it for a long time, if ever.

Gomes was devastated. This had been a big opportunity, and he'd blown it.

He had no idea how things were about to change.

PART II

BOLSHEVIK IN RESIDENCE

The wicked are wicked, no doubt, and they go astray, and they fall, and they come by their deserts: but who can tell the mischief which the very virtuous do?

—WILLIAM MAKEPEACE THACKERAY,
THE NEWCOMES

CHAPTER 6

The Girl with the Legs

DENNIS GOMES OFFICIALLY BEGAN HIS INVESTIGATION OF BALLY SALES, a distributor for Bally Slot Machines, on February 24, 1971, with a surprise raid on the company's offices, located just off the Strip in the heart of the city's warehouse district. The glitz and glitter of Las Vegas didn't extend into this labyrinth of industrial headquarters, where layers of soot decorated the once-white buildings.

Bally Sales was the first target that Gomes selected specifically because he suspected that this company had ties to organized crime. Bally Manufacturing Corporation was a separate company that built slot machines. Bally Manufacturing was allegedly linked to the Mob; however, because they did not do business in Nevada, they were not subject to any investigations or licensing requirements. Gomes suspected that if Bally Manufacturing were a Mob company, they would use distributors— such as Bally Sales—as fronts in order to appear clean.

"Are you ready?" Gomes asked Sam Rosenberg as they pulled into the parking lot of Bally Sales a little after nine in the morning. "This is going to be a long day. I want every single document in that office."

"Yep—let's get it over with," Rosenberg said.

They both sensed that this would be a rather uneventful raid. With any luck it would be merely a long, tedious day of collecting, recording, organizing, and packing documents. Then again, luck had not always been on their side, and Gomes had seen enough to know that any situation could quickly turn volatile. Rosenberg grabbed a stack of unfolded file boxes from the trunk and they calmly walked into the office.

"Well, hello. I wasn't expecting anyone today. How can I help you?" This greeting came from a cheery, rosy-cheeked secretary with an uncanny resemblance to Mrs. Claus. Her workspace was littered with small animal figurines.

Other than the secretary's menagerie, there was not much to the office—just a couple of slot machines and a beige couch flanked by a brown coffee table.

"My name is Dennis Gomes. I'm a division chief with the Gaming Control Board. Is Mr. Wichinsky here?"

"Sure. I'll go get Mickey right away." The secretary scurried over to an office just past the greeting area. Within seconds a round, little old man, balding, with just a thin splay of white hair, shuffled out. He looked up at Gomes from behind the spectacles perched on his nose.

"I'm Mickey Wichinsky. What can I do for you?"

"I'm Dennis Gomes, and this is Sam Rosenberg. We are with the Gaming Control Board. We're conducting an audit investigation of your company, and we need to temporarily seize all of your documents."

"Really? Well, okay." Wichinsky furrowed his brow. He was obviously a little shaken by this, but too nice of a guy to complain.

Gomes kept a pleasant look on his face. "If you could just show us where everything is, we'll get started. We'll be out of your way as quickly as possible."

Wichinsky showed Gomes and Rosenberg the files and made sure they had whatever they needed. After hours of sifting through a seemingly endless series of records, and fending off the occasional offer of coffee from Mrs. Claus, they gathered all of the relevant documents and took them back to division headquarters.

On the drive back, Gomes began to question his selection of Bally Sales for an investigation. Wichinsky seemed like a genuinely nice guy. It was difficult for Gomes to believe that he could be involved in the rotten business of *La Cosa Nostra*. Gomes had to remind himself that it wasn't Wichinsky he was after, but rather, what he suspected Bally Sales was funding—the Mob.

After reviewing the documents, Gomes discovered that Bally Sales was never actually licensed by gaming authorities to distribute slot machines in Nevada, although it did hold a current gaming manufacturer's license. Consequently, Gomes was able to require that Bally Sales and its owner, Michael "Mickey" Wichinsky, go through the entire licensing and related investigative process.

Normally, the Investigations Division would handle the background/licensing investigation. However, because Gomes's division had opened the official investigation into Bally Sales, Phil Hannifin mandated that Gomes's team handle the entire inquiry.

The licensing investigation began in September of 1971. The background review was conducted in Las Vegas, Los Angeles, Chicago, New Jersey, and New York. This operation would lead to the acquisition of important allies.

During the course of the Bally Sales investigation, Gomes developed one of the most valuable informants of his law enforcement career—a man by the name of Herbert Itkin. After realizing the scope of Gomes's investigation, a New York law enforcement agency placed Gomes in contact with Mr. Itkin in return for a copy of the investigation report once it was completed.

Itkin was a former New York lawyer with strong ties to the Mafia who, according to a federal affidavit, had penetrated the inner sanctum of organized crime in the United States. Itkin had been a confidential informant for the FBI and CIA for fourteen years. At the time of Gomes's investigation, Itkin was under federal witness protection, which made it difficult to establish initial contact. However, Gomes was not one to shy away from difficult situations. Thanks to his persistence, he was able to arrange a clandestine meeting with Itkin at a dingy hotel just outside of Los Angeles. This meeting had one stipulation: Gomes and his agents were instructed by federal marshals to come with concealed weapons due to the constant threats facing the man. The more Gomes learned about Itkin, the more eager he became to interview him.

Gomes was in his office preparing for their meeting when he received a surprise visit from Enforcement Agent Jim Chaney.

"Have I got a girl for *you*," Chaney told Gomes.

"Hey, Jim. What girl?" Gomes had no idea what Chaney was talking about.

"She has a friend, a dancer. She wants to set you up with her."

"Oh, yeah?" Gomes scratched his head. "That sounds good. When?"

"What about tomorrow?"

"Shit, I can't. What about Friday?"

"Sure," Chaney enthused. "Friday it is."

Now Gomes had another meeting that he couldn't believe he had lucked into: a dancer from the French spectacular, the Folies Bergere. It was the first time in a really long while that Gomes had felt butterflies in his stomach. Excited and nervous, he still needed to clear his mind, focus, and prepare for his meeting with Herbert Itkin.

Gomes, Rosenberg, and Iannone made the one-hour flight to Los Angeles early on the morning of October 1, 1971. Gomes knew that they were to meet Mr. Itkin in a shabby old motel, but this place was far worse than he could have imagined. It had been a dive back in the 1950s, when it was first built, and by 1971, it should have been condemned. Gomes drove by the motel three different times thinking that it was abandoned, and only realized it was the place when he pulled into the empty parking lot to check his map.

He drove around to the back of the building, broken glass and battered pavement crackling under his tires, and parked the car. Rosenberg and Iannone slowly emerged from the vehicle and took stock of their surroundings. This was one hell of a meeting place, and Gomes felt his senses instinctively shift into alert mode.

They cautiously made their way to the designated room and paused to listen for any voices or unusual sounds before knocking on the door. A federally appointed guard opened the door, checked everyone's credentials, and then let them in.

The stale smell of mold and rot was enough to make Gomes stop breathing for fear of causing damage to his health. Finally, when he couldn't take it any longer, he took shallow little breaths through his mouth.

The inside of the place clearly hadn't been touched since it was built twenty years before. Frayed brown bedspreads covered two very small beds that flanked a white plastic table, which held a phone and a King James Bible. There were stains on the faded blue carpet, and more on the peeling pink-and-green-flamingo wallpaper. Gomes was determined to avoid wondering what had caused them, or how they had gotten there.

In the back of the room were two open doors on opposite sides—one leading to the blue-tiled bathroom, and the other to a connecting room with more peeling flamingo wallpaper and more stains.

At a small, wooden round table sat Herbert Itkin. The federal marshal stood off to the side.

"Mr. Itkin, I'm Dennis Gomes, division chief with the Nevada Gaming Control Board, and this is Sam Rosenberg and Rich Iannone, audit division agents. Thank you for agreeing to meet with us."

"No problem. I'm glad to help." Itkin spoke in a harsh, New York–bred, tobacco-cured voice. He was in his early fifties, and well-dressed in a designer suit. His dark hair was nicely groomed. This stylishly professional look was topped off with a little too much Aqua Velva, but at least it covered the nauseating smell in the room.

"You have a very impressive history," Gomes commented. "You were a government informant for an amazingly long time. That's a very difficult life to maintain."

Itkin met his gaze.

"We are investigating Bally Sales," Gomes announced, "a slot-machine distribution company owned by Michael Wichinsky. We suspect that he is a front for the Genovese crime family. Because of your familiarity with this family, we were hoping that you might be able to help us with this investigation."

Itkin nodded. "Yeah, I know Wichinsky. He's a nice guy. I was in Cuba with Mickey."

"Is he associated with the Mob?" Gomes asked.

"Oh, yeah. He's close with some of the top bosses. I mean, he's not a bad guy, but he's in business with some of the worst."

Gomes heard a rattling sound and turned to notice the doorknob to the room shaking. Before Gomes could turn back around, the federal marshal grabbed Rosenberg, who was closest to him, and shoved him in the bathroom. Gomes was all too aware that there was an open hit order on Itkin, which gave any thug with a gun, knife, bomb, or bare hands an incentive to kill the man on sight.

Instinctually, Gomes practically lifted Itkin out of his seat and passed him to the marshal, who shoved him into the adjoining room. The marshal pulled his gun, aimed at the door, and stood just behind the threshold that connected the two rooms.

Time stopped.

The doorknob gently turned from side to side. In one swift movement Gomes and Iannone dove behind the bed farthest from the door. Gomes looked over at the marshal and drew his .38 Chief's Special, aimed at the door, and cocked his weapon. He heard the *click, click, click* of the other guns readying. The knob rotated a few more times until the lock finally disengaged.

The door opened an inch and froze. Then, it opened more, inch by inch, still revealing nothing. Gomes strained to get a glimpse into the narrow void, poised to fill the gap with bullets, but saw only a sliver of darkness beyond. Suddenly, a little old Chinese man with a thatch of white hair and a badly faded red uniform poked his head into the room. His eyes tripled in size when he saw the arsenal of weapons aimed at his head.

"So sorry—must have wrong room." He practically ran from the room, but the marshal was quicker. The Chinese porter was stopped, ID'd, and questioned. Twenty minutes later he had cleared his inspection and was freed.

—◆—

Gomes and his agents interviewed Herbert Itkin for more than six hours, the federal marshal allowing Gomes free rein over him for the entire time. Itkin knew that Wichinsky had spent a month in Cuba between 1957 and 1958, at the Cuban Riviera Hotel, with one of the owners, George Hyman Levine, aka George Lewis, a gangster and a close associate of Salvatore Granello, aka Sally Burns. Along with Granello and Levine, Itkin also linked Wichinsky to a slew of Mob associates, including Meyer

Lansky, and members of the Lucchese crime family, as well as Gerardo Catena, who was capo de capo of the Mafia in the United States, and also head of the Genovese crime family.

Herbert Itkin was confident in his knowledge that Wichinsky was very much a part of organized crime on a personal and business level. Gomes believed him, and left the meeting with a notebook full of information to further corroborate his story.

The worm was turning.

The past several years had taught Gomes to accept nothing at face value. So despite the mountain of testimony that Herbert Itkin had provided, the following morning, Gomes had his agents hard at work searching for evidence to substantiate and document Michael Wichinsky's alleged Mob associations. Duane Noyes had already managed to pull together some impressive intelligence reports. In a report on Cuba's gambling, Gomes found it astonishingly ironic that during the island's gambling heyday, the only legitimate place for high rollers to gamble was the Montmartre Club—a Meyer Lansky joint.

"Hey, Gomes. How goes it?" asked Enforcement Agent Jim Chaney after barging in on the busy office full of accountant cops.

"Hey, Jim. I'm good now that I've seen you two times in one week."

Chaney grinned at the jab. "Ha! Yeah, I think 'document runner' has been added to my job description. Anyway, I'll meet you at the Tropicana lounge tonight at a quarter to nine. Okay?"

"What?" Gomes asked.

"Joanie, my girl."

Gomes stared blankly at Chaney.

"The wild dancer. She's bringing her girlfriend to meet you tonight."

"Oh shit, I totally forgot. And, man, I'm so busy. I don't know. Besides, no Las Vegas dancer is going to like a recently divorced guy with two kids."

"Stop making excuses. They're counting on you. You can afford an hour or two for a couple of drinks."

"Well," Gomes said, "what's she look like?"

As if on cue, Chaney, a little too enthusiastically, said, "She's twenty-five, one of the principal dancers in the show. She's about five-seven, has long black hair, a knockout body, long, beautiful legs, and a face like an angel."

Gomes almost couldn't answer fast enough. "All right. I'll see you at the Trop."

The Tropicana was known as the "Tiffany" of the Strip. It was luxury all the way. It sat on acres and acres of manicured land, boasting extravagant fountains and pools. It was built in the 1950s, but had been continually added on to, creating an ageless decadence. It was a favorite of the rich and famous.

The casino was busy that night, and Gomes had to claw his way through the dense crowd of tourists and regulars. The Vegas party people were out in force. This was one group of people that Gomes didn't understand. Though he liked to have a good time as much as the next guy, he just couldn't grasp the concept of your entire life revolving around a doomed attempt at maintaining an everlasting party. It seemed like such a vacuous existence to him. Gomes usually tried to avoid the Vegas party crowd. It wasn't his scene, and it made him very uncomfortable on this night.

These dancers are probably all big partyers, Gomes thought. *We're going to have nothing in common.*

Navigating his way through the endless stream of platform shoes and sequins, Gomes finally found Chaney sitting at a small table in the lounge.

"I was getting worried," Chaney said as he greeted Gomes. "I thought you were going to back out. Sit down."

"I don't know about this. You know me; I'm not a big partyer. What am I going to do with some wild girl?"

"Dennis, man, you need to lighten up. You really want me to tell you what you can do with a wild girl?"

A willowy, long-legged beauty, with thick, dark hair cascading past her shoulders, floated toward Gomes. At first, Gomes thought she might be a mirage. She was the most remarkably beautiful woman he had ever seen, even in her heavy show makeup. Those petite red lips, high cheekbones, and big brown eyes were exaggerated to epic proportions by the makeup and fake eyelashes. Gomes had barely noticed the other girl until they were at their table.

"Dennis, this is my girl, Joanie," Chaney said, gesturing to the other girl. "Joanie . . . Dennis."

"So nice to meet you. Jim has told me all about you." Joanie reached out and shook Gomes's hand. He was relieved that the brunette was not Jim's girlfriend. Joanie was pretty, too; she had a cute little body and dirty blonde hair pulled back.

"Nice to meet you," Gomes replied.

"This is my friend, Barbara," Joanie said. "Barbara—Dennis, and Jim." Barbara shook their hands and sat down next to Gomes. The two of them easily fell into conversation. Barbara was so soft-spoken and sweet, Gomes could have talked to her all night.

Chaney was craning his neck, scanning the room. "Where is this cocktail waitress? Can I get you girls a drink?"

"No, thanks," Barbara answered.

"You're not going to have a drink?" Gomes asked.

"No, we have another show to do tonight."

"You guys can stay and watch it from the light booth if you want," Joanie said. "We just added five new numbers. It's basically a new show."

There was no arm-twisting necessary. Gomes and Chaney gladly stayed and watched the Folies Bergere from the light booth. They had a perfect bird's-eye view. There was not one beehive in their way. Everything was pitch black. The orchestra played "I Love Paris." Then the light-booth operator counted down: "Three, two, one . . ."

A single spotlight shone on a lone dancer. It was easy for Gomes to recognize the dancer as Barbara. The image of her perfect body was forever burned into his memory. Barbara had on an impossibly tight, all-black, latex bodysuit. The only thing peeking out were her big brown eyes, cute nose, and red lips.

Thank you, God, Gomes thought.

So began a burgeoning romance. Much to Gomes's relief, he quickly learned that Barbara was not the wild partyer he'd been expecting. She was, in fact, a serious and dedicated performer who was easily as focused on her career as he was on his.

Barbara was Gomes's escape from everything, and they saw each other often. Gomes would take nightly breaks from his surveillance and meet Barbara for a late dinner, or they would meet at a lounge for a quiet drink. In the beginning of their relationship, Gomes would always bring Barbara to dance clubs.

She's a dancer, he figured. *She must love to go dancing.*

Eventually, Barbara told him that since she danced all day and half the night, the last thing she wanted to do during her downtime was dance. That was fine with Gomes. No matter where they went or what they did, they always had a great time together.

Gomes needed a haven away from the vile individuals he investigated. He needed Barbara. She was the only thing that brought balance to his life. This was a good thing for him, because it was getting more and more difficult at work.

After long hours of research, phone calls, and meetings, Gomes and his agents were able to prove beyond a doubt that Michael Wichinsky was in fact associated with organized crime. They delivered a report of their Bally Sales investigation, which led Hannifin and the other Board members to summon Michael Wichinsky for a formal hearing. Wichinsky's lawyer responded by immediately filing a request to cancel the hearing due to the pending sale of the client's interests in Bally Sales. Gomes suspected that this transaction was merely an attempt to take the heat off of Wichinsky. But, because Wichinsky still held two other gaming licenses for smaller companies, he was called into a licensing hearing anyway.

Backed into a corner by the evidence that Gomes's hard work had produced, Wichinsky had no choice but to admit to associating with various mobsters. According to Nevada Gaming Commission Regulation 5.011: "Catering to, assisting, employing, or associating with, either socially or in business affairs, persons of notorious or unsavory reputation" was grounds for disciplinary action.

As far as Gomes was concerned, this should have been a slam-dunk case.

Although the Gaming Control Board members all agreed that Wichinsky's actions were not acceptable, they were only willing to hand the admitted mobster a formal warning and send him on his way, free to conduct his business as he always had, while retaining his gaming licenses.

Gomes was furious. All of his and his agents' hard work, the cold, solid proof of organized-crime involvement, resulted in a "warning" letter. The State basically told Wichinsky, "Handle your business better" (wink, wink).

Gomes wondered what it would take to get these politicians to act decisively to rid Nevada of organized crime. He was determined to find out.

CHAPTER 7

Rules of the Game

"I KNOW THE MOB IS INVOLVED IN THE ALADDIN DEAL," GOMES TOLD Phil Hannifin one November day in 1971, in the section chief's cluttered office. "You have to let me handle the financial part of the licensing investigation. I'll be able to trace the funds of this sale back to the Mob."

"All right, Dennis. I agree—you should handle this investigation. But are you ready to deal with the other divisions?"

Gomes knew that this move would be viewed as an encroachment on the territory of the other two Gaming Control Board divisions. However, he felt strongly that his division's financial acumen was needed in the licensing investigation of gaming applicants. Hannifin agreed on both fronts, and told Gomes to be prepared to deal with the implications of this decision.

The catch? Hannifin told Gomes: "You only have one month to complete your investigation."

All Audit Division agents had received Gomes's memo announcing the mandatory meeting, and the conference room was full. The smell of strong coffee filled the room. The only thing more noticeable was the loud, caffeine-fueled banter between agents speculating on the reason for the meeting.

Gomes was the last person to arrive. "Everyone, listen up," he said. "We will be conducting a financial investigation of the Aladdin purchasers. Moving forward, the Audit Division will now be handling the financial phase of licensing investigations."

Several of the agents nodded their approval.

"This is the first time in Nevada's thirty-year gaming-regulation history that a financial phase will be included in a licensing investigation of this magnitude, and it's the first time in this division's history that we will be involved in the licensing process. The Aladdin is in a very precarious financial situation, and Delbert Coleman is threatening to close it if this sale doesn't happen quickly. As such, I want this investigation to be your main priority, as we only have one month to complete it."

"*What?* Did you say *one* month?" a frantic Dick Law asked.

"Yes, one month," Gomes replied.

The room erupted in protest. When it came to following a paper trail, these accountant-cops knew that rushing this sort of investigation was just about impossible. Some of the more-pessimistic agents even suggested that this assignment might be a setup to fail. However, despite these dissents, Gomes and his entire division also loved their work. At this point in time, they felt like their work was making a direct contribution to society. Because of this, Gomes was able to persuade his division that the risk in this instance was worth the reward, and through sheer focus, they would be able to tackle it in under a month.

"Look," Gomes went on, "right now you all have your own assignments and investigations that you're working on. What do we have—five investigations going on right now?"

"Seven, if you include the audits," Jacobson said.

"Okay, so, seven different investigations. I want every single one of you to put some focus on the Aladdin investigation for the next month. Don't completely ignore your other assignments; just spend a good portion of the day on the Aladdin. We are going to have a daily meeting to go over this case. This division is going to operate like a machine for the next month. We will be a team. I realize one month is not much time, but it's not impossible."

"What about the Investigations Division?" Iannone asked.

First and foremost, Gomes instructed his agents to not share any information pertaining to this investigation with anyone outside of the Audit Division. His lack of trust had developed quickly, thanks to Enforcement Division agents such as Will and officers like Sergeant Mack. However,

Gomes still needed to maintain a working relationship with the other divisions. Consequently, Gomes planned to work with Tom Carrigan, the chief of the Investigations Division, on the licensing phase, but mandated that he would be the only person to have contact with the other divisions regarding the Aladdin licensing investigation.

"Sam, you will be in charge of delegating the assignments here," Gomes said. "I want you to meet with everyone at ten a.m. every day. I will call you at nine a.m. to fill you in on what needs to be done."

Gomes concluded the meeting, and the agents rushed back to their desks to clear out their schedules for the next month.

Returning to his office, Gomes began poring over the legal documents for the proposed Aladdin sale. The deal had been orchestrated by Sorkis Webbe, a powerful lawyer and politician out of St. Louis, and involved a total of five investors from St. Louis and Detroit, and one from Las Vegas. Webbe was not considered part of the investigation because he was not one of the purchasers. However, he was the originator of the deal, and thus, the logical place for Gomes to begin. Furthermore, five out of six of the potential purchasers in the Aladdin deal were based out of Detroit and St. Louis. So, Gomes decided, that's where he, Law, and Iannone would begin their investigation.

At one point that day, Gomes called Sorkis to set up a meeting with him in order to gather all of the related documents.

"This is Sorkis," came the voice on the other end of the line.

Gomes introduced himself and got right to the point. "I am conducting the financial background investigation for the Aladdin licensing investigation."

"What financial background investigation? There's never been a financial background investigation."

"The Nevada Gaming Control Board has initiated a new phase in licensing investigations, focused on the financial background. I'm looking forward to your cooperation in this matter. I will be in St. Louis tomorrow, and I'd like to meet with you in order to gather all documents relating to this purchase deal."

"The licensing hearing is one month away," Sorkis cautioned. "This is an extremely rushed deal, because if it doesn't happen quickly, the Aladdin will close, and thousands of your fellow Nevada residents will be out of their jobs."

"I know, and my division has made arrangements to complete this investigation prior to the hearing."

"That's ridiculous. It's impossible."

Gomes assured Webbe that he would be working with a team of highly trained agents with very strong financial backgrounds. And, in a nice way, Gomes explained to Webbe that without this investigation, there would be no license, and hence, no deal. Webbe eventually conceded to a meeting at his St. Louis office.

Later that day, Gomes received a call from Hannifin.

"Dennis, I just want to go over a few things before you leave. I know you spoke to Sorkis Webbe. It's fine for you to pick up documents from him, but you cannot question him."

"What? Why not?"

"Because, for one thing, he is not getting licensed, so he's not subject to our investigation."

"But he put this whole deal together. I need to ask him some questions."

"Dennis, we will ask him any questions you may have. You can be abrasive, and I don't want you to piss him off. He is not subject to our investigation, so tread lightly around him."

"But—"

"Dennis, I will take you off the licensing investigation if you do not agree."

"Fine."

The walls of Webbe's law office were coated in beige, the desks were heavy, dark wood, and there was marble wherever possible.

As soon as Gomes got there, he and his fellow agents were greeted by the receptionist, an attractive blonde with a statuesque figure and a sway in her walk, who whisked them to the nearest conference room.

Sorkis Webbe walked in almost immediately, smelling of expensive aftershave. He looked exactly as Gomes had pictured him, sporting a pricey haircut and wearing a tailor-made three-piece suit. Webbe showed Gomes, Law, and Iannone a warm welcome. He firmly shook each of their hands, and even managed to appear happy to see them. He led them over to the conference-room table, where a pitcher of ice-cold water was waiting, along with the files Webbe had that pertained to the Aladdin purchase deal.

Gomes momentarily felt like he was catching up with an old friend. There was no vestige of the uncooperative man he had spoken to yesterday.

"Is it okay to make copies of these documents?" Gomes asked.

"Sure—just give them to Sally, and she'll copy anything you need." Webbe was one of those guys who made you feel you've known each other forever. He was so good, in fact, that it almost frightened Gomes.

"Unfortunately, I have to leave," Webbe said. "Do you have any questions before I go?"

Gomes thought about this for a moment. *Yeah, as a matter of fact I do have questions for you.*

"No," Gomes said finally. "I think we have everything. Thanks again."

"Great. Guys, it was nice to meet you," Webbe said. "I'll be around all week; you know where to find me." And with that, he left.

Sorkis Webbe had an uncanny ability to take over a room. People just seemed to like him. This trait did not fool Gomes, however; if he hadn't gotten a taste of the passive threat Webbe had implied during their previous phone call, he might have been fooled.

Sorkis Webbe was born and raised in St. Louis, Missouri. Webbe's family had been politically involved in the St. Louis community for many years. Webbe was one of the youngest state senators ever elected in Missouri. He served in that position for seven years, until he sought and won the elective office of St. Louis public administrator in 1963. At the time of the Aladdin license applicant investigation, Webbe still held this position. He was also a practicing lawyer with the firm of Rooney, Webbe, Davidson, and Schulter, whose law office had hosted the day's meeting.

According to Webbe, the majority of his law practice was in the field of labor negotiations. In particular, he represented the St. Louis Plumbers

& Pipefitters Union Local 562, a union that was well known for its violent and notorious history. Furthermore, according to federal sources, Sorkis Webbe was known to associate with Anthony Giordano (reputed head of the St. Louis Mafia), James (Jimmy) Michaels Sr. (reported head of the St. Louis Syrian mob), and many other lesser-known hoods.

Gomes, Law, and Iannone spent hours sorting through and making copies of the necessary documents. During this process, Gomes learned that the Aladdin purchase deal involved six investors; three from Detroit: Charles Goldfarb (46 percent), Irwin Goldfarb (3 percent), and George George (15 percent); two from St. Louis: Webbe's brother, Peter Webbe (15 percent) and Richard Daly (15 percent); and one investor from Las Vegas, Sam Diamond (6 percent). Gomes would later assign Duane Noyes the job of looking through various intelligence files for anything relating to any of the investors; by this point Gomes and Noyes had developed one of the best intelligence units in the state of Nevada.

Following the meeting with Sorkis Webbe, Gomes, Law, and Iannone spent time with members of the St. Louis and Detroit organized crime bureaus.

"You want to know about Charles Goldfarb?" Detective Sykes* asked in a booming, rock-salt voice. "I can tell you all about that son of a bitch."

Detective Sykes from the Detroit Organized Crime Task Force had fists that looked like mallets, a neck as thick as a barrel, and a flattened nose. The man proudly wore his official uniform, which was covered with so many badges and stripes, Gomes couldn't possibly have guessed what they all stood for. He looked more like a cop from 1920 than 1971. And the office did nothing to belie the image; it was a spartan, off-white labyrinth of file cabinets and metal desks.

Sykes explained that Charles Goldfarb was a Detroit bail bondsman, whose father-in-law was Art Caplan. In 1963 the US Senate Select Committee on Improper Activities in Labor and Management (also known as the McClellan Committee) described Caplan as a higher-echelon member of organized crime in the Detroit area. Charles Goldfarb and his

---

* Pseudonym

brother Irwin hung around a lot of made guys. Whether or not they were officially made, Sykes wasn't really sure.

"One of Goldfarb's closest friends is Louis 'Rip' Koury," Sykes said. "We have placed them together on numerous occasions. Rip is a lieutenant in the Licavoli-Bommarito combine."

"Koury, Koury—right." Gomes said, sitting forward in his chair. "We found a recent transaction where Charles borrowed ten thousand dollars from him, then paid Koury's son five thousand."

"That stupid son of a bitch. I can't believe that he's applying for a gaming license."

"He wasn't counting on my investigation. The State just added it," Gomes said, then asked, "What about his brother, Irwin?"

Irwin Goldfarb was in that same group. His closest associate was Frank Ryan, a lay-off bookmaker for the Detroit-area Mob.

The last applicant from Detroit was named George, Gomes recalled, but he needed the detective's help with the man's full name.

"You must be talking about George George," Sykes said.

"Oh, right." Gomes smiled. "How could I have forgotten that name?"

George called himself a businessman, Sykes explained, but it just wasn't legitimate. He had a bunch of business and social relationships with various members of Detroit's crime family. His foster brother and business partner was James Tamer, classified as a non-Italian member of the Detroit Mafia. He'd been arrested around forty times for everything from bookmaking to bank robbery to murder, but he'd been difficult to convict because witnesses tended to go missing, or turn up dead.

Gomes nodded.

"Tamer was convicted for his role in operating a multimillion-dollar interstate gambling ring," Sykes said. "And we found him holding a hidden interest in the Melody Gardens Night Club."

"Right. That interest was fronted by George. We also found a real-estate transaction with Phil Peters that George left off of his application," Gomes said. "Can you tell us anything about him?"

"Phil Peters is a member of the Licavoli-Bommarito combine," Sykes explained. "He's been arrested fourteen times, with six convictions."

"This is so helpful," Gomes marveled. "We really do appreciate your help."

"Here's one more little tidbit of information: George's sister, Dolores, is married to Sam Monazym. And Sam's brother is Charles Monazym, a major racketeer."

Gomes's smile widened.

— —

It was all coming back to Nevada's gaming statutes (specifically Statute 5.011, item 5), which stated: "Catering to, assisting, employing, or associating with, either socially or in business affairs, persons of notorious or unsavory reputation" are grounds for the denial or revocation of a gaming license.

With regard to the Detroit investors, Gomes had found his smoking gun. However, when it came to the St. Louis applicants, there was a lot of smoke but no gun. For example, Sam Diamond was a local Vegas guy who had worked for numerous mobsters in various positions. The other two investors, Peter Webbe and Richard Daly, really didn't have much of a record to speak of, either legitimate or illegitimate. This led Gomes to believe that they were merely clean "fronts" that Sorkis Webbe and the St. Louis Mob had managed to find.

Armed with lots of dangerous information, Gomes, Law, and Iannone questioned the six applicants. Unfortunately, nobody seemed to know anything about anybody.

— —

Gomes and his men returned to Vegas on a high. The applicants had not admitted to anything, but they didn't need to; playing dumb was not a valid entry on their application.

Gomes and his agents put together a tight investigative report of their findings, which clearly linked the Detroit investors to various members of the Detroit organized-crime family in both social and business dealings. They distributed the report to the three Gaming Control Board members and to Tom Carrigan, chief of the Investigations Division.

Satisfied with his work, Gomes was ready for a night out with Barbara. He made a late reservation at the Golden Steer Steakhouse, a favorite of the Rat Pack, celebrities, and gangsters, telling Barbara that he would pick her up at the Tropicana after her show.

In the meantime, Gomes went over to Linda's house to see Doug and Mary.

"Why are you all dressed up?" Linda asked him the moment he walked into the tidy little bungalow.

"I'm going to the Golden Steer," Gomes replied.

"Fancy. By the way, I heard that you're dating a dancer."

"Who told you that? What's it matter?"

"It doesn't; I was just curious. Well, are you?"

"Yeah."

Linda didn't come out and say that she wanted Gomes back, nor did she say that she was bothered by his dating life; nonetheless, he had the distinct impression that she wasn't completely at peace with the idea that he was moving on. This conversation reminded him of all the problems that went along with being married. Linda had filed the divorce papers; for Gomes, there was no coming back from that.

Gomes left Linda's house confident in his decision to never get married again. He wasn't in the best frame of mind, but one sight of Barbara in her soft shift dress, belted at her tiny waist, with bouncy ruffles that danced around her gorgeous legs, and Gomes was thinking about something totally different than marriage. Barbara had her hair pulled into a low bun, accented with a flower.

"You look beautiful." Gomes's grin was enormous. "I love how you always have flowers in your hair."

She had taken off her show makeup, which left the lightest stain of red on her lips.

"Really? Thanks. You look nice, too. So, where are we going?"

"The Golden Steer. Is that okay?"

"Oh my gosh, I've wanted to go there ever since I moved here!"

A short dash down the Strip, and they were having drinks at the Golden Steer's dark oak bar while their table was prepared. Gomes noticed a few of Vegas's more notorious characters hanging around the restaurant, but he had left his badge at home this night. Gomes and Barbara were seated at a burgundy-leather corner booth.

"I'm going to be in the very first performance of the Nevada Dance Theatre, Las Vegas's first ballet company," Barbara told Gomes, the candle on the table flickering in her eyes. "You should come to our performance."

Barbara's sweet-natured excitement made Gomes feel bad that he was not going to marry her, or anyone else.

"Look, Barbara, I don't want to give you the wrong idea," Gomes said as he clasped her hands in his. "Marriage is not part of my plan for the future, nor will it ever be. I will never get married again."

Barbara took a moment and looked at Gomes like smoke was coming out of his ears. She tilted her head as if she couldn't quite believe what she had just heard.

"What are you talking about?" Her gaze bored into him. "First of all, what makes you think that I would ever marry you? Second, how do you presume to think that I have even thought about it? As far as I can remember, the word *marriage* has never been in any of our conversations." Her hands slipped out of his grasp.

"Anyway," she went on, "I was talking about the ballet. Vassili—I work with him in the Folies—he's such an amazing ballet dancer and choreographer. I'm so excited that I get to be in it. This is a dream for me."

"That's incredible. You must be so busy, both with the Folies and putting together a ballet." Gomes was thankful that Barbara had pranced right over his embarrassing faux pas.

"Well, I don't mind. I love ballet. And this will bring some good culture to the city. You should really come to the performance."

"Yeah, I would love to."

They spent several hours at the Golden Steer—lost in conversation, in each other's eyes, in their own world—until they finally realized that there was literally no one else in the restaurant. Gomes tried to pay for their dinner, but Barbara insisted on splitting the bill. They drove to her house holding hands the entire way. Barbara laid her head on his shoulder and Gomes could smell the flower in her hair. She kissed him good night, and he watched her impossibly long legs glide away.

Phil Hannifin walked into Gomes's office a few days after the Aladdin financial background reports were distributed to the board. "Dennis, you just proved me right!" he exclaimed. Gomes beamed.

Later, even Carrigan told him, "Gomes, this is really good. I'm going to use it to support the background investigations my division did. This may be the start of a good working partnership."

As a result of Gomes's report, the Gaming Control Board decided to deny the licenses of Charles Goldfarb, Irwin Goldfarb, and George George. The Board did, however, approve the licenses of the three remaining applicants.

After hearing about the decision, Gomes told Hannifin that he didn't believe any member of the deal should have been licensed. By virtue of being in the Aladdin purchase deal with the Mob-tainted and denied Detroit applicants, Gomes believed that they too were in business with "unsavory characters," and therefore not suitable for a license.

Hannifin backpedaled, explaining that there was lots of politics involved, and how he received calls every day telling him to make sure that the Aladdin didn't get shut down.

"So it's better to have the Mob funneling money to their crime operations than to let the Aladdin close for a while?" Gomes replied. "You might as well just put up a billboard inviting the Mob: Calling all gangsters . . . Nevada welcomes you."

"You have to think about this," Hannifin said. "We denied the license of sixty-four percent of the investors. It's highly likely that the deal will fold."

"You don't know that."

"If we would have denied all of the licenses based on the clear evidence, it would be much easier for the Nevada Gaming Commission to overrule our decision as biased. They cannot deny that the Detroit applicants are involved with the Mob, but they could question the St. Louis applicants."

Gomes still thought the whole deal was corrupt, and if it went through, the Mob would only become further entrenched in Las Vegas.

How can I find a way around this ridiculous dance? he wondered.

CHAPTER 8

Unholy Pact

GOMES NOTICED THE FAINT SMELL OF VARNISH AS HE ENTERED THE Nevada Gaming Commission hearing room. He was certain that no amount of varnish would be enough to cover all the tainted decisions that had been made here.

He was the first person there on that cold December morning, so he occupied his time by studying the Great Seal of the State of Nevada, located directly behind the elevated table from which the commissioners ruled. ALL FOR OUR COUNTRY, it read, which brought a smirk to Gomes's face. The Great Seal of the State of Nevada was chosen to immortalize the mining industry. Nevada was born out of the discovery of gold and silver by the forty-niners on their way to California during the great gold rush. Now, in the twentieth century, Nevada was the first state that had figured out a way to lure visitors in search of a very different kind of gold strike.

That fateful December day in 1971 was the first time Gomes had ever been in this room, almost exactly one year after accepting the position as the Gaming Control Board's Audit Division chief.

Nevada's gaming regulations were based on a two-tier ruling body— the Gaming Control Board, for which Gomes worked, and the Gaming Commission. The Gaming Commission was comprised of a five-person lay panel appointed by the governor, and the Gaming Control Board worked as the enforcer of the Commission's judgments. The Commission had the final say on all licensing matters, and the responsibility to act on the recommendations of the Board. However, the Commission also had the power to veto a decision made by the Board through a unanimous vote of its members.

The denial of gaming licenses to the three Detroit applicants inter-ested in buying the Aladdin created a tremendous problem when the mat-ter reached the Commission level. If the Commission followed through on Gomes's recommendation and the applicants were denied, the deal would likely fold and the Aladdin would close.

That day, the room went from completely empty to filled beyond capacity in a matter of minutes. The Board members (Phil Hanni-fin, Shannon Bybee, and Jack Stratton) rushed in and took their places opposite from the elevated five-person panel's desk. The Aladdin gaming applicants sat in the gallery with the other spectators, a few benches down from Gomes, and avoided all eye contact with him. Sorkis Webbe and his representatives took their place at a small desk opposite the panel.

Tom Carrigan, chief of the Investigations Division, was one of the last to enter. Carrigan saw Gomes, shook his hand, and sat down next to him.

"Great job, Gomes," Carrigan whispered. "Your financial phase of the investigation is really going to help us."

Three knocks of the gavel called the meeting to order, and the Com-mission members filed in. The hearing began with Phil Hannifin present-ing his recommendation to the Commission members: the denial of the three Detroit applicants.

The following are comments from two of the Commission members, excerpted from this December 16, 1971, hearing. The text is taken from the confidential "Report of Investigation Relating to Possible Organized Crime Involvement in the Aladdin Hotel," conducted by the Audit Divi-sion of the Nevada Gaming Control Board and Dennis Gomes:

Commission member Mr. Diehl: *"Well, this is what concerns me. From this background that we have, and with his background [refer-ring to Sam Diamond], to be very frank with you, to me this whole thing is tainted and it worries me. Now, we're not talking about a few minor arrests in these situations; we're talking about some high echelon people in the underworld . . . but to me the whole thing was tainted. It worries me."*

Chairman Turner: *"I'm going to make a motion in favor of the licensees and those are the two, R. DALY and PETER WEBBE. Mr. SORKIS WEBBE is not technically an applicant, and therefore we have no jurisdiction over in his regard, and we're not in a position where we could even, in fact, investigate him adequately. I have some reservations because of the fact that his name appears so often. Should it become later known that his affiliations are adverse to the State of Nevada, I would be willing to move for removal of these two."*

Commission member Mr. Diehl: *". . . I still have some reservations here for reasons that I've already stated and won't go into them now, and I think that I know you well enough [Herb Jones, representation for the applicants] that you will certainly advise your people of our concern with these certain individuals and their associations, and, of course, we'll be keeping a watchful eye on the establishment."*

Following this discussion the Commission took the following action:

1. *Approved the application of the entity ALADDIN HOTEL CORPORATION and the applicants: DIAMOND, P. WEBBE, and DALY.*

2. *Denied the applications of Charles Goldfarb, Irwin L. Goldfarb, and George J. George based upon their unsuitable background and unsuitable associations.*

3. *Conditioned the approval of the license under the following terms: that the approved principals in the corporation secure an additional $200,000 to relieve capitalization deficiencies resulting from the denial of the prospective shareholders captioned above.*

Gomes left the hearing furious. He arrived back at his parents' house and walked in to find his mother and father in the kitchen washing vegetables that they had just picked from their garden.

"Denny, Linda is dropping Doug and Mary off," Mildred Gomes told her son. "They are going to spend the night."

"Fine, Mom."

"You're home early," Steve said. "How did the hearing go?"

"It's such fucking bullshit. They—"

"Denny!" His mother gave him a mortified look. "What has gotten into you? Go outside! We do not use language like that in this house. . . ."

Mildred and Steve had been in Las Vegas for close to fifteen years by this point, and they were well versed in its unique politics. Gomes's father Steve was in the building trade, and he knew the power of unions firsthand. He also knew that the unions contributed to the politicians. As a result, when the unions spoke, the politicians listened. No one wanted to see the Aladdin close, particularly when that would mean a large number of union employees would suddenly be unemployed. However, that didn't necessarily mean an end to Gomes's investigation.

"Denny, if you know that the Aladdin is a Mob operation, investigate them and catch 'em in the act," Steve said, as Linda's car pulled in and Doug and Mary jumped out and ran up the driveway.

By midnight that evening, Gomes had already called a late-night, closed-door meeting with Dick Law, Rich Iannone, Sam Rosenberg, and Larry Clark.

"We're going to investigate the Aladdin," Gomes announced in the fluorescent-drenched conference room at headquarters, surrounded by bleary-eyed agents and full pots of strong coffee. "We're going to prove that the Mob really is running things there, but we have to be extremely careful about how we do this. We have to make it look like a routine audit. You know, like nothing out of the ordinary. So no one, not even our own agents, can know what we're doing."

"Detroit and St. Louis obviously hold a hidden interest in the Aladdin," Iannone said. "But if they already approved the license, why do you think that an investigation would make any difference?"

"The money that's being skimmed is funding God only knows how many prostitution rings, drug empires, and crime syndicates," Gomes said. "We can't just sit here and pretend that that's okay."

Gomes was in a difficult situation. He had just completed an investigation of the Aladdin purchasers, so if he immediately started another investigation of the same individuals, he could face some serious consequences. Namely, the Board would not allow it, and the recently licensed purchasers could easily make a case for harassment. However, Gomes knew the Mob was involved in the Aladdin and could not let that go. He also knew that part of the Audit Division's core responsibility was conducting routine audits of each casino in Nevada. Gomes decided that he would conduct an investigation of potential organized-crime interests in the Aladdin under the guise of a routine audit. The Aladdin purchasers knew Gomes, Law, and Iannone, so they had to keep their distance—at least initially. So Gomes instructed Sam Rosenberg to go in during the day, as if he was conducting a routine audit, and to make copies of every document he could get his hands on. Gomes instructed Law and Iannone to collect the documents and review them at headquarters.

"They don't know Larry," Gomes added. "So, Larry, I want you to become a regular at the Aladdin. And we need to start changing our looks as drastically as possible."

Gomes had experimented with his appearance before. Sometimes he would let his hair go ungroomed, or grow a mustache. That cold day in January 1972 would be the last time Gomes would shave or style his hair for months. Within a few weeks, Gomes looked frighteningly similar to Al Pacino's character Frank Serpico in the film that was only a few months away from becoming a blockbuster.

Gomes wanted to test his disguise. Looking like a man too beaten by life to care about his appearance, he went into the Aladdin in tinted glasses, wearing a trucker's hat over his messy hair, and sporting a scraggly beard. No one placed him. Even Sam Rosenberg failed to recognize him when he walked by with a briefcase full of documents.

Considering this test a success, Gomes went home. He knew he had a lot of late nights at the Aladdin in his immediate future, so an early night with a home-cooked meal would serve him well.

When Gomes got home, his younger brother Geoff, who was eighteen years old, was watching TV in the living room.

"Oh man, you look like a grit," Geoff said, nearly doing a spit-take. "What happened to you?"

"Long story. Has to do with catching bad guys. Is that today's paper?" Gomes took the paper from Geoff and sat down on the couch next to his little brother.

"Well, good job—you look like a bad guy. Larry told me you took him along with you on surveillance before he was an agent. Can I go with you sometime?"

"Yeah, sure," Gomes responded absently. The headline on the front page was about the inaugural performance of the Nevada Dance Theatre. The paper reminded Gomes of Barbara; weeks had passed since he had spoken to her.

"All right! Can we do it Friday?"

"Do what?" Gomes pulled his attention away from the paper.

"Surveillance," Geoff repeated.

"Oh, I don't know."

"Come on. You just said I could."

Gomes shrugged. "Okay. Fine. I'll pick you up around five on Friday."

The sound of banging woke Gomes from a restless sleep on Friday morning.

"Denny, are you awake?" Gomes's bedroom door creaked open, and Geoff peered in, ready to go.

"Geoff, what time is it?"

"Six-thirty. I'm leaving for work, but I wanted to see what time we're going tonight?"

"I'll meet you here at five."

"Okay. Sorry I woke you up. See you tonight."

Gomes tried to fall back to sleep for another hour, but all he saw was his beautiful ballerina doing *grand jetés* across the backs of his closed eyelids.

Gomes thought he would be the first person to arrive at the office, but he bumped into Rosenberg in the hallway.

"Hey, Dennis," said Rosenberg. "Here, I wanted to bring these to you before I went in today. It's the hotel register from the last couple of weeks. There are a lot of comps, and I'm sure they're all hoods."

Gomes took the file folder from Rosenberg, started to thank him, then saw there was more.

"Here's the casino list," Rosenberg said. "I haven't had a chance to really compare the two, but based on my initial examination, most of the comped patrons show very little or no play in the casino."

Gomes was delighted. "This is great. We'll start looking it over today. Have you heard or seen anything else?"

"Everyone there looks and talks like a thug. But I've mostly been locked away in a little office, so I haven't made any positive identifications."

Gomes smiled. "You didn't notice me the other day, did you?"

"What? When?"

"I was at the Aladdin. You walked right past me."

"Huh?"

"Never mind."

Gomes settled into his office, spread the files in front of him, and began to look through the hotel register. He instantly noticed a large number of comps, and began writing down the names and addresses of every guest that had received one. The phone rang and startled him.

"Hello."

"Could I speak to Dennis Gomes?"

"Speaking."

It was an unexpected call from a fellow LEIU member, a detective out of Chicago. This detective wanted to check in on Tony "The Ant" Spilotro. They were investigating a murder in Chicago, and suspected that Spilotro had played a role. Gomes explained that Spilotro was keeping a relatively low profile. Other than the gift-shop concession he owned under a fake name at the Circus Circus, he'd been quiet.

"Thanks, man. And, hey, keep in mind that Spilotro is not the type to maintain a low profile. He's demented—a real loose cannon."

Gomes hung up the phone. The day hadn't even officially started, but he was already in the thick of it.

Within an hour, Gomes had Law, Iannone, and Noyes neck-deep in the Aladdin's hotel log. Before the magnifying glasses were even out, the red flags were unfurling. The three Detroit applicants who had been denied a license were fully comped on numerous occasions for stays lasting up to three weeks. James Tamer and Phil Peters, both known crime associates, had been comped as well. The family members of James "Jimmy" Michaels and John Vitale had also been catered to and fully comped.

Gomes was feeling the familiar rush of adrenaline. He was gathering photos and information on the Detroit and St. Louis Mafia, so now, when he went undercover on surveillance, he would know who to look for. He zoned in on James "Jimmy" Michaels Sr.

"Horseshoe Jimmy," as Michaels was once known, had cut his teeth with the Cuckoos Gang. He was arrested in 1929, at just nineteen years old, for the 1925 robbery of the Illinois Central Freight Depot. He then jumped bond, but was captured a year later and sentenced to ten years to life. He was briefly released, but arrested again for a series of gangland killings, for which he was never convicted. He served thirteen years for the robbery, was released, and quickly found his way back to his criminal life. He worked his way up to capo of the Syrian faction of the St. Louis Mob, and wielded a great deal of control over the local labor unions.

Gomes found a picture of old Horseshoe Jimmy. He had a full head of white hair, beady coal-black eyes, and a chewed cigar holding up his lips. His face was twisted into a scowl, making him look very, very unpleasant. Even though he was now close to seventy, Gomes could tell he was one tough son of a bitch.

"Hey, Dennis, can I come in?" Noyes filled the office door.

"Yeah, sure. What's up?"

"You are not going to believe this. I think the gods split the clouds and shone a light down. I just happened to come across this."

Noyes, clearly excited, pushed a document in front of Gomes. This was the first time that Noyes had ever allowed any sort of emotion to disrupt his formal appearance.

Duane Noyes had discovered that James "Horseshoe Jimmy" Michaels had been staying at the Aladdin, fully comped, under three aliases: James Anthony, James Ponti, and Francis J. Marcus. Noyes had made this discovery quite simply because "Horseshoe Jimmy" was using his real address each time he registered under an alias.

Gomes's phone rang. Noyes whisked out of the room so that Gomes could have some privacy. The voice on the other end of the line was his brother's.

"Denny, I thought you were going to pick me up at five."

"Oh shit; I lost track of the time. Sorry, Geoff." Gomes looked at the clock—it was a quarter to six. "On my way."

Gomes traded Horseshoe Jimmy's LEIU file for Tony "The Ant" Spilotro's, picked up his little brother, and made his way to the Strip.

"So, what's the plan?" Geoff asked as their car skimmed over neon-drenched streets and past garish billboards.

"We're going to check in on an enforcer for the Outfit—Tony Spilotro."

"What's the Outfit?"

"It's Chicago's organized-crime syndicate."

Gomes looked over at Geoff as he pulled into the Circus Circus parking lot, wondering if bringing his brother along was a good idea. Geoff seemed to be having a similar reaction. Gomes instructed his visibly nervous little brother to just stay calm and act natural.

With the slightest bit of enjoyment, Gomes told his little brother, "I have my gun; I'm protected. I don't know what you're gonna do. I guess if I were you I'd probably run as fast as I could—and make sure you run in zigzags. It'll make you harder to shoot."

Gomes had to fight back his laughter. He knew nothing would happen; the Mob would never do anything to disrupt their goose with the golden eggs. But, you're never too old to tease your little brother.

"Maybe this isn't such a good idea," Geoff said softly.

"You'll be fine. Just remember to zig and zag, zig then zag."

Gomes could see the beads of sweat forming on Geoff's brow.

The Gomes brothers walked through the front doors just as the sun was setting behind the valley's mountains. Inside they were met by blaring horns, jugglers, high-flying trapeze aerialists, carnival games, and a carousel bar. Gomes enjoyed this vaudevillesque surveillance; it reminded him of playing with a jack-in-the-box toy as a little kid. The music was going, the crank was spinning . . . When would Tony "The Ant" pop up?

Ta-da. The drumbeat echoed with a slap on the cymbal, and the aerialists took their bow. From off to the left came the loudest cackle Gomes had ever heard. As if on cue, Tony Spilotro walked right by Gomes and Geoff.

Gomes felt like a huge Band-Aid had just been pulled off. Any fun he was having quickly drained away as the sting of reality took hold. Spilotro may have been only five-foot-five, but he held enough rage in that compact body to scare the biggest man. This was the first time that Gomes had seen Spilotro in person. The killer's dead eyes chilled him.

Time seemed to be moving in slow motion as Gomes watched Spilotro walk by. His hair looked more like a helmet—thick, hard, and rubbery, all covered in greasy tar. He looked Gomes right in the eye. *Don't look away. You can't look away.* An eternity seemed to crawl by before Spilotro blinked and moved on.

"Dennis, was that him? He's so short." Geoff asked.

"Yeah, come on—let's go." The reality of this evil was suddenly tangible. Gomes did not want anyone from his family exposed to such darkness.

"He was looking at you."

"I know."

"Do you think he knew you were a cop?"

"Probably. Come on . . . fun's over."

From that point on, Gomes vowed to not stop until the Mob was completely out of Nevada. It wasn't about his job anymore; it was black and white, right and wrong.

Gomes pulled into his parents' driveway, anxious to return his brother to normal life. "Geoff, I'll see you later."

"Denny, what are you doing?" Geoff asked.

"I have some more work to do. I'll see you tomorrow."

"More work tonight?"

Gomes nodded.

"Be careful," Geoff added. He closed the door and watched his brother screech out of the driveway.

Gomes made his way to the Aladdin with the speedometer never going below seventy-five miles an hour.

—⟶ ⟵—

The Aladdin looked like Ali Baba had moved the forty thieves' treasure to a nice spot on the Las Vegas Strip. Inside the place, incense and cigarette smoke lingered at nose level.

Gomes went straight in and took a seat at a slot machine close to the table-games pit. A cocktail genie took his order and quickly returned with a beer from her magic lamp.

Above the bar, a huge lit-up oil lamp sat in full view—at once both gaudy and beautiful. Gomes saw Sorkis Webbe blatantly giving directions to a casino shift boss. Technically, it wasn't illegal for Webbe to be at the casino, but it *was* illegal for him to work at the Aladdin without a gaming license. What was worse, Gomes recognized the casino shift boss as the nephew of reputed Detroit mobster Charles Monazym. The nephew shared the same name and some of the same criminal record; he had multiple arrests and convictions, and, like his uncle, two were for bank robbery. Now, he was illegally employed at the Aladdin watching over huge bundles of cash.

"Would you like another beer?" the cocktail genie asked Gomes, who had been so focused on Webbe and Monazym that he hadn't realized he'd finished his beer.

"Yeah, all right. Thanks." She returned with another beer right away.

Gomes had seen enough for one night. He felt like his eyelids had been ripped off. Anger put a tight vise around his chest, and he could feel the pressure building. If Gomes didn't leave soon, there was a good possibility he might explode. He guzzled his beer and left.

—⟶ ⟵—

Sunday couldn't have come quickly enough. Gomes needed an escape—needed to bury his sorrows in the arms of his ballerina, if she would have him. He found the prettiest bouquet, bought a ticket, and went to the ballet.

He didn't know what to expect. He had never been to a ballet before, and if it weren't for Barbara, he probably never would have. He didn't have any trouble finding the Judy Bayley Theatre, right on UNLV's campus. Still looking disheveled, he felt slightly self-conscious around this cultured crowd. Women in fur coats and men in suits were milling and air-kissing around the entrance.

The building was new, and still looked it. The massive glass wall that greeted the patrons at the entrance reflected the glittering crowd in such a way that Gomes felt like a lump of coal in a sea of diamonds. There were floor-to-ceiling glass windows. The exterior and interior walls were constructed of a textured concrete, which combined soft curves with rigid lines. The faint smell of fresh paint and just-cut wood made everything smell new, combining nicely with the onslaught of expensive perfume.

Gomes expected to be the only man there, but he wasn't. There were quite a few other, far more stylish men carrying bouquets. He hoped they weren't there for Barbara.

An usher led him to his seat as the lights were going down. The music began, and Gomes let out a deep, relaxing sigh. Then the stage lights came up, and standing in the center of it all was Barbara. Every muscle in her toned body served a higher purpose. She was living, breathing art. An angel not confined by earthly limitations. She twirled, she pique-turned, she leapt, and grand jeté'd with otherworldly grace.

Gomes was hopelessly, insanely, permanently in love.

The ninety-minute ballet seemed to last no more than ten; it was an hour and a half of pure relaxation, like meditation. Gomes didn't think about work. Not even once.

After the curtain closed, Gomes made his way through the well-dressed crowd to where the other men with flowers were waiting.

"Dennis. Dennis!"

Gomes turned and was surprised to see Linda and his daughter Mary.

"Mary! Hi, sweetheart." Gomes gave her a hug. "Linda, what are you doing here? I didn't know that you were coming."

"I thought it would be good for Mary," Linda replied.

"You're right; I'm glad you brought her. Mary, what did you think?"

"It was good. Daddy, wook what I do." Mary put her arms up and twirled with the adorable awkwardness of a four-year-old.

"Wow, sweetie—that was incredible! How did you learn to dance so well?"

Mary laughed and gave her dad a big hug.

"So, which dancer are you dating?" Linda asked while Gomes threw Mary in the air, hugged her, and sat her down.

"Did you notice the dancer that was all in white at the very beginning?"

"Her?"

Gomes nodded.

"Oh my God, she's beautiful," Linda marveled. "She was the star of the whole show."

Gomes wasn't sure how to reply. He was also desperately hoping that they were, in fact, still dating.

Dennis gave Mary a hug and a kiss, and Linda and Mary left.

———

When Barbara finally came out, a stylish, clean-cut man with perfectly coiffed, sandy-blond hair and designer duds gave her a huge hug and a bouquet. Gomes was crestfallen.

Dammit! I knew it! he thought. But just before Gomes could throw away his own flowers and storm off, Barbara's male dance partner came out and this same gentleman gave the male dancer a bouquet, and the two men exchanged a loving, longing glance that gave Gomes hope. Barbara kissed them good-bye and continued walking.

"Barbara—congratulations!" Gomes said, standing before her with his flowers. She looked into his eyes for a long moment.

"Dennis?"

"Oh, yeah, sorry. It's for work."

She laughed and rubbed his beard. "Oh my gosh, I didn't recognize you. I didn't think animals cared how you looked." She giggled under her breath.

"What animals?"

"You have to promise to never make fun of me for this, but when Joanie first told me that she was going to fix me up with a Gaming Control Board agent, I thought you worked for some wildlife organization, or Parks and Recreation. This was more the guy I was expecting." They shared a laugh. "Anyway, what did you think of the ballet?"

Dennis was simply in awe of Barbara, and he told her exactly that. They easily fell into conversation and decided to grab a bite to eat. Dennis was so relieved that Barbara was still single, he promised to never let that much time go by without a phone call ever again. Barbara laughed off his apology and they left the theater arm in arm.

CHAPTER 9

Sledgehammer

"Will you marry me?"

"What?"

"Barbara, will you marry me?" Gomes was sitting on his couch, covered in a blanket, running a temperature, drained with exhaustion. He held a bowl of soup, which this beautiful creature had just brought for him.

"Are you serious?"

"I'm completely serious. I love you."

"You're not just saying this because you're delusional and sick, are you?"

"I'm not that sick. I want to marry you," Gomes said.

After a pause, Barbara said, "Can I tell the girls at work?"

"That depends; what's your answer?"

"Yes. Oh my gosh, yes, yes, yes, yes!" she exclaimed between fusillades of hugging and kissing.

Gomes managed an enormous grin. "Well, then, yes, I guess you can definitely tell the girls at work."

"Oh, I don't want to leave now, but I have to. I love you so much."

"I love you too. How about we go buy a ring tomorrow?"

"Okay—great! I love you. I'll see you tomorrow. Feel better." Barbara kissed Gomes and practically floated out the door.

The wedding date was set: May 26, 1973—a small, intimate ceremony at the Methodist Church on Maryland Parkway, which would be followed by a reception gladly hosted by Gomes's parents at their home.

Gomes always felt a little guilty for not putting more effort into the proposal, but Barbara didn't mind. She had no interest in the "proper" way to do things.

Barbara never bothered Gomes with any of the wedding planning. She knew he couldn't have cared less whether the napkins were blue or yellow.

━ ━

One night, not long after the proposal, Gomes picked up Doug and Mary and started the drive across town.

"Dad, are we going to meet our new mommy?" Doug asked.

"What? Doug, is your seat belt on?"

"Mommy doesn't make me wear my seat belt," Doug replied.

"Well, I do. So put it on now."

"That's not fair," Doug, now six years old, whined. Gomes felt something drip on his pants. His hands were sweating so profusely that beads of salty moisture were running down the steering wheel and onto his lap.

What if Barbara doesn't like kids?

"Dad, Mary's hand is on my side!"

I've never seen her around any kids.

"Daddy, Dougie hit me hand!"

How could I marry someone that doesn't like kids?

"Doug, stop it. Keep your hands to yourself. Don't make me pull this car over."

"That's not fair," Doug complained.

What if Doug and Mary scare Barbara away? Gomes's mind was racing.

Barbara was outside when he pulled up to the curb.

"Dad, why is that lady waiting outside?" Doug asked. Gomes took a deep breath. He and Mary got out of the car first, then watched Doug bolt from the vehicle and take off running down the street.

"Doug, get back here!" Gomes yelled.

"I'll get him!" Barbara said. She ran down the street and caught up with him a few houses away. Gomes couldn't hear what she said, but after a brief conversation they walked back to the house holding hands. Gomes felt utterly solid at that moment—glad that he had listened to his gut and proposed. Secure that he could take on anything, as long as he had Barbara to come home to.

Gomes brushed Barbara's long, thick, silky hair behind her shoulder and kissed her, lingering in her flowery scent. "Barbara, you've met Doug. This is Mary."

Barbara beamed at the little girl. "Hi, sweetheart. I love your dress. You are just the prettiest little princess I have ever seen."

"Tank you. Wook, I do ba-yay!" Mary twirled and Barbara applauded.

"That was beautiful. Mary, if you'd like, I can teach you more ballet, and I can put your hair in a bun just like a ballerina."

"Yeah, yeah, yeah. Pwease, pwease."

———

The Aladdin's corrupt comps kept rolling in. There was no sign of this train slowing down. Sam Rosenberg documented everything. Gomes spent Wednesday nights conducting surveillance, and Larry Clark and Rich Iannone alternated the remaining nights. Not surprisingly, it didn't matter which night he and his agents were at the Aladdin; there was always a buffet of hoods.

Gomes had plenty of documentation to prove that the Aladdin was catering to organized-crime members. However, he wanted to take this investigation a stage further. Gomes wanted to catch an organized-crime member illegally involved in the business operations of the Aladdin. The only way to accomplish this was with a surprise raid in order to catch them in the act.

The week leading up to a raid was always nerve-wracking for Gomes; he always worried about the possibility of a tip-off. All of the investigative work would have been for nothing. The Aladdin's resident thugs were so supercilious and brazen, however, that Gomes wasn't worried about them pulling back on the illicit activity, even if someone there did receive a tip.

Still, the Aladdin was gnawing on his nerves on a deeper level. Everything about the place, and the thugs who ran it, bothered him at his core. The very fact that the State had blessed this bullets-and-blood factory clamped the vise around his guts a little tighter each day.

By Thursday, Gomes had lost his appetite. On Friday, he spent a good portion of the morning in the bathroom. This unfortunately made him late to work that morning. When he finally got to the office, there was an urgent message from Phil Hannifin waiting for him.

"Shit. Fuckin' shit. Dammit!" Gomes blurted out as he settled behind his cluttered desk and studied the note.

"Everything all right, chief?" Iannone said as he peeked his head into Gomes's office.

"I hope so. Come back in ten minutes and I'll let you know. Close my door, would you?"

Gomes put his hand on the phone but couldn't bring himself to pick it up.

Hannifin must have found out about this investigation, and he was calling to stop it. Someone at the Aladdin had probably complained about Sam. This is such fucking bullshit. One fucking day before I had those assholes. I just won't call him back.

Gomes reconsidered and picked up the phone and dialed.

"This is Hannifin," came the voice.

"Hey, Phil, it's Dennis; you wanted to talk to me?"

Hannifin had just received a request from the Ways and Means Committee. They were about to formulate the annual budget in a public meeting the following week, and they wanted to hear from Gomes. The Audit Division had quadrupled in size over the past two years, and the Ways and Means Committee wanted to see how that investment was performing. Hannifin instructed Gomes to prepare a formal presentation on the Audit Division's state of affairs and to wear his best suit.

On the one hand, Gomes was relieved that his Aladdin investigation had not been corrupted. On the other hand, he was worried that his division's ability to get results was becoming a threat to the State—the same state that had recently welcomed a boatload of Midwestern thugs . . .

Whatever, Gomes thought. *I'll worry about this next week.*

Gomes spent the rest of the day studying the pictures of the mobsters and cheats whom he suspected he would find at the Aladdin. Iannone,

Law, and Clark were set to arrive at the casino between 9:00 and 10:00 p.m. that night.

Later, back home, Gomes put on his lucky jeans, holstered his gun, and made his way out. The neon night seemed to stream past his car like a dream, the passage of time juiced up by his nerves.

When he arrived, the casino was crowded. There were lamé suits, micro minis, and thugs thronging the bars, slot machines, and table games. Gomes immediately picked out Sam Guccione and Sam Bartolotta, suspected associates of the Giordano crime family. Gomes took a seat at the casino bar near a group of girls with feathered hair and dresses that should have been shirts.

They have to be from LA, Gomes thought, and then overheard their conversation.

"What a groovy place to get married."

"I know. I wish we could get into the suite that Elvis and Priscilla were actually married in."

Gomes remembered when Elvis and Priscilla had gotten married at the Aladdin. It was all the press had talked about for days.

Gomes easily pulled his attention away from the girls, feeling slightly stupid for listening in the first place. He began to scan the casino for anything irregular. Then he noticed Jay Vandermark, a notorious casino cheat, walking through a row of slot machines before disappearing into the funhouse maze of flashing lights that offered the lure of a big payout.

What's he doing here? Gomes thought.

⸺

Bob Griffin, an ex-Metro officer, and a genuinely smart and practical guy, founded Griffin Investigations in 1967. In time, they began publishing the "Griffin Book"—commonly referred to as the "black book"—a compilation of gaming offenders, which included slot cheats, table-game cheats, card counters, and any other illegitimate casino actor. Griffin's private investigators would gather all of the information from various casinos and law enforcement, and their compilation included pictures and backgrounds of the various offenders. The Griffin Book placed this valuable information in one central location, for law enforcement and casino security to use. George Jay Vandermark was listed in the Griffin Book as a notorious "slot cheat."

How stupid could he be? Gomes wondered that night, hunkered down at the Aladdin's bar. *If the Mob catches him trying to cheat their casino, they'll probably kill him.*

Gomes checked his watch. It was 11:45 p.m. He suspected that the earliest the count would take place would be 1:00 a.m. He had time to take a quick walk around the casino to check up on Vandermark.

Beer in hand, Gomes made his way to the slot-machine aisle, down which Vandermark had slunk. George Jay Vandermark, who went by Jay, was a "crossroader"—a professional casino cheat—who specialized in taking coin from slot machines. Gomes caught a glimpse of his tall, lanky frame just as he turned down an intersecting aisle. Vandermark looked like a weasel. He had a long, skinny neck that imperceptibly merged with a head topped with a frizz of light hair. He had close-set, shifty, light eyes, a pointy nose, and a thin, crooked smile.

Gomes saw him make an abrupt turn down another aisle. He gave chase, still sipping his beer and trying to look as casual as he could under the circumstances. Gomes thought he was just about to catch his prey when he realized that Vandermark was gone—as though he'd just vanished into thin air.

Gomes checked a few different aisles, but Vandermark was nowhere to be found. Checking his watch again—12:05 a.m.—Gomes decided he better return to the table-games pit. He navigated his way through the vast intersecting aisles of one-arm bandits. *Like ants falling into the casino's web*, Gomes thought, as he fought his way through the tide of tourists moving in the other direction. In a casino every single detail is planned, including the layout. Strategically, slots are placed in rows that theoretically make it easier for customers to venture in and more difficult for them to venture out. This could involve a main curving aisle that circles through the casino but never out. At any rate, it seemed to be working at the Aladdin. Gomes respected the clever development of casinos in this respect.

Gomes returned to the casino bar and found an open seat that offered a clear view of the main cage and the table-games pit. From this vantage point he would see the drop collection as soon as it started. Iannone and Clark were nearby, playing a couple of slot machines. Then Law grabbed a seat a few away from Gomes at the bar. Everyone was converging on the pit, getting ready for the drop collection to begin.

The ringing of the slot machines and the overemphasized sounds of meager payouts started to shear Gomes's nerves. He had no idea what to expect in tonight's raid. *Could the Aladdin executives really be stupid enough to have mobsters in the sanctuary?* He hoped so, because that's all he needed to tie up this investigation. *But, what if there are no wolves in the henhouse? Do I really need the linchpin? With the upcoming Ways and Means meeting, yeah, I need everything I can get!*

Suddenly, an entourage of money counters, escorted by Security, emerged from the back of the house and rolled a rattling cage toward the pit. Gomes watched as the team collected each drop box and secured it in the cage on wheels—in essence, a mini armored car.

Flashing their credentials, Gomes, Law, Iannone, and Clark intercepted the money train just before it vanished back into the depths of the casino.

"We're with the Gaming Control Board," Gomes told them, "and we're here to do a routine inspection of your count-room operations."

"No problem," replied a bucktoothed, pale, middle-aged, greasy-haired man. "I'm the count manager on this shift. Follow us back."

The four other count clerks were different versions of this guy, more or less. Two security guards that could have doubled as Vikings escorted them. The guards said nothing to Gomes.

They passed by a kitchen employee pushing a cart of raw meat that spilled blood every time the wheels shook, leaving a brownish-red trail in his wake. Just as they passed the carnage, they must have been somewhere near the garbage-collection site, because a rotten, stomach-churning scent assaulted Gomes's nose, and vomit rose up, burning the back of his throat. He had to swallow hard to keep it down.

They reached a locked door. On the other side could be the key to this investigation.

One of the count clerks flipped through his key ring until his thick fingers landed on the one he'd been groping for. He slipped the key in the lock, turned and jiggled it, and slowly opened the steel door. A plume of cigarette smoke escaped. The door opened and Gomes immediately recognized the smoker—Jack Joseph. Gomes had to clench his jaw to keep it from hitting the floor.

Jack Joseph at that time looked like nothing more than a crumpled, gray heap of an old man. A cigarette dangled from the corner of his downturned mouth. His dark-rimmed glasses looked more like they were used to hold up his drooping brow than to help him see.

"Who are you?" Jack growled with a gravelly, worn-out voice.

I know who you are, Gomes thought before he said, "We are Gaming Control Board agents, and we're here to monitor the count."

Joseph grumbled something and shuffled over to the table.

Jack Joseph had been arrested fourteen times in the St. Louis area between 1951 and 1968. In 1958, he was subpoenaed, along with John Joseph Vitale, reputed underboss of the St. Louis faction of *La Cosa Nostra,* to testify in the US Senate Labor Rackets Committee hearing. The committee was investigating the criminal control of the jukebox and vending-machine business in St. Louis. This investigation was prompted by the violent bombing of several companies, the murders of operators, and the obvious struggle for control of the vending business—and Joseph had been very much a part of it all.

During the Senate Labor Rackets hearing, Robert Kennedy had charged that Jack Joseph was nothing more than a front man for Vitale's vending-machine outfit. It was also well known that Jack Joseph was a close friend of Vitale's, and boss Anthony Giordano.

"Before we get started, we need to check everyone's ID, along with your sheriff's work card," Gomes announced.

The count team set the cage in place and handed their IDs over. The agents checked and documented the count team's identities and recorded that information, along with their role in the count. Each team member then took their turn providing the details of their work history, how long they'd been working at the Aladdin, and what they did in the count.

"Mr. Joseph, could you please explain your role in the count?" Gomes asked.

"I represent the management." Joseph stared at Gomes.

And, what management would that be? Giordano? Vitale? Gomes thought, but said, "Could you be more specific?"

"I monitor the count to make sure it's done right and then sign off on it," Joseph stated flatly.

"Is this your only position within the casino?"

"No, I am also a casino host."

Tell me something I don't know, Gomes thought. "How did you get your position at the Aladdin?" Gomes asked.

"I applied," Joseph grumbled. Gomes could tell he was not going to get anything out of Jack Joseph here, and the fact that he was in the count room was really all he needed anyway.

"We're going to need to borrow all the count-room logs. Mr. Joseph, as management representative, we will need you to come downtown Monday for a few more questions."

"Did I do something wrong?" Joseph said with an unaffected smirk.

"Not to my knowledge. We just have some more questions, and we don't want to take too much time away from the count."

"Anything to help the State." Jack managed to twist his lips into a smile that seemed sincere. "So, are we good to start the count?"

Gomes nodded, and the well-oiled machine took off.

Jack Joseph stood in the corner with his arms crossed for the entire count. He calmly watched everything without the faintest hint of emotion.

"Everything okay?" Joseph asked at the end of the process.

"The procedure was fine," Gomes said.

"Great. I'll see you Monday," Jack said with a cold smile.

Is this asshole taunting me, or is he being helpful? Gomes could not get a read on this old bull of a man.

Gomes left the Aladdin satisfied. He had his linchpin. He slept well that night, and most of Sunday.

He was ready.

—◆—

Refreshed and energized on Monday morning, Gomes started working on his report. He had to get everything on paper, in black and white.

Larry Clark poked his head into Gomes's office. "Dennis, Jack Joseph is here to see you."

"What time is it?" Gomes asked.

"About 10:20."

Gomes stretched his weary neck. He was a little surprised that Joseph had actually shown up.

"It's early. Show him to the small meeting room and grab a pad. I want you to note everything. I'll get Dick and meet you there."

Gomes had adopted the white-walled meeting room, which was hardly ever used for meetings, as an interrogation room. The room had one cheap wood-composite table with four plastic chairs. Gomes had only used it a couple of times. He had turned a few low-level snitches there in the past, guys he had caught pocketing a few bucks from a casino here or there, misdemeanors. They were always easy to intimidate. They would come in thinking they were real tough guys, but they'd be eating out of Gomes's hand after five minutes. All he had to do was threaten to press charges, and they were usually glad to offer up any bit of information they could.

"Hi, Jack—thanks for coming in," Gomes said after entering the room with his cadre. "This is Agent Clark and Agent Law."

"I remember," Joseph replied with a terse nod.

"Can we get you a coffee, water?"

"No, thanks."

"Okay, I'll get right to the point. How did you get your job at the Aladdin?"

"I applied."

"Who hired you?"

"I don't remember. I ain't no good with names."

"Let's go further back. What were you doing prior to taking a job at the Aladdin?"

"I worked at a vending company."

"Where?"

"St. Louis."

"Are you referring to the Jack Joseph Vending Company?"

"Yeah, like I said on my work-card permit. I was self-employed in my own company."

"Well, that's kind of funny," Gomes said. "Because according to our information, the Jack Joseph Vending Company changed its name to Automatic Cigarette Sales in 1957, and merged with the Anthony Novelty Company. Then it was sold way back in 1965."

"So?"

"Well, how can you work for a company that doesn't exist?"

"The company exists, just by a different name." Joseph looked calm, even snide. "Am I under arrest for using the wrong name?"

"No, let's keep talking about your vending company. At one time, were you in business with John Vitale, Anthony Giordano, and Ralph Caleca?"

"Yeah. Is there a problem with that?"

"Dick, can you explain what that problem is?" Gomes asked the man to his right.

"Sure." Dick Law leveled his gaze on the subject. "You see, Giordano, Vitale, and Caleca are all members of the Mob. In fact, Giordano is the boss of the St. Louis outfit."

"You're kidding me," Joseph exclaimed with a straight face.

"You do realize," Gomes chimed in, "that in the state of Nevada, it's illegal for anyone associated with the Mob to work in certain positions in a casino."

"That sounds like it's probably a good thing."

"You're associated with the Mob. You were in the count room. And, you don't have a casino license. That's a problem."

"Look, I ain't gonna lie. I know Tony, John, and Ralph. But I ain't got no idea what they do on their own time. I never seen 'em do nothin' bad. As far as I know, they're stand-up guys."

Law interjected: "In business, it's your responsibility to know what your partners are affiliated with."

Joseph shrugged.

Gomes added, "If you're not associated with organized crime, why were you called to testify at the Senate Labor Rackets Committee hearing, and why did you take the Fifth?"

Jack Joseph looked at him with those old, lidded eyes. "You know, I've never been able to figure out why they called me to testify, and I took the Fifth 'cause I hate public speaking."

"Come on, Jack. You don't fucking expect us to believe this bullshit?"

Joseph lifted up both wrinkled old hands and said, "I'm an old man. I've got nothing to hide."

"What brought you to Las Vegas?" Gomes asked.

"I had a bronagal condition."

"Excuse me?"

"A bronagal condition—for my health, my breathing."

Gomes, Iannone, and Law realized that Jack meant to claim that he had a bronchial condition, and had to fight to stifle their laughter. They also realized that if Joseph really had a bronchial condition, he would have known the right word.

Gomes had had enough. "Jack, we're trying to help you. You can get in some serious trouble. We know that the Detroit and St. Louis organized-crime families hold hidden interests in the Aladdin. You seem like a nice guy. We would hate for you to get dragged down in this mess."

"You're talking to the wrong guy. I wish I could help you out, but I'm just a host. I needed a job. I don't know nothin'."

Gomes burned his gaze into the old man. "We don't need your help. We have everything we need. Tell me about Charles Monazym."

"He's a pit boss."

"Where's he from?"

"I don't know. Ask him."

"He's from Detroit," Law said. "He's the only other name that signed off on the count as the management's representative."

"He's a convicted felon, and he's heavily tied to the Detroit mob," Gomes said. Charles Monazym, who changed his name to Monassum, had an uncle, also named Charles Monazym, who was a well-known Detroit thug and associate of James Tamer. Both the uncle and nephew had long arrest records, which included bank robbery.

"Fellas, I don't know what to tell ya," Joseph said at last.

"We know what's going on," Gomes declared. "The St. Louis and the Detroit Mafia families hold a hidden interest in the Aladdin. What were you really doing in the count room?"

"I told you, I was representing the management."

"Who asked you to take on that role?" Law asked.

"I think one of my managers did. I can't remember now; it was a while ago. I'm an old man. I forget things."

"Come on, Jack. You know who put you there."

No answer.

Gomes sat back. It was obvious that nothing ruffled Jack Joseph's feathers. He was the real deal. This was the first time Gomes had witnessed the difference between a real gangster and some low-level thug. Nothing affected Joseph. He remained calm and pleasant.

"These are low-life pieces of shit you're working for," Law said.

"I needed a job. I just go to work and go home. Am I under arrest for that?" Joseph gave them another agreeable smile.

"Nope. Jack, we just wanted to talk to you," Gomes said. "You've been very helpful. Thanks for your time."

"Wait." Dick Law seemed frustrated. "This is your last fucking chance to come clean before you go down with the rest of them. You've already been arrested fourteen times; you have a record."

Again with the smile, the old man said, "I'm not sure what you mean. But if you are going to continue asking me questions, I'm going to have my attorney come down."

"We're finished." Gomes shook Jack Joseph's hand.

Gomes spent the next three days locked in his office, buried in LEIU files and reports from Duane Noyes. When he finally emerged, he had a forty-four-page report that detailed every aspect of the Aladdin deal. Beginning with its origin in the hands of Morris Shenker, Jimmy Hoffa's former attorney and suspected underworld kingpin, to every mobster that was comped at the Aladdin, to the gangsters that were employed there. This report detailed everything—just in time for the Ways and Means Committee meeting.

Gomes told no one about the report. He had Rich Iannone hand-deliver it to Phil Hannifin on Friday. Gomes was too busy preparing for the Ways and Means meeting that was only days away.

—◆—

Monday morning, while Gomes was in his office preparing his comments, his phone rang. "This is Gomes."

"Dennis." Hannifin's voice was ebullient. "This Aladdin report is fantastic and terrible at the same time. Great job!"

"Thanks."

"The Commission and Board are meeting this week—actually, the day after the Ways and Means Committee. We'll figure out what to do about this. Really great job! Are you prepared for the Ways and Means?"

"I'm getting there."

"I know you won't let me down. I'll see you in Carson City. Nice work."

—◆—

The dread of public speaking was building within Gomes, which, oddly, made time seem to go by extraordinarily fast. Before he knew it, he was dressed in his suit, boarding the early flight to Reno.

One of Gomes's Reno-based agents picked him up from the airport and drove him thirty miles to the capitol building in Carson City. It was March 7, 1973. Phil Hannifin was waiting outside.

"Jesus Christ, Dennis." Hannifin eyed Gomes from the top of the steps into the capitol. "You look like a hippie in a suit. I can't believe you didn't shave or get a haircut."

"It helps with surveillance. Do I really look that bad?"

"Nothing you can do about it now. Come on. By the way, I gave the hearing members your Aladdin report. Since this is a public meeting, you cannot specifically refer to any casino or mobster by name; still, the committee will know what you're talking about."

Gomes was too nervous to appreciate the colonial beauty and grandeur of the all-brick State building surrounded by lush greenery. He followed Hannifin past the four massive white columns, through the double door, under the brass chandelier, and into the marble entranceway. Built in 1870, this capitol building was the second oldest still in use west of the Mississippi.

Hannifin motioned for Gomes to wait just outside the double white doors to the hearing room. Hannifin quietly slipped in, and Gomes sat on the wooden bench just outside. He pulled out the handkerchief his father had given him and used it to dry his sweaty hands, nervously rubbing them against the white cotton cloth. All the dread Gomes had ever experienced about public speaking had formed into an anvil weighing on his chest.

The door opened and a clerk looked out. "Mr. Gomes, they're ready for you."

Gomes instantly jumped up, getting a little dizzy in the process. He shoved his sweat-soaked handkerchief in his pocket, grabbed his briefcase, and walked in.

The second Gomes set foot into the hearing room, he wanted to turn around and sprint as far away as possible. But the massive room seemed to suck him in. He walked down a narrow aisle between rows of benches packed with spectators, all staring at him. His legs felt numb, but somehow continued to carry him toward the colossal, solid-wood, curved desk, where fifteen Nevada legislators were seated, intently watching him. There was a small oak table with a microphone and two chairs that faced the massive desk.

Hannifin was seated at the table. He twisted in his chair to watch Gomes approach. To the far right—Gomes hadn't even noticed it at first—sat another small desk occupied by a suited man whose nameplate stated he was the budget supervisor.

Gomes finally made it to the open chair next to Hannifin. "I'd like to introduce my Bolshevik in residence, Dennis Gomes, the Gaming Control Board's Chief of Audit."

Nervous titters filled the room. Gomes couldn't believe that Hannifin had introduced him as a "Bolshevik" to a body of government officials.

"Go ahead, Denny."

Gomes looked up to see a smiling Eileen Brookman, a Nevada senator, and a close family friend of his parents. Gomes leaned toward the microphone. He'd had a catch in his throat, and now he felt like his throat was going to close up entirely.

He took an awkward sip of water, then began painting a picture of the Teamsters' Pension Fund, its organized-crime ties, and its major role in Nevada's casinos.

Gomes had asked Duane Noyes to put together a report that focused on the Teamsters' Pension Fund and Allen Dorfman. This fund had tens of millions of dollars invested in Nevada's casinos, and showed no sign of slowing down. Gomes, as well as many others, suspected the fund was controlled by organized crime.

Allen Dorfman, the adopted son of a lieutenant for Al Capone, and a close ally of Jimmy Hoffa, controlled the fund. Dorfman had been convicted of embezzlement of the fund in 1970 and had served one year in jail; nonetheless, he continued to manage the fund.

"I have to admit that this is frightening," a committee member commented. "What do you propose to do about this?"

Although Gomes was still nervous, adrenaline kicked in big-time, and he really started talking . . . and talking. And talking.

———

Gomes told the Ways and Means Committee everything that he and his agents had uncovered, and it must have sounded good, because everyone was wide-eyed, listening intently.

"What do you need?" a committee member asked.

"What do I need?" Gomes was not sure what they were referring to. What he needed was for them to not cut any of his agents.

"How many more agents do you need?" the chairman asked, in an apparent attempt to clarify his previous question.

How many more agents? Okay . . . they'll probably give me half of what I ask for, Gomes thought.

"I could use fifty more agents." It was a shot in the dark. Phil Hannifin had a coughing fit and looked like he might pass out.

"Wait a second." The budget director for the governor had chimed in. "That's way above the twelve new hires we had allotted for in the budget."

Gomes sat there silently, worrying. *Dammit. I should've thrown out a lower number.*

"I don't think it matters," Eileen Brookman spoke up. She made a motion for the allowance of fifty new agents for the Audit Division.

"I second that," a different committee member declared.

Is this really happening? Gomes wondered, his mind racing.

The vote was unanimous.

On their way out of the capitol, Hannifin whispered to Gomes under his breath, "Dammit, Dennis! Do you know how much explaining I'm going to have to do to the governor?"

Gomes didn't know what to say. He was stunned as he followed Hannifin toward the parking lot. It was a crystal-clear spring afternoon in Carson City. There was still a small coating of dirty snow at the tree line, but Dennis could feel the warmth creeping in.

"But, it's well worth it. Great job!" Hannifin gave Gomes a hearty pat on the arm. "I'll go call your office and have them send someone to pick you up and take you back to the office"

"That's all right. I think I'll walk."

Hannifin looked at him. "Are you sure? It's a couple miles."

"Yeah."

"Okay, I'll see you on Friday. I'll be back in Vegas."

"Sounds good. Thanks."

Gomes walked just until Hannifin was back inside the building. Then he ran. He ran the entire three miles, cheering like a kid. He got more than one sideways glance, but he didn't care.

Friday morning, March 23, 1973, Gomes went to Hannifin's Vegas office to find out what the Commission had decided to do about the Aladdin.

"Are they going to revoke the Aladdin's license?" Gomes asked.

"Well, no."

"No? So, what are they going to do?"

Hannifin looked down. "Nothing."

"What?"

"Nothing," Hannifin repeated flatly.

"I don't understand. Did you just say that *nothing* is going to happen?"

"Nothing is going to happen to the Aladdin or its license holders."

"Didn't they read the report?"

"Yeah."

"And they're still not going to do anything?" Gomes blanched. He felt like the air had been sucked out of his chest.

Hannifin was as surprised as Gomes. According to the Commission, they did not want to tarnish Las Vegas's image. Neither Hannifin nor Gomes could find the logic in this decision. However, Hannifin's hands were tied. He was legally obliged to follow the Commission's final ruling in all gaming matters.

But this just wasn't good enough for Hannifin, and he surprised Gomes with a suggestion. "Hand your Aladdin investigation over to the feds, and then leak it to your guy in the press."

"Really?"

"Yeah. This is bullshit; something needs to be done. But no one can ever know that I suggested this."

Gomes said nothing, just nodded, thinking, *Whatever it takes.*

CHAPTER 10

Crash Course

THE COMMISSION'S DECISION TO BLATANTLY ALLOW MOBSTERS TO WORK
and play on the Vegas Strip wore on Dennis. It was the first time that he'd
had a bitter taste of injustice.

"What am I even working for?" Gomes complained one night to Barbara as they sat up in her small bed, its adjacent window looking out over
the desert valley. "This is such bullshit. It doesn't make any sense. Why
wouldn't they do something? What am I supposed to do now?"

There were no answers to these questions, and Barbara didn't try to
force any. She simply reinforced the fact that Dennis was doing the right
thing, and that was reason enough for him to continue on. Besides, Barbara and Dennis were a matter of days away from becoming husband and
wife—there was no need to waste time in bed talking.

Little did they know (or care at that moment) that Barbara was
about to get more involved in Gomes's work than either of them could
have ever expected.

❦

Gomes might have been tired the following day, but he felt renewed. That
afternoon, when he was poring over intelligence files, madly searching for
his next target, his phone rang with an unexpected caller.

"My name is Don North," the caller began. "I'm a local field agent for
the FBI. I was hoping to set up a meeting with you."

"Yeah, sure. Is this about the Aladdin?"

"That, and other things. I'd like to meet as soon as possible. You
wouldn't happen to be free for lunch today, would you?"

Gomes didn't hesitate. "I am."

—◆—

They met at the French Café, a funky little place in a strip mall on Maryland and Flamingo, right by UNLV—always packed with academic types. It was a safe place, and just a fifteen-minute drive for Gomes from downtown. He spent the time contemplating all the reasons the FBI might have for wanting to talk.

The French Café was easy to find, like most places in the well-planned Las Vegas city grid. Gomes checked his watch—11:59. He took a deep breath and willed his feet to walk him into the place. He tried to ignore the smell of freshly baked goods and the rumbling in his stomach as he looked around, not really sure what he was looking for. In the small dining area, he made eye contact with a light red–haired guy who looked to be in his late twenties, sitting at a corner table facing the door. He gave Gomes a slight nod and Gomes made his way over.

"Dennis?"

"Yeah."

Don North was not an imposing figure; he was on the small side, and rather skinny. But he was definitely someone you would not want to cross. North had a reputation for using innovative strategies to fight crime. He had attacked the Mob as an organization rather than individual criminals.

Gomes and North both sat down so they were facing the front entrance.

"Thanks for meeting me on such short notice," North said, getting right down to business.

"No problem."

The waitress came over and took their order.

"Thanks again for the Aladdin investigation," North said after the waitress had trundled off. "It was really well done. I also wanted to meet with you today because I think that we can form a mutually beneficial partnership."

Gomes agreed.

North then surprised Gomes with another request. A new undercover agent was moving to Las Vegas and needed some help acclimating.

This agent was just getting into the scene. He was operating as a sort of pimp, running girls. North asked Gomes if he would be open to meeting with this undercover operative at Gomes's home on a monthly basis. However, North cautioned Gomes that he could not breathe a word of this to anyone. Gomes agreed.

They finished their lunch and Gomes returned to his office with a sense of satisfaction. It felt good to know that his and his agents' hard work hadn't been completely in vain. And he was about to get a phone call with some more pleasing news.

"This is Dennis Gomes," he said, answering his phone that afternoon.

"Dennis, Shannon here." Shannon Bybee was the Gaming Control Board member stationed in Las Vegas. "I just wanted to give you a heads-up. Your Aladdin investigation was great, and I'm with Phil. What the Commission did was bullshit. But, listen, we're going to require that Jack Joseph and Charles Monazym file for gaming licenses as key employees."

"They'll never do it."

"Exactly. Then we can mandate that the Aladdin fire them or we can take formal action. I know that seems inadequate, but at least it's something."

As soon as Gomes had hung up the phone, he called his inner circle into his office. Rich Iannone, Dick Law, Larry Clark, Sam Rosenberg, and Duane Noyes knew the drill by that point. The first ones to come in took the chairs. The others dragged in plastic chairs from the open area. And, the last one in—usually Clark—got the corner of the desk as a seat. These were the agents Gomes trusted with the division's most important investigations. There were always other investigations and audits going on that were important, but this was Gomes's closed-door crew.

"We need to get our next major investigation started," Gomes began. "After this week, I'll be out for two weeks. I want something solid to come back to. Ideas?"

Circus Circus and Caesars were both suggested. It was likely that organized crime held hidden interests in both those properties, but Gomes wanted to find a target that was new, and likely to get a good reaction out of the Commission.

"Well, there's been a lot going on at the Trop," Law suggested. "What about—?"

"Perfect!" Gomes nodded. "Start monitoring the Tropicana now."

<hr/>

This warm May day in 1973 was a good day for Gomes. He had a new target. He was back in the game. After work, he rushed to his parents' house to pick up some of his things. He was slowly moving into Barbara's place, and wanted to get there before she left for work.

Gomes managed to get to Barbara's at 6:00 p.m. Normally this would have given them a half-hour, but not tonight.

"Where are you going?" Gomes asked. "It's only six."

"I know. I'm sorry—I got called in early."

"Really? Why?"

"I don't know; just a preshow meeting. This is such a drag. Sorry. I love you."

"Love you too."

"You can just leave your stuff in the living room and I'll put it away tomorrow." Barbara kissed Gomes and ran out the door.

It didn't take Gomes long to unload his belongings. It was surprising how little he actually owned. A few rickety boxes held all of Gomes's possessions. Some would look at this as a bad thing, but not Gomes at that particular moment. *Who needs baggage, anyway?*

<hr/>

The following morning, Duane Noyes rushed into Gomes's office: "I have some information that I think you'd like to hear."

"Okay, Duane, sit down. I'm all ears."

"I have an informant at the Tropicana who told me there is an inordinate amount of bad credit."

"How reliable is your snitch?"

"Very."

Gomes called Rosenberg and Law into his office. Without waiting for them to sit down he said, "We're going to raid the Tropicana's casino cage and credit office tonight."

——◆——

Gomes, freshly shaved and with a clean, clipped coif, picked up Clark, Law, and Noyes in an unmarked State car.

"Babyface Gomes is back," Larry jabbed.

Gomes shook his head.

The mood was easy, workmanlike, almost casual. Unlike most raids Gomes went on, there wasn't much on the line with this one—not yet, anyway—and there wasn't going to be any tortuous waiting. If they didn't find out anything with this raid, no big deal; there had not been a lot of work invested in this case yet. There was no surveillance; they didn't need to wait and watch for the count. They would park the car, walk in, identify themselves, and examine the records. This type of raid was commonplace for all of Nevada's casinos, so the folks at the Tropicana wouldn't think anything of it. Typically Gomes wouldn't even go along on such assignments. These raids rarely turned up much of anything. So, this was just going to be fun—more like a game than work.

It was a slow time of day, as well as a slow day of the week for a casino—a Tuesday, at 4:30 p.m. Gomes found a parking spot right by the door. His team walked straight through the casino and converged on the casino cage just before 5:00 p.m., right when the shift change was about to take place. Gomes hoped this would make it more difficult for the employees to focus on exactly what the Gaming Control Board was looking at.

The casino cage at the Tropicana resembled a teller window at an upscale Manhattan bank from the time of John D. Rockefeller. Gold bars, rich, dark hardwood, and marble counters completed the look.

"Gaming Control, right?" asked the cage clerk, an attractive woman with short black hair.

Gomes nodded.

"GCB is here!" she yelled to a back office.

A voice: "They're here now, at five o'clock?"

"Yes, they are."

A buzzer signaled the unlocking of a side door for Gomes and his crew to get into the cage.

A middle-aged, overweight man with thick glasses and a bad comb-over scurried out of the back office. He had a mustache and a perpetually runny nose, which he wiped with a handkerchief. "I'm the cage manager. What can I do for you?"

The agents flashed their credentials. "We're here to do some routine assessments," Gomes announced. "We just need to check and copy some of your cage and credit records."

"Follow me. I'll show you where the files are."

—◆—

Something didn't seem right. Nobody could put a finger on exactly what it was, but the information the cage manager had given them just seemed slightly incomplete. Typically, markers—accounts of indebtedness by a player to the casino—contain a thorough background record of past casino credit. The big ones, especially, tended to include this information. Many of the Tropicana's markers, however, barely listed names and addresses. And the sheer fact that the unpaid markers for the year were topping out at $1 million—which, in the 1970s, was an exceptionally high amount for any casino—raised red flags.

Things just didn't seem right. Then they found the rep totals sheet and discovered that the $1 million in unpaid markers came from one casino rep, Edward "Baldy" Sarkisian, and his Detroit Junketeers. A casino rep is an individual that brings customers to a casino in return for compensation either in the form of a commission or a salary.

Gomes seethed. *Here we go again.*

They made copies of all unpaid markers and went about their business as if nothing was out of the ordinary.

—◆—

During the Aladdin investigation, Gomes had become familiar with the Detroit *La Cosa Nostra* family. Detroit's could arguably be considered the most successful organized-crime family in the United States. And *family* they were, both criminally and genetically.

In the 1970s the sons and nephews of the founding members were ascending the throne. The second-generation Toccos and Zerillis were entering the crime world with college degrees and a propensity for murder. Law enforcement considered the Detroit Mob particularly difficult to infiltrate because of their strong blood ties.

The Detroit Mob was suspected in a multitude of murders that spanned decades (and would be suspected in the murder of Jimmy Hoffa in 1975), but no one from the crime organization had been convicted of a single murder since the 1940s. According to intelligence files, the Detroit family was one of the biggest distributors of heroin in the United States. In fact, Detroit's Charles Goldfarb, one of the denied Aladdin applicants, was a close friend of Nicky Barnes, the famed drug kingpin out of New York. On one occasion, Goldfarb, a bail bondsman, flew to New York to bail Barnes out of Rikers Island. The Detroit Mob, through its connections with the Teamsters Union, used truckers to move heroin across the country.

Gomes suspected that the Detroit Mob was using credit as a way to funnel money out of the Tropicana, which meant that they likely held hidden points in the casino. Now, Gomes just needed to prove it. Doing so would require weeks of footwork. Each marker had to be reconnoitered. Knowing how much time and dedication would be required to investigate all of the Tropicana's markers, Gomes handed the reins over to Duane Noyes so that he could get married.

It was—and would continue to be—a busy year.

Gomes woke up in a cold sweat on the morning of May 26, 1973. He was more nervous than he had been in a long time. More nervous than he was for the Zimba's Casino raid, and even the Aladdin raid. Gomes's guts were twisted in knots. The butterflies were at war and shredding his insides. The second that he sat up in bed, the first rush came. Gomes barely made it to the bathroom.

He was marrying Barbara in a matter of hours (that is, if he could get out of the bathroom). Deep down, Gomes wasn't nervous about *being* married. He was nervous about *getting* married. Standing in front of a hundred of his closest friends and family while declaring his love for Barbara sent massive waves of anxiety through his core, turning him into mush.

On that morning, once he had nothing more left inside his stomach, he took a shower and looked in the mirror. He was pale, and his already-thin frame looked somehow even scrawnier. *I just have to get through the ceremony. I just have to get through the ceremony.* Gomes was sure he was going to pass out; at least he'd have his younger brother Geoff and Larry Clark up there to catch him.

Gomes dressed in his rented black tuxedo with its gray-striped ascot. Everyone was in the living room waiting for him. It was unanimous; Gomes looked like he felt. The guys took bets on when Gomes would pass out.

The over/under was set at "I do."

Gomes's mother Mildred put a quick stop to the taunting and handed Gomes, Geoff, and Clark white carnations to pin on their lapels. She put a carnation on little Doug's suit. He looked adorable all dressed up. Mary had spent the night with the girls, and Gomes knew she would show up looking like a life-size doll. The guys and Mildred piled into three cars and drove straight down Sahara to Maryland Parkway, and were at the Methodist church in ten minutes.

The pastor met Gomes in the front and brought him to a back room where he would sit and wait until everyone had arrived.

Gomes's wobbly legs managed to get him to the altar. He stood frozen in place as the members of the wedding party made their way in. Then the music switched and Barbara and her father, George, stepped onto the aisle. The bride was completely covered from head to toe in lace. She looked as if she had just stepped out of a Tissot painting. She was stunning. The second Gomes saw Barbara, his nerves calmed, and the wedding flew by. Before he knew it he was kissing the bride.

Gomes felt good walking out of the church a married man. He felt secure. As the rice poured down on him and Barbara, any trace of anxiety faded.

They drove to Los Angeles that night and stayed at the Century Plaza. Barbara's friend had arranged for a bottle of champagne to be waiting in their room. Gomes and Barbara spent the next ten days driving up the coast of California. Gomes had a great time; he'd needed to get away.

Nevertheless, throughout the trip there was a nagging pit in his stomach. He was anxious to get back into work.

———

The answer to an epic cliffhanger was sitting on Gomes's desk when he got back to work at the headquarters building. The Detroit Junketeers, led by "Baldy" Sarkisian, had accumulated more than $1 million in bad credit in about a year. Gomes discovered that most of the bad markers were registered to phony names and bad addresses. This amount of bad credit was rapidly increasing; it was draining the Tropicana dry.

This was credit fraud, plain and simple—a criminal offense.

———

The Tropicana executive offices were upscale, lavish, like the rest of the property. Lots of rich hardwood, green plants, and comfortable leather chairs. Still, under the florescent office lights the Tropicana's age was starting to show; the wood varnish was faded, and the carpets were fraying.

A pretty blonde receptionist greeted Gomes. She had a bouquet of roses on her desk, scenting the office. She phoned Deil Gustafson, the barrel-chested owner of the Tropicana, to let him know his appointment had arrived.

"*Send him in!*" boomed a voice from a few offices down.

Gustafson was a blowhard, and an acutely loud one at that. He had one of those deep, guttural voices that echoed and reverberated off of any surface with which it came in contact.

Gomes found Gustafson sitting behind a massive oak desk like a Viking ruler on his leather throne.

"Thanks for meeting with me," Gomes said.

"Anything for the Gamers."

"I wanted to talk to you about some troublesome information we came across."

"Go on."

"For the year, the Tropicana has over a million in bad credit from the Detroit junket program."

"So, why is this a concern to you?"

"Because, we suspect a credit fraud is taking place."

"No. No way. We just haven't collected on those debts yet."

"Well, you probably haven't collected because the markers are registered to fake names. I think Sarkisian is operating this credit scam, which means your casino manager, Tom Corrigan, would have to be in on it too."

Gustafson raised his eyebrows. "No, they're not. I know what goes on in my place, and I completely trust Tom and Ed."

"Well, it just doesn't add up. No one could legitimately give out that much bad credit."

"Look, Gomes, I fucking told you that nothing is going on. Tom knows what he's doing. You have bad information."

"I'm just trying to look out for you and the Tropicana."

The steam was building. "I don't appreciate you coming into my fucking place and acting like you know what's going on. I told you there is nothing for you to be concerned about."

That was that. Gustafson's reaction told Gomes everything he needed to know.

———◆———

"This needs to be sent to Robert List, Nevada's attorney general, for proper jurisdiction," said the Las Vegas district attorney. "We just don't possess the financial expertise to prosecute a case of this complexity," the Las Vegas DA explained. "I would hate for us to blow this case. The attorney general can convene a special grand jury to prosecute cases that the county is unable to. Talk to Bud Hicks; he's the deputy attorney general. He'll help you out."

Gomes felt like he might be getting the typical bureaucratic runaround; fortunately, he was a good runner. He immediately sent the credit fraud investigation to Bud Hicks.

Hicks was impressed by what he heard and formally recommended taking action to List.

Unfortunately, exactly one week after his initial conversation with Gomes, Hicks called Gomes's office.

"Dennis, I'm sorry, but Bob has declined this request. He refuses to convene a special grand jury to try this case. He thinks it's too sensitive of an issue."

"What?" Gomes squeezed the receiver. "That doesn't make sense. This is a blatant crime, and no one wants to do anything?"

"My hands are tied. I wish I could help you out. I think this is total bullshit, but I can't do anything about it. Listen, you can never repeat this—I don't know how true it is, and I've never seen any evidence myself, but some feds told me that List is dirty."

Whether Nevada Attorney General Robert List was "dirty" made no difference to Gomes at the time. The fact was, a crime was taking place, and no one was doing anything about it.

CHAPTER 11

In the Red

DENNIS GOMES DEEPENED HIS CREDIT-SCAM INVESTIGATION OF THE Tropicana and discovered that there was more bad credit than he'd previously thought, and it was going to more cities than just Detroit. To Gomes this meant there was a distinct possibility that other Mafia families also held points in the Tropicana and were skimming money.

These various credit scams were creating a problem for Tropicana owner Deil Gustafson. They were rapidly draining the casino of necessary operating funds. Consequently, the "cash on hand"—the cash levels in the casino cage—were abysmally low.

According to Nevada Gaming Statute 6.150, casinos are required to maintain a minimum amount of money to ensure that the casino could cover any potential winnings. Knowing that the state of Nevada would not want to tarnish its image with a casino that couldn't cover the action, Gomes reported the Tropicana's lack of casino-cage funds to the Board.

"How did it get that low?" Hannifin asked Gomes over the phone one day.

"All the bad credit."

"Do you realize how bad it would look if a Nevada casino could not pay out some winnings?"

"Right," Gomes said, wondering if he were the only one who saw how ridiculous this was.

"We are going to immediately require that the Tropicana raise their cash level by one million."

This requirement was exactly what Gomes wanted. When that $1 million came into the Tropicana, the Audit Division would be called in to investigate the source of funds—the open door Gomes needed.

Still, this whole situation bothered Gomes for other reasons. *Why had the Tropicana allowed itself to get into such a precarious financial situation? If various organized-crime families held points in the Tropicana, why didn't they lessen their skimming to get the casino back on its feet? Was each family entitled to a predetermined skim amount? Or, was each family competing to see who could loot the most?*

Was Gustafson really in charge, or was he just a blowhard serving as the front for an elaborate crime?

Gomes did not have to wait long for an answer.

On September 28, 1974, a loan for $1 million was reported to the Gaming Control Board. Carefree Travel, Inc. and Edward LaForte secured the $1 million from Valley Bank through the sale of real estate. In return for the loan, Edward LaForte was promised a 10 percent interest in the Tropicana Hotel and Country Club at some future point ("Of course, after he is licensed by the GCB," Gustafson assured Gomes).

Gomes learned that the loan for $1 million was actually first received in payments between May 24 and July 19, 1974, from Edward LaForte. Then, on August 6, 1974, the full $1 million was repaid to Edward LaForte. And on August 28, 1974, the Tropicana received a loan from Carefree Travel and Edward LaForte, which was restructured for tax reasons.

The Audit Division discovered that Carefree Travel was a subsidiary of Imperial Worldwide Group Tours, Inc., which operated primarily as a holding company for Carefree Travel. Imperial had been formed on April 27, 1972, with Edward LaForte as the sole stockholder, but he gave roughly 7 percent of the corporate shares to two employees, and 9 percent to his brother, Giuseppe (Joseph) Joe "The Cat" LaForte.

Gomes knew that he needed to go to New York in order to learn more about the LaForte brothers and Carefree Travel. But to do this, he needed approval from a Gaming Control Board member. While it was far from a sure thing, he got the okay.

The Stardust was one of four casinos owned by Argent Corporation, a business that Dennis Gomes investigated for suspected criminal activities. Argent Corporation was owned by Allen Glick, a California businessman, and was funded by the Teamster's Pension Fund. PHOTO COURTESY OF THE LAS VEGAS CONVENTION AND VISITORS AUTHORITY/LAS VEGAS NEWS BUREAU

Frank Rosenthal was a well-known sports betting handicapper and an associate of the Chicago Outfit. Rosenthal held numerous positions with Argent, including CEO and entertainment director. However, Gomes suspected his true function was running the entire gaming operation on behalf of the Chicago Outfit. PHOTO COURTESY OF THE ASSOCIATED PRESS

At one time the Tropicana was considered the "Tiffany of the Strip" and a hotbed of criminal activity. The Tropicana was the focus of Dennis Gomes's investigations on numerous occasions. It also happened to be the place of employment of Barbara—his girlfriend and future wife. PHOTO COURTESY OF THE LAS VEGAS CONVENTION AND VISITORS AUTHORITY/ LAS VEGAS NEWS BUREAU

Born Vincenzo Pianetti in Italy, this Kansas City mob associate (center) assumed the name Joseph Vincent Agosto after he immigrated to the United States. He purchased the Follies Bergere show in 1975 and used the production as a guise to run the mob's operation at the Tropicana. PHOTO BY AND COURTESY OF ANDREA WALLER

Dennis Gomes's investigation of the Aladdin resulted in the denial of three gaming license applicants from Detroit. Despite this denial, well-known mobsters were regularly catered to at the Aladdin. Gomes suspected that the St. Louis and the Detroit mobs held hidden interests in the Aladdin. PHOTO COURTESY OF THE LAS VEGAS CONVENTION AND VISITORS AUTHORITY/LAS VEGAS NEWS BUREAU

Tony Spilotro (front, left) was a well-known enforcer for the Chicago Outfit and a close friend of Frank Rosenthal. He ran a multitude of criminal activities in Vegas and was known to have a penchant for torturing his murder victims. PHOTO COURTESY OF THE ASSOCIATED PRESS

Larry Clark was Dennis Gomes's best friend from college. He joined the Nevada Gaming Control Board following his service in Vietnam and after obtaining a master's degree. PHOTO COURTESY OF CHARLENE CLARK

During interviews for the writing of this book, Rich Iannone—second from the left and pictured here with his wife (Barbara), Barbara Gomes, and Dennis Gomes—said "during my time on the Audit division everyone felt good, like they were making a difference. It was fun." Iannone was part of Gomes's most trusted inner circle and operated by the same moral code. PHOTO COURTESY OF RICH IANNONE

Dick Law, pictured here with his kids, was a public school–bred liberal while Dennis Gomes was a Catholic school–bred conservative. However, the colleagues in the Nevada Gaming Control Board's Audit Division shared a vision of right and wrong. Gomes and Law worked in the name of justice and were dedicated to their families.
PHOTO COURTESY OF DAVID LAW

Dennis Gomes had a great deal of admiration for his boss and friend Shannon Bybee. As members of the ruling body of the Nevada Gaming Control Board, Bybee and Phil Hannifin worked hard to clean the mob out of Nevada's casinos. Bybee continued to influence Gomes's career long after his tenure with the Gaming Control Board.
COURTESY OF NORMA BYBEE

In 1968, at just nineteen years old and long before she met future husband Dennis Gomes, Barbara moved to Las Vegas to pursue a dancing career. She used this photograph as a publicity shot. PHOTO COURTESY OF BARBARA GOMES

In 1972, Vassili Sulich, a principal male dancer in the Follies Bergere, formed the Nevada Dance Theatre and presented the company's first ballet. This photograph of Barbara Gomes with her dance partner, Wayne Clemons, was used for promotion. PHOTO COURTESY OF BARBARA GOMES

This photograph of Barbara Gomes with Bonnie Schreck was taken during a special performance of *Jubilee* to benefit the Nathan Adelson Hospice. PHOTO COURTESY OF BARBARA GOMES AND FRANK SCHRECK

Dennis Gomes, pictured here during college, sought an accounting degree with the ultimate goal of using it to help him join the FBI. However, just before Gomes found his way to the Bureau, he interviewed for the position of chief of the Audit Division for the Nevada Gaming Control Board. PHOTOGRAPH COURTESY OF BARBARA GOMES

Dennis Gomes and Barbara were married on May 26, 1973, just nine months after their first date. PHOTOGRAPH COURTESY OF BARBARA GOMES

State of New Jersey
DEPARTMENT OF LAW & PUBLIC SAFETY
DIVISION OF GAMING ENFORCEMENT
This is to certify that

Dennis C. Gomes

Is attached to this office in the
Capacity of

Chief, SIB

For office use only

After leaving his position with the Audit Division of the Nevada Gaming Control Board, Dennis Gomes took a brand-new position as chief of the Special Investigations Bureau for the New Jersey Casino Control Commission. New Jersey passed the gaming referendum in 1976, and Gomes moved to the Garden State to lead the investigation of the first gaming applicant, Resorts International, which officially opened its casino on May 26, 1978. PHOTOGRAPH COURTESY OF BARBARA GOMES

Dennis Gomes was very focused on his career, but never at the expense of his family. This photograph was taken just after Gomes's resignation from the Nevada Gaming Control Board, as the family was planning its move to New Jersey. PHOTO COURTESY OF BARBARA GOMES AND MARY (GOMES) SWAIN

Dennis and Barbara with the Gomes kids: Danielle, Mary, Gabrielle, Aaron, and Doug. The casino business ran thick in the Gomes blood, and each Gomes sibling worked in the industry at one point. As of this writing, Gabrielle is cutting her teeth as a casino analyst and Aaron is the Managing Director of Jupiter's Casino on the Gold Coast of Australia, overseeing a multi-million-dollar expansion. PHOTO COURTESY OF BARBARA GOMES

Dennis Gomes retired from law enforcement for good in 1979 because, according to Gomes, "the guys I was chasing weren't as bad as some of the judges and politicians I was working for." He went on to have a very successful career helping to operate casinos, accomplishments for which he would eventually be enshrined in the Gaming Hall of Fame. Yet Gomes never sacrificed family or health. He led a life of balance. He was a devout student of the martial arts, for example, a Master fifth-degree black belt in Tang So Doo, and a second-degree black belt in Hopkido.

LEFT PHOTO COURTESY OF BARBARA GOMES.
TOP PHOTO COURTESY OF BARBARA GOMES
AND DAVE SIROTA

Gomes took the red-eye to JFK Airport in December of 1974. The first hints of daylight were turning the black sky to a glowing navy as he made his way to the rental car pickup. He grabbed every map he could get his hands on and wrote down specific directions to get him to the west side of Manhattan, then jumped on the Van Wyck Expressway.

Gomes was struck by the sheer amount of concrete and steel. *Why would anyone live here?* he wondered. There wasn't a single inkling that anything natural existed under the layers of concrete.

The sun was just coming up as Gomes found the Grand Central Parkway. It wasn't until he crossed the Triborough Bridge that his view of New York changed—literally. His heart fluttered. The beauty of New York's architecture was like nothing he'd ever seen before.

Just being in New York City was electrifying. It was hardly dawn and the streets were already jumping. It was a sort of energy—much different than that of Vegas—Gomes had never experienced before. The height of the buildings and the narrowness of the streets seemed to condense an unseen energy source into a tangible current.

He checked into a small but decent hotel on the Upper West Side. If he weren't so keyed up he might have taken a nap. Instead, he walked a few blocks, inhaling the vibrancy of the city with each step—blaring horns, angry voices, and carbon fumes, which somehow seemed mildly pleasant here.

The building that housed the NYPD Criminal Intelligence Unit was like any other law enforcement headquarters Gomes had ever been in. Basic industrial furnishings, lots of people trying to look busy. But unlike what Gomes was accustomed to, this building seemed ancient. Gomes wondered how long detectives had been going after criminals in this place, plotting their demise within these walls.

A New York investigator and LEIU member greeted Gomes outside a large cubicle. Gomes had worked with this detective a few years ago during the Bally Sales investigation, and knew the man was a hard-nosed detective who had worked his way up by walking the beat.

"Thanks for meeting me today," Gomes said, shaking the big hand offered to him.

The detective led Gomes back to his office. A plain wooden desk with three chairs sat in the middle of a white room covered in piles of files. Decorating this spartan space were massive charts of various Mob families, illustrating the structure of each family with names and photos.

"Wow! Who did those charts? They're incredible," Gomes exclaimed.

"Our unit did. You want them? I'll get you copies."

"Yeah. That would be terrific."

"By the way, thanks for the Wichinsky investigation. It was great," said the detective.

"No problem."

"I went ahead and made copies of everything we had on Joe LaForte. His brother Edward is clean on paper, but we have some information on him, and who he spends time with."

Joe LaForte was a known member of organized crime. His brother, Edward LaForte, was not a known associate, but spent a great deal of time at Luna's Restaurant in Little Italy with some Gambino associates.

"Listen," the detective warned, "I know you don't know your way around town. So when you leave, make sure that you don't head west from here. It turns into a really bad part of Harlem. An unmarked cop was driving through a few days back. He was stopped at a light, and a group of guys walked up to his car, popped his hood, unplugged the spark plugs so he couldn't drive. He was armed, and when he flashed his badge, they took off. But it's a rough neighborhood."

"Okay, thanks."

"My office is yours for the day."

The detective brought Gomes a large bag for the files and copies of the Mob charts he had on his walls. Gomes couldn't wait to hang them up in his office.

❧

Gomes spent the entire day studying the files the detective had left for him. He was thoroughly impressed with the New York unit. There was so much interconnected information, and it was all perfectly organized.

Edward LaForte did not have a criminal record, but he associated with many suspected mobsters. Anthony "Tony West" DeLutro, an alleged soldier in the Carlo Gambino crime family, was one of Edward's closest friends. He also associated with Paul Castellano and Carmine Lombardozzi, both suspected capos in the Gambino family.

Joseph LaForte's file was not so simple. Born Giuseppe, he went by Joseph, and was known as Joe "The Cat." Joseph LaForte was reported to be the boss of policy rackets (numbers), narcotics, and loan-sharking for all of Staten Island. Joe "The Cat" was listed as a member of the Gambino crime family, and worked directly under capo Paul Castellano. Joe LaForte had been arrested eight times between 1934 and 1948 on charges of bookmaking, felonious assault, petty larceny, rape, and allowing and permitting illegal activities.

Gomes glanced up and noticed that it was dark out. He was surprised by how long he had been swimming in the files. He was tired. He gathered up the documents, left the building, found his car, and headed back to the hotel, looking forward to a good night's sleep.

Everything looked so different at night, but just as vibrant. Gomes navigated the city streets. One wrong turn led to another, and things weren't looking right. The hustle-and-bustle crowd had turned into dead ringers for zombies. Drugged-out wisps of human beings that were absentmindedly limping from corner to corner all seemed to notice that Gomes didn't belong there. The first-floor windows on all of the businesses had bars. No lights were on anywhere. Gomes drove by a housing project that looked like a bombed-out ruin from some science-fiction rendering of America after World War III.

Whatever you do, don't head west.

Finally, Gomes came to a gas station with a light on. He pulled the car over right by the door and darted in. If a record had been playing it would have scratched to a sudden halt. A group of African-American men deep in a poker game simultaneously glared over at Gomes.

"What can I do for you?" an older man growled from the table.

Gomes suspected that this was the station owner, and that he was hosting the poker game. He was a big guy with white hair, wearing grease-stained overalls.

"How are you doing? I'm not from New York and—and—" Gomes stammered.

"No kiddin'. You lost?" a younger guy asked. He looked like a younger, albeit bigger, version of the station owner.

With a shrug Gomes admitted, "Yeah—I have no idea where I am."

"Where are you trying to get to?" the older man asked.

"I think the Upper West Side. Around West Eighty-first Street."

"Oh boy. You're definitely lost. Al, get me a piece of paper . . ."

———

Gomes returned to Vegas with renewed energy. With a significant amount of information that tied Joe "The Cat" LaForte to the Gambino crime family, the next step would be to prove that Joe was financially linked to his brother Edward and Carefree Travel. This became the focus of the financial investigation of Carefree Travel.

The link was not difficult to establish. For starters, Joe LaForte owned 9 percent of Imperial Worldwide Group Tours, Inc.—the parent company of Carefree Travel. He drove a Mercedes-Benz that was a gift from Vacation Ventures (a sister company to Carefree Travel, also under Imperial Worldwide). A few months prior to the start of this investigation, Joe began to receive a paycheck from Carefree Travel for $800 per week. He apparently was working as a salesman, but that could not be substantiated. The only other salesman for the company earned $300 per week.

Then, there was the issue of a loan of $60,000 from Edward LaForte to Joe LaForte, so that the latter could invest $100,000 in an entertainment production company, headed by Joseph Agosto. However, as soon as the Audit Division initiated an investigation into Carefree Travel and the LaForte brothers, Joe pulled the money out of Agosto's production company.

Finally, Joe and Edward were the only two authorized persons on two safety deposit boxes utilized for Carefree business purposes.

While the investigation of the $1 million loan from Carefree Travel was under way, Gomes wanted to put some extra pressure on Gustafson, and test Nevada politics in the process. In addition to the Tropicana, Gustafson also owned a very small downtown casino, the Sundance West. It was a real crap joint, a locals' sort of place.

Gomes wasn't sure if they were going to find any evidence of corruption there. He wasn't sure what to expect at all. It was a complete shot in the dark. The Audit Division initiated round-the-clock surveillance on the Sundance West, continuously rotating two agents on four-hour shifts, so as not to arouse suspicion. Gomes took as many of the shifts as he possibly could. At the end of the three-day surveillance period, he and eighteen of his best agents, including, of course, his inner circle, raided the casino, including the hard-count (where coin is counted) and the soft-count (where cash is counted) rooms.

Beginning with the surveillance leading up to the raid, Gomes and his agents documented the Sundance West Casino violating just about every gaming regulation on the books. Undocumented cross-fills (money/chip exchange from table to table), irregular count times and procedures, and unapproved individuals inside the count rooms were among the major casino-procedure regulations that the Sundance West had broken.

But Gomes found no evidence of higher-level criminal activity.

He took the information to the Board and the Commission, curious to see how they would react. If they gave only minor warnings to mobsters that used casinos to conduct criminal activity, you would expect them to not even acknowledge a small casino that was not properly operated.

Not the case.

Nevada Gaming authorities took the sledgehammer out and came down hard. They stripped Gustafson's Sundance West of its casino license, which he surrendered without so much as a peep.

Just as the Sundance West went down, Gomes completed his investigation of the Carefree Travel $1 million loan. His report clearly linked Carefree Travel, Edward LaForte, and Joseph LaForte to organized crime. Gomes recommended that the Gaming Commission exercise its authority pursuant to Regulation 8.130, and order that the $1 million loan transaction be rescinded and the funds repaid.

Much to Gomes's surprise, the Commission did, in fact, find the $1 million to be from an unsuitable source, and they ordered the loan to be repaid.

This was the first loan recession in Nevada's gaming history.

Not long afterward, Gomes read in the papers that Gustafson had sold a majority of the Tropicana.

—— ❦ ——

In early 1975 the Audit Division was called in to investigate the Doumani brothers, Ed and Fred, whose investment in the Trop was fronted by Mitzi Stauffer Briggs. The Doumani brothers were longtime Las Vegas residents and the owners of El Morocco, a smaller casino on the Strip. The Doumanis had a reputation around town as being honest, well-liked businessmen with no hint of any organized-crime ties. Gomes began to think he had run the bad guys out of town—or at least the Mob out of the Tropicana.

Gomes was ecstatic. *The Tropicana's just the first step. One casino at a time, and soon there'll be no bloodsucking crooks draining Nevada of its lifeblood.* Gomes could see the big picture; he would have the Mob out in no time.

The investigation of the Doumanis and Mitzi Stauffer Briggs was relatively easy. Everything looked clean. All funds could be clearly traced to legitimate sources. Things were going well, even though Mitzi was not the easiest woman to deal with.

Stauffer Briggs had inherited a multimillion-dollar fortune after the death of her husband, and while she was certainly a nice-enough woman, she was certifiably insane. Well, maybe not certifiably. She was a religious fanatic of epic proportions who had visions of being the Blessed Mother incarnate. Gomes considered most religious zealots insane, so someone like Mitzi topped the charts. In a town that, in truth, amounted to a cacophony of vice, Gomes found it surprising that someone like Mitzi Stauffer Briggs would immerse herself into its culture.

The only dark shadow on Gustafson's sale of the Tropicana now appeared to be Paul Lowden. A former lounge performer, Paul Lowden had become a local businessman. Gomes suspected him of being in with the Mafia, but hadn't been given the opportunity to call Paul Lowden forward for a formal investigation. However, Lowden pulled out of the Tropicana purchase deal just before Gomes's investigation commenced.

So, all seemed good; two esteemed Vegas brothers and a religious fanatic purchased the Tropicana.

Unfortunately, this pretty picture that Gomes so desperately wanted to believe quickly began to crumble.

—⁓—

A fresh wave of trouble rolled in when Gomes received a call from an informant he had developed while investigating Gustafson and the Tropicana. When the woman called Gomes, she was working as the secretary to a high-level executive in the Doumani regime.

"I'm so glad that you're in," she said softly on the other line one day as Gomes began to pace his office, his phone welded to his ear. "I needed to talk to you before I went to work," the lady informant explained.

"Did something happen?" Gomes asked.

"Well, not really. It was just this guy that came into the executive offices; there was something up with him. He scared me."

"Did he threaten you?"

"No. No, nothing like that. He just seemed evil, and he was so rude to me. Then, I overheard him talking to my boss about Ed and Fred."

"The Doumani brothers?"

"Yeah, those guys."

"What did he say?"

"He said that they're good boys, and that they're going places. Oh, and he also said that they were *good* businessmen who could be trusted."

"Did he talk to either Fred or Ed?"

"No, he said that he would just catch up with them later."

"Did you get his name?"

"Yeah, he signed in with me. His name was Richard Allen."

"Did you say Richard Allen?" Gomes instantly recognized the alias of John Joseph Vitale, the acting boss of the Italian faction of the St. Louis *La Cosa Nostra*.

"Yeah. Richard Allen. Like I said, I wrote it down."

Gomes's heart accelerated. "Can you stop by my office tonight after work? I'd like to show you some pictures."

Precisely at 5:30 p.m., Jane* walked into Gomes's office, escorted by Iannone and Clark. They tended to go out of their way when pretty girls were around. Jane was cute, in a somewhat mousy way, a pixie with short, dark hair and big brown eyes.

"Thanks for coming in. I really appreciate it," Gomes told her. He laid four mug shots out on his desk: Edward LaForte, Joseph LaForte, John Joseph Vitale, and Paul Castellano.

"There, that's him. I'm one hundred percent sure of it. I'll never forget those beady eyes. He was horrible."

Gomes pointed to the picture of Vitale. "Just to be clear, he signed in as Richard Allen, with the intention of meeting with your boss?"

"Yeah, he walked in like he owned the place, and was irritated that I had the nerve to make him sign in. Then my boss rushed out and brought him straight into his office."

Gomes told her who it was.

She shuddered. "I knew there was something not right about this guy."

Jane was a good person. She wasn't a snitch that Gomes had to turn; she was simply motivated by wanting to do the right thing. If Nevada had a good citizenship award, Gomes would have nominated her.

The last time Gomes had shaved was when he turned in his investigation of Carefree Travel. Changing his look had become part of the job, something he and everyone around him were used to. Gomes donned his oldest blue jeans and a sweatshirt from the roofing company he'd briefly worked for. Then he headed to the Tropicana for a little informal surveillance.

Dressing like a construction worker had another benefit beyond simple disguise. Large casinos often had some sort of construction maintenance going on, so Gomes would be able to blend into the "back of the house" and check things out.

Roaming the Tropicana's back of house was no different than any other casino's employee area. It was plain, plain, plain. Like most casinos,

---

* Pseudonym

the Tropicana had a lounge exclusively for the casino workers, such as dealers, pit bosses, and shift bosses. The Tropicana's casino employee lounge was secluded from other areas by a half-wall. There were some couches, a coffeemaker, a refrigerator, a TV, many ashtrays, and a haze of smoke seeping into the common areas.

As luck would have it, Gomes saw John J. Vitale in the exclusive casino employee lounge talking to a group of casino managers.

What the fuck is he doing there? A bomb of rage exploded in the pit of Gomes's stomach. *This asshole knows about the Aladdin. He knows we went after his crew for holding points there. Is he really so arrogant that he would run around this place like he owns it? If St. Louis has points here, why would he be so stupid? The damn State is to blame! They allowed this bullshit to happen at the Aladdin! It's a disease.*

"Are you looking for the cafeteria?" an older woman in a housekeeper's uniform asked Gomes, startling him out of his raging stupor.

"Yeah."

"First left, first right, and you're there. Are you working on the new tower?"

"Ah, yep."

"What are you doin' over there? Wait, let me guess . . . you're a carpenter, right?"

"You guessed it. Thanks for the directions." Gomes had to get out of there. He could feel unwanted eyes staring.

Gomes made his way out to the casino. He checked his watch. He had an hour until he was going to meet Barbara in the lounge between her shows. He headed toward the baccarat pit. There was some heavy action going on, guys betting upwards of $10,000 a hand.

Gomes was completely consumed by the action, fueled partially by his disgust with the fact that some of this money would probably end up in the hands of rotten human beings, like John Joseph Vitale. The amount of action in the baccarat pit was staggering. Guys were losing $10,000 in a matter of minutes, and then throwing down another. Completely surrounded by beautiful women. Everyone was laughing and drinking. Gomes watched as one heavyset gambler lost more money in fifteen minutes than Gomes made in an entire year. The man would throw his head back, laugh it off, and fish-lip wet sloppy kisses on the two girls flanking him. Gomes couldn't help but watch. That was until the *What the fuck?* moment.

Right in the middle of the action, dressed to the nines, emerged Joey Cusumano. Joseph Vincent Cusumano was well known by Nevada law enforcement to be the kingpin of loan shark collection activities in Las Vegas. He was a thug out of Chicago, and a good buddy of Tony Spilotro's. *He must have brought the girls for this rich fuck.* Gomes couldn't see the gambler's face, but he suspected that the guy was some gangster from Chicago.

Joey Cusumano was a good-looking fellow with a sense of style. He was always tan, always well dressed, and always surrounded by a gaggle of seemingly adoring fans. Gomes noticed that Cusumano was within the designated pit area—a line that no one (other than casino employees licensed to be there) crossed.

Gomes gaped. *I can't believe the pit boss is allowing this!* Gustafson had just lost his Sundance West casino license for regulatory infractions that weren't as severe as this. But then Gomes saw Cusumano approve a credit extension to a baccarat player and realized that the baccarat pit boss *was* Cusumano.

If the Doumanis had hired Cusumano, then the Chicago Mafia probably held points in the Tropicana.

Gomes had awakened that morning thinking he had made a difference—that at least one casino on the Strip was going to be a clean operation, thanks in part to him. It had been the most satisfied Gomes had been with his work in a long time. Now, to have it all completely disintegrate in a matter of hours left Gomes on the brink of despondency. He couldn't think about it anymore. He went to the casino lounge, ordered a martini with three olives, and waited for Barbara.

He waited, and waited. Gomes began to worry. It was not like Barbara to forget. She never forgot anything. Forty-five minutes of the hour Barbara had between shows had come and gone when she suddenly rushed into the lounge.

"Where were you? Did you forget?" Gomes asked.

"No, no. I'm sorry. This new producer keeps calling all of these last-minute meetings. It's starting to get annoying." Barbara kissed Gomes, leaving red lip marks on his cheek.

"Is he going to change the show or something?"

"I don't think so. Apparently he loves the show. I don't think he even really knows anything about dancing. I think he just likes to talk to the girls."

"Really? What a jerk."

"He's nice enough. A short Italian guy. Sometimes I can barely understand what he is saying. But, I have to go back. I'm sorry, sweetheart. I love you."

The martini relaxed Gomes. He watched his beautiful ballerina bride run off. *Thank you, God, for her.*

CHAPTER 12

The Gamer's Wife

IT WAS MARCH 1975, AND EVERY AGENT IN THE AUDIT DIVISION WAS crowded into the unit's debriefing room.

"I want you to examine every single book and record the Tropicana has," Gomes announced from the front of the room. "I want everyone in this division to focus some of their time on the Tropicana investigation. Lindsey, you will head up the audit team."

"Okay," Jacobson replied.

"I want to have two agents at the Tropicana twenty-four hours a day conducting surveillance. Rich and Duane, I want you to work on developing some informants there."

"Wait . . ." Rich Iannone broke in. "So, the Doumanis aren't the clean boys everyone thinks they are?"

Gomes sighed. It wasn't an easy question to answer. "I think they're good guys who are on the brink of getting caught up in a very bad situation."

This was debatable, and the audit agents went ahead and debated. Can you get caught up in a bad situation that you didn't invite in?

At any rate, this didn't change the task at hand, which was organizing around-the-clock surveillance at the Tropicana. Gomes knew there were a multitude of investigations going on, but he wanted the Tropicana to be a priority for every single one of his agents.

⁓

"Hi, Dennis, it's Jane," the voice said after Gomes answered the phone in his underwear in the kitchen of Barbara's condo shortly after 12:00 the next night. "I'm not sure if this is anything bad."

"That's all right. Any information you can provide is appreciated."

"I heard Nick and Fred talking about getting some money through someone named Agosto. I think his first name was Joe, but I'm not sure."

"Just to be clear, you're referring to Nick Tanno and Fred Doumani, right?"

"Yes."

"And the conversation was pertaining to bringing additional funds into the Tropicana?"

"Yes."

"From Joe Agosto?"

"Yes. Is this helpful information?"

Gomes grinned in spite of his exhaustion. "Very helpful. Thank you, Jane. You're doing the right thing."

Gomes immediately recognized Joe Agosto's name. It had surfaced before when Gomes was investigating Joseph "The Cat" LaForte. Joe LaForte had invested in Joe Agosto's entertainment company, and then had withdrawn his investment at the start of Gomes's investigation. Because of this, Gomes did not investigate Agosto's dealings at that time.

The day after Jane's phone call, back at the office, Gomes asked Duane Noyes to check and see if there was any intelligence out there on Joseph Agosto. As usual, Noyes promptly returned with a detailed report of existing intelligence. There wasn't much on Agosto. He didn't have a criminal record, but he did have strong social and business ties to known organized-crime associates, including Nick Civella, boss of the Kansas City crime family.

The very next day, Gomes took the background information on Agosto to Board member Shannon Bybee, who immediately called a meeting with Ed Doumani. During the meeting, Bybee told Doumani that Joe Agosto would not pass muster as a gaming licensee. Ed Doumani thanked the Board for their consideration and warning. Gomes assumed the matter with Joe Agosto had ended.

That night, Barbara had dinner ready for Gomes when he got home. The Folies was dark, and she didn't have any rehearsals for the ballet. Doug and Mary were there most nights, now. Linda had decided to try her hand in the workforce, and felt that Gomes and Barbara had a more stable home for the children.

"Smells good. I'm starving," Gomes said as he walked through the door with his briefcase full of larceny and deception.

"Hi, honey. Perfect timing." Barbara gave him a kiss. "Wash your hands before you sit down."

"Daddy," Mary spoke up. "Don't you know you have to wash your hands before you eat?"

With a chuckle Gomes said he was well aware of this fact. He playfully ruffled the girl's hair and went to wash up. Barbara fixed plates for everyone and cleaned up the kitchen before sitting down to eat.

"Sweetheart, I want to run something by you," Barbara said as Gomes eagerly shoveled food into his mouth. "I was thinking about leaving the Folies and doing the ballet full-time. Nevada Dance Theatre has enough funding now to bring on a few paid dancers, and I want to be one of them."

"That's great!" Gomes said.

There were a few drawbacks to Barbara leaving the Folies—in particular, a cut in pay—but that didn't bother Dennis. As long as they could cover their bills.

———

Barbara's retirement from the Folies did not last long. She was asked to return after another girl moved away. Barbara agreed because the ballet season was only five months long, and she wanted to work. Also, Barbara really liked the Folies choreographer.

Gomes and Barbara were right back to their normal routine, with lots of late nights.

One night, shortly after the Agosto phase of the Tropicana investigation had quieted down, Gomes was reading in bed, waiting for Barbara to get home from work. The few short months that she wasn't working these late hours were such a tease. It was nice to return to a real home, with a wife, and dinner ready. Still, Gomes had known that he wasn't marrying a housewife when he'd taken his vows.

Barbara quietly came in. She was happy to find Gomes still awake.

"Guess what?" she said, taking off her earrings. "I'm not an employee of the Tropicana anymore."

"Great. You can focus on the ballet full-time now."

"Oh, no, I'm still in the Folies . . . but now I work for a guy named Joe Agosto. The show was sold."

Gomes stared at her. "You're fucking kidding me. Keep your distance. He's got ties to the Mob."

The next morning, after a sleepless night, Gomes told Shannon Bybee about this latest development. Bybee had Ed Doumani in a meeting that afternoon. The two men faced each other down like gunfighters in a secure conference room. When questioned about the sale of the Folies Bergere to Joe Agosto, Ed calmly replied, "The Tropicana sold the Folies to Agosto, and we're leasing it back. But this matter doesn't fall under the Board's jurisdiction anyway."

"As far as I'm concerned, this is a sale and lease-back arrangement, a matter specifically provided for in the Commission regulations," Bybee explained icily. "Therefore, the Board *does* have jurisdiction to investigate this transaction, as well as the purchaser/lessor. And, as a matter of fact, we are requiring that Production Leasing come forward for a finding of suitability."

Joe Agosto, as owner of Production Leasing, was immediately subpoenaed to attend a closed hearing with Shannon Bybee, Phil Hannifin, and Dennis Gomes. During the hearing, Joe Agosto reluctantly gave the Board permission to examine his company's books and records. The Board gave Agosto three weeks to provide Gomes with everything he needed.

Maybe it was a matter of timing, or maybe Shannon Bybee and Phil Hannifin had finally tired of Nevada's politics, but this was the first moment since Gomes had started going after the "big fish" that he felt like he truly had the Board behind him.

Turning "inside snitches"—those informants who were deeply embedded within organized-crime families—was no simple matter. Most of Gomes's contacts were either good people uncomfortable with certain situations, or low-level crooks on the fringe who just wanted money or some inconsequential charge dropped. So when one of these inside snitches approached Gomes, he was skeptical.

While he was waiting out the three-week period Agosto was given to deliver his company's records, Gomes received a phone call from a man named Tom,* claiming to be a true insider.

"I have some good information on the Tropicana that I think you'd like to hear," said the man on the other end of the line. "I know things—I can help you. But I'd rather not talk over the phone."

With the phone pressed to his ear, Gomes walked to his office door and gently clicked it shut. "Well, can you come down to my office?"

"No, I'm afraid that won't be possible. There's a little bar on West Sahara and Charleston. Meet me there at nine tonight. I'm valued . . . if you catch my drift. You can check me out. I've helped some others."

Gomes agreed and hung up. Then he immediately tracked down Duane Noyes, who was doing some background work with Gene Butler (Tom Carrigan's intelligence officer). Gomes asked Noyes to put a temporary hold on that work and check out Tom.

As it turned out, California law enforcement agencies valued Tom as a credible informant. Gomes returned to his office almost giddy with excitement, wondering what kind of information this Tom character had. But before he could even sit down, his phone was ringing again.

"Dennis—for God's sake! What's this I hear about you causing a major disturbance in California?" Phil Hannifin's voice was so loud that Gomes had to hold the receiver away from his ear.

"What?"

"Carrigan called me and told me that you were talking to a high-level informant, and the California law enforcement agencies are pissed off."

"They're pissed off? He contacted me, for chrissake!"

"Dennis, this is a valuable informant with highly detailed, sensitive information. Apparently he's difficult to handle, so the California agencies have restricted all contact with him to one investigator out of the DA's office. And now they're pissed off at us."

---

* Pseudonym

Gomes took a deep breath. He instantly knew that this was Gene Butler's handiwork. He suspected that they were mad that this informant had contacted Dennis and not Butler, or maybe even Carrigan.

Hannifin didn't care; he forbade Gomes from having any further contact with this informant until he figured out what was really going on. But Dennis didn't plan on listening to Hannifin. He wanted to find out what this informant wanted to talk to him about.

Luckily, Hannifin worked his magic less than an hour later.

"All right, Dennis. You're cleared to use him as an informant. You just have to share any information with his handler, and you have to use the utmost caution when dealing with him."

Deal!

Like many dive bars in Las Vegas, this hole had no noticeable name. The smell of smoke lingered in the air, and peanut shells crunched under Gomes's feet as he walked in.

A few regulars were at the bar. The burly, red-faced bartender watched Gomes make his way across the room. Tom was in a corner booth, chowing down on a big basket of deep-fried drumsticks. In Gomes's intelligence-file pictures, Tom had looked heavy, but in person, stuffed into a booth, he was more than just fat. One prick from a pin and he was liable to pop.

"Hey, Dennis," the man said as Gomes approached. "Ha! What are you, like fifteen years old? I pictured you a lot bigger and a lot older for someone that scares the shit outta so many guys. Sit down. Thanks for meeting me."

Gomes scratched his chin and sat down. "We have a lot of things to clarify."

"No problem." Tom brushed his hands off and held them up in a surrender position. "I'm an open book."

"All right. The first thing I want to know is why you contacted me; what do you want out of this?"

That was simple. This informant wanted a legitimate job in a casino. However, because of his criminal record, he would not be able to get a gaming license.

Gomes let out a sigh. This was something that he could arrange—with a few stipulations. First, the informant needed to prove that he actually had valuable information. Second, if Gomes ever found out that this informant had provided him with any false information, Gomes would "annihilate" him. Finally, if this informant was ever to stop providing information after he was licensed, Gomes would stop protecting his identity as an informant.

The man shrugged. "No problem," he said.

The informant took his assurance a step further and called Joe Agosto right then. Tom told Agosto he was in Vegas and ready to get to work.

"No problem," Agosto told Tom. In fact, for a $250,000 "investment," he had just set up Raymond Patriarca—the New England crime boss—with a junket program for a 5 percent hidden interest, and his boy Johnny was running it.

"I'll see you there tomorrow. Thanks, Joe."

"Yeah, Tommy. See you tomorrow."

Click.

❦

Gomes was buzzing with excitement when he left the bar. The tawdry Vegas jungle, with its infestation of underworld kings and jokers alike, was all a drain on Gomes. But nights like this were his drug.

Capping off this perfect night, Barbara was getting home as Gomes pulled in. She and the new Gomes home on Newcomer Circle—a cute little split-level—comprised the man's foundation.

"Guess what happened at work tonight?" Barbara asked before she'd even closed the door behind her. She wore her beautiful sequined skirt over her leotard. "After the show, all of the girls were introduced to Joe Agosto, and when Jerry got to me, he introduced me as 'Barbara Robertson—I mean, Barbara Gomes.' Right, so Mr. Agosto goes, 'Gomes—you're not related to Dennis Gomes, are you?' And I'm like, 'Yeah, he's my husband.' So he goes, 'Huh . . . funny. Well, you were great in the show.'" Barbara wasn't smiling. "Isn't that crazy?"

Gomes wasn't smiling either. "Yeah. Keep your distance from him."

The following day, Gomes switched much of his manpower back to the credit-scam investigation of the Tropicana.

Sure enough, the new director of casino junkets was Johnny Bryan, aka John Barborian—a known associate of Raymond Patriarca (boss of the New England faction of the Mafia). Under Johnny's lead the Tropicana continued to extend credit to fictitious names and addresses. In other cases, credit was extended without any confirmation. Then, there was the situation of "lost" markers. Although these activities pointed toward skimming, there was still a lack of absolute proof.

Gomes needed something (or someone) to tie the skims to organized crime, and then to the casino. He continued to monitor the credit situation at the Tropicana, but redirected his focus to Joe Agosto, whose three-week time limit was up.

At 9:00 a.m. on April 15, 1975, Gomes told Agosto, "If Production Leasing Limited's records are not submitted by noon, I will have them seized."

By 11:30 a.m., the financial records were on Gomes's desk.

During the initial review of the records, Gomes's agents found something astounding, if only because of its brazenness. Production Leasing Ltd.'s records indicated that a major source of funds utilized by Agosto to purchase the Folies came from Joseph LaForte. Further examination indicated that some additional funding was provided by a close associate of Kansas City crime boss Nick Civella. The remaining funds for the purchase of the Folies somehow just "mysteriously" appeared in Production Leasing Ltd.'s bank account.

Joe Agosto couldn't have been taller than five-foot-five. He had a thick crop of black hair and bushy eyebrows. What Joe Agosto lacked in stature, he more than made up for with personality. He was a compact, loudmouth Italian with a thick accent and a great sense of humor—a real character.

Unable to find any evidence of legitimate funding used to purchase the Folies Bergere, Gomes was curious to know how Joe Agosto would explain it all. Gomes met Agosto at the new headquarters for Production

Leasing Ltd., the Tropicana, where Agosto had a small office by the showroom. There was nothing in it except for a small desk, two chairs, and a mess of paper. It looked unused.

Gomes sat down across a cluttered desk from the diminutive Italian and opened up the conversation.

"Joe, I wanted to talk to you about some major problems with the funding used to purchase the Folies."

Agosto looked completely unfazed. "No problem. I'm sure it's just a misunderstanding."

"To start, some of the monies came from Joe 'The Cat.'"

"Who? I don't know no Joe Tecat."

"Joseph LaForte."

"Oh, LaForte. I thought you said Tecat."

"That's what he's known as—Joe 'The Cat.'"

"I don't know nothing 'bout that. In fact, I don't really know him. A friend just said I got this guy, wants to invest, so what am I gonna say— no? If it's a problem I'll just give the money back to LaForte."

"It's a problem."

"Not anymore. I'll take care of it first thing tomorrow. See, Gomes, we can work together. Speaking of work, I just met your wife. Quite the talent."

Gomes stared at the man. "Thanks, but there are other issues with the funds."

"Dennis, for such a young guy, you're wound too tight. We'll take care of everything, don't worry."

"Where did the rest of the money come from? There is no source. As far as we can tell, the money just appeared in Production Leasing's account."

"Well, it was always there."

"How did it get there?"

"It was just there."

Gomes sighed. "It doesn't work like that. We need to know where the money originated from."

Agosto made a noncommittal motion with his hands. "Hey, I'm no accountant. I can't keep track of these things. But I'll look into it. The Folies is a step up for my company. My last show, the girls weren't so first-class. Know what I mean? I took my blind uncle backstage and he thought he was in a fish market."

Gomes laughed. He knew he wasn't going to get anything out of Agosto, but at least the man was enjoyable to talk to. It was almost hard to believe that such a friendly man was in with the Mob.

At that point, though, it didn't matter what Agosto said; Gomes already had plenty of documentation of bad funds. He just wanted to make this case irrefutable. He suspected that Agosto was the Mob's guy on the inside. Nominally, he was just the owner of the Folies, but Gomes had a hunch that Agosto was overseeing the points, the skim, and maybe even managing the casino.

Gomes had assigned his agents to twenty-four-hour Tropicana surveillance, and they reported back that Joe Agosto was routinely in the casino, giving orders to various personnel and generally acting like he owned the Trop. Gomes confirmed it all with his snitch. In a brief conversation, Tom told Gomes that Agosto was indeed giving orders.

A couple days after that conversation, toward the end of April, Tom called Gomes back.

"Dennis, if you come in right now, you'll find Joe signin' checks."

"How do you know?"

"He just sent a secretary to pick up checks."

"Where is he?"

"His office. You know, the entertainment—"

Gomes didn't wait for Tom to finish. He'd hung up and was already out the door, in his car, pushing a hundred miles per hour on the 95. He made it to the Tropicana in less than ten minutes, parked in the back, and ran directly to Agosto's office.

"Dennis, hey—nice to see you. What are you doing here?" Joe said while calmly but quickly slipping everything into his desk drawer.

"Oh, just wanted to stop by and talk to you. What are you up to?"

"Just signing some show checks."

"Great; can I take a look?"

"Whaddya wanna see those for?"

"Just to tie some loose ends together."

Joe reluctantly opened his desk drawer, pulled everything out, and handed it to Gomes.

"Joe, this signature stamp has Nick Tanno's name on it, and these are checks from the Tropicana."

Still the little Italian seemed unruffled. "Oh, the Folies' checks are mixed in. The secretary screwed up the piles. I was just going to bring them back to her all at once."

Gomes fixed his gaze on the man. "Joe, these checks are dated for today, and Nick's out of town. And that still doesn't explain why you have his stamp. Do you want to tell me what the fuck is going on?"

"What can I say, Dennis?"

"This is a felony, Joe. You will do some serious time for this."

"Dennis, come on . . . work with me."

Gomes felt his spine tingle. "Joe, you broke the law. I'm not sure what I can do. Unless . . . never mind."

"Unless what?"

"Look, Joe, I'm not after you. I think you're a spoke in a bigger wheel. Am I right?"

After a beat of silence: "Yeah, of course." He leaned toward Gomes and lowered his voice a little. "But, I know that wheel. You know what I'm saying?"

Gomes had to work hard not to grin.

That was it. Gomes had flipped Joe Agosto. They obviously couldn't talk at the Tropicana, so they arranged a meeting at a small bar later that night. Gomes made copies of the checks that Agosto was signing and got Agosto to sign the back of the checks as "signed by Joe Agosto"— that way, Agosto would think that Gomes had "the proof" on him and wouldn't dare back out of their arrangement.

On the way out of the Tropicana, Gomes bumped into Ed Doumani, current operator of the Tropicana, and they decided to go get a cup of coffee. Gomes and Ed shared many of the same values, and if the situation had been different, the two men could have easily been friend

They talked for a couple hours that day, about business and family. Ed was an intelligent businessman and a good family man. Gomes admired how much Ed loved his younger brother, Fred, even though Gomes suspected that Fred was one of those guys who liked to rub elbows with the Mob. Gomes suspected that Fred had convinced his brother to take a bad money loan in order to buy the Tropicana—the deal that had landed them in this predicament. Gomes had no real desire to get the Doumani brothers in trouble, but he couldn't ignore the fact that the Mob controlled the Tropicana.

Gomes left the Trop that day reeling with anticipation.

For his clandestine meeting with Agosto, he had to drive way off the beaten path to a bar on the north side of town. Driving there, Gomes couldn't help but wonder if every thug in Vegas had his very own dive bar to escape to.

He was surprised by how big the joint looked from the outside. It was unmistakably a cowboy bar. Gomes could hear the country music from the parking lot. *This can't be the right place*, Gomes thought. There was a crowd of cowboys checking out a new Ford pickup. *Agosto better not be playing any fucking games.*

The cowboys didn't notice Gomes walk in. *Maybe I don't look as out of place as I feel*, he thought. Stale beer, the scent of pine . . . everything inside the place made of wood. There was a dance floor with a few drunk girls dancing, or rather, attempting to dance. A handful of cowboys were sitting on bar stools, two beers to a man, one for spitting and the other for drinking.

Where the fuck is he?

Gomes maneuvered his way past the other patrons to the corner of the bar and ordered a Pabst from the well-endowed, blonde bartender.

Soon, Agosto walked in and pulled up a stool at a high-top table at the opposite end of the dance floor. Gomes made his way over.

"Joe, what the hell made you pick this place?"

"I love country music."

"I hope you have some good information for me. I know you're running the Tropicana for the Mob."

"I'm not running it; I'm just trying to help out Nick. He's overseeing everything."

"Come on, Joe—that's bullshit," said Gomes, who knew Agosto was referring to Nick Tanno. "I know you're running it. What families have points? Who's skimming?"

"I ain't doin' nothin' wrong. If there's skimming, I don't know about it."

Gomes was getting angry. "Joe, quit the fucking bullshit. I know Detroit was skimming through the junkets."

Agosto shrugged. "From what I hear, they had a little when Baldy was doin' junkets, but they're out now. They got enough on their plate with the Aladdin."

"I know there are other credit scams for different families going on."

"Yeah, you're right. Ash Resnick and his junket guys oversee all of that. I heard rumors that they're in with Patriarca, outta New England."

"What about the Doumanis?"

"Fucking idiots . . ."

The conversation continued on like this, Agosto repeatedly proclaiming his innocence while asserting the guilt and stupidity of everyone around him. He claimed that the Doumanis were working for St. Louis, but Gomes suspected that he was lying. Gomes basically knew that Agosto was running the Tropicana for the various organized-crime families that held points in the casino. Gomes brought up Agosto's criminal associations with Kansas City, and again Agosto talked in circles. He admitted to knowing Nick Civella, Kansas City's crime boss, but not to having any real association with him.

"Joe, I've had enough fucking bullshit for one day. I'm going to give you a little time to think about what you're doing. I hope you have better information for me next time."

"Dennis, I ain't doin' nothin' wrong. But I'll keep telling you what I hear."

Gomes left.

Gomes knew Agosto wasn't being totally up-front, but at least he had ratted on some of the others. *What a screwed-up situation. I bet there's some internal power struggle brewing*, Gomes thought as he drove home that night.

The second Gomes got home, he called his snitch, Tom.

"Yeah, there's been friction buildin' for a while," Tom reported, "between Agosto and—I call 'em the Doumani brigade—Ash Resnick, the casino manager, and Barborian, director of junkets. Agosto is tryin' to bring in a new casino manager, Carl Thomas, but the Doumani brigade is fightin' it. From what I hear, Carl Thomas is bringin' in some money from the Teamsters' Pension Fund."

This brought Gomes back to the botched raid at Circus Circus. Carl Thomas, then the casino manager at the Circus Circus, had been tipped off by Metro, allowing him to stop his skimming just hours before Gomes's planned raid. The resentment that he carried from that early career snafu had never gone away. Thomas's hiring was like putting a kettle on an open flame. Anger boiled and spilled into every square inch of Gomes's being.

⸺ ⌣ ⸺

Carl Thomas quietly became the Tropicana's new casino manager in 1975. Gomes called Joe Agosto and set up another meeting at the same cowboy bar.

"Joe, tell me about Carl Thomas. Who hired him?"

"Nick Tanno told me it was his idea. Thomas is a smart guy."

"I know, he's very intelligent. He's also very adept at cheating."

"Oh, I don't know about that. If you want to go after someone, you should go after those Syrian idiots, the Doumani brothers. They deal with some very bad people."

"Like who?"

"Bosses from St. Louis. And Ash is very close to the Patriarca family."

"And what about you?"

"I just run the Folies. I was helping Nick."

"I'm fucking sick of you ratting on everyone else. I know you're overseeing everything." Gomes got up and left.

⸺ ⌣ ⸺

Gomes had expected this much from Agosto—ratting on everyone else, giving just enough information to appease the authorities without implicating his own interests. Now Gomes wanted to put Agosto on the edge.

That night, Gomes arrived home to a dark and silent house, except for one light over the kitchen table. Littering the table were his daughter Mary's construction paper and crayons. Gomes sat down at the table, picked up a crayon, and began using the skills he'd learned in the link-analysis course at the LEIU convention back in 1971.

On the piece of paper, each name written in a different color, Gomes wrote the following names:

Joe Agosto—Red

Irving "Ash" Resnick—Blue

Joey Cusumano—Orange

Doumani brothers—Green

Joe LaForte—Yellow

Gomes made the simple connections first: Resnick was a suspected associate of the Patriarca crime family out of New England/Boston. Cusumano was a known associate of Tony Spilotro and the Chicago crime family. Gomes knew the Doumani brothers had met with John Joseph Vitale, the underboss of the St. Louis crime family. Joe LaForte was a known associate of the Gambino crime family out of New York. Finally, Agosto was closely tied to Nick Civella and the Kansas City crime family. Gomes thought about including Edward "Baldy" Sarkisian, but he was no longer running junkets, so Gomes suspected that the Detroit crime family no longer held points in the Tropicana.

Then, Gomes began connecting the dots. He drew lines based on business/work relationships, financial relationships, and social relationships. When Gomes was finished, he had a chart that linked Agosto to each family, placing him in the center of the Tropicana's operations.

Next, Gomes would go to work on writing up his formal investigative findings for the Tropicana.

❧

He didn't stop for two days. The result was a report that revealed the presence of five organized-crime families that held "hidden points" in the Tropicana: Kansas City, St. Louis, Chicago, New England/Boston, and New York's Gambino family. Gomes identified each organized-crime associate who was a Tropicana employee, detailed the surveillance work that found Vitale in meetings with executives, and revealed the fact that he believed Joe Agosto was running everything. In this report, Gomes recommended that the Nevada Gaming Commission issue a large fine and cite the Tropicana under Regulation 5.011, for "operating in an unsuitable manner," with a possible revocation of their gaming license.

But before the Gaming Control Board went to the Commission and took any formal action, Gomes wanted the Board to call forward Joe Agosto for a "finding of suitability" hearing, and require him to file for a gaming license. This would allow Gomes to further investigate Agosto.

At their next meeting the Board agreed that it was all a good idea. They were stunned by Gomes's investigation. During a break Hannifin took Gomes aside out in the corridor.

"Dennis," Hannifin whispered, "how in the world did you catch Agosto signing Tropicana's checks as Nick Tanno?"

"I walked into his office at the right time."

"We completely agree with your suggested course of action. We just have to consult with Bob List to find out how to proceed."

"What? Why do you need to talk to List?"

"Dennis, it's our policy. We need to do everything within the proper means."

Right.

———

Gomes never saw evidence of this himself, but he had heard more than one rumor that Nevada Attorney General Bob List was "dirty," so he was less than thrilled that the Board had to run the Agosto plan by him. On the other hand, the evidence of Agosto's involvement in the operations of the Tropicana was undeniable, and there was plenty of documentation of organized-crime involvement, so there was no way List could stop this investigation from proceeding.

After Gomes had returned to his office and was waiting to hear back from Hannifin, his snitch Tom called him with a particularly juicy bit of information.

"Dennis, you ain't gonna believe this. I was in Joe's office, right? And in walks Carl."

"Carl Thomas?"

"The very same. So, Carl sits down and we're just bullshittin', you know, 'bout nothin' in particular, right? So then Joe goes, 'So, Carl, what's the situation? What can we do?' You know, I had no idea what he was talkin' about. You followin'?"

"Yeah. Keep going."

"Okay, so then Carl tells Joe that the situation's different here than in his place, right? 'Cause all the people belonged to him over at his place. But there's definitely potential here."

"Potential for what?"

"That's what I'm gettin' to. Potential to skim. Carl started tellin' Joe about what'll work here and how to do it."

"What did he say?"

"To be honest, I couldn't really follow. Somethin' about needin' a hand, or a couple of hands, in the count. And I think he said the Trop should skim outta the slot coin; it's easier to do it on the sly. But, I ain't totally sure."

"Carl wants to skim out of the hard count as opposed to the soft count?"

"I think so . . . but like I said, I ain't sure. It was kinda over my head. Anyway, Joe told Carl that they were gonna take a trip, and that he would need to explain all this to the bosses."

It all confirmed what Gomes had suspected. Once he had complete access to all of Agosto's personal files, and clearance to investigate him, Gomes knew he would be able to prove that organized crime controlled the Tropicana.

Gomes would never get that opportunity.

A call from Phil Hannifin on January 15, 1976, demolished everything.

"Dennis, Bob List said that we don't have the authority to call Agosto forward for any sort of gaming licensing, and suggested that we don't move forward with any sort of formal action."

Gomes made a fist around the phone receiver. "The case is strong, Phil."

"He just said it's out of our jurisdiction."

"That's bullshit. The Board should ignore List and move ahead anyway."

"You know we can't do that."

"Listen . . . I have an informant who just told me he was in a meeting with Carl Thomas and Agosto, and Thomas was telling Agosto how to skim."

"Dennis—no. Listen to me: It's out of our hands now. Do you understand?"

Gomes said nothing.

———

Gomes left his office early that cold January day, not talking to anyone. He gathered everything he had on the Tropicana case, drove to the FBI's field office, and turned it all over to Don North.

Then he went home and puked his guts out.

Once there was nothing left inside of him, Gomes sat in the dark, contemplating his situation. He lost track of time. *Those goddamn politicians are a fucking rotten bunch. Pieces of shit, all of them.*

The quiet rage went into the night, until Gomes heard the front door open. Doug and Mary were at Gomes's parents' house for the night. He had no idea what time it was, or how long he had been sitting in his dark living room. He flicked on a lamp as Barbara was walking in.

"Dennis, you scared me. What are you doing?"

"What time is it?"

"It's close to two-thirty."

"Two-thirty in the fucking morning? Where the fuck were you?"

"Dennis, what's wrong with you? Don't talk to me like that. I told you I was going out after the show for Joanie's birthday."

"Where did you go?"

"The Aladdin."

"You told me you were going to Caesars. Why are you changing your story?"

"I thought we were, but then everyone wanted to go to the Aladdin."

"Everyone. I thought it was just a few girls."

Dennis proceeded to interrogate Barbara as if she were a criminal. There was absolutely no reason for him to even be angry, and somewhere deep down he knew that. But something had snapped, and Dennis couldn't control himself.

Barbara started crying. When Gomes saw her tears, whatever synapse had snapped fused back together. He felt terrible, but it was too late. She was already out the door and driving away.

Gomes sank back into his chair. A lecture from Philosophy 101, a quote from Friedrich Nietzsche, taunted him: "Whoever fights monsters should see to it that in the process he does not become a monster. And when you look into an abyss, the abyss also looks into you."

Part III

Wolves in the Henhouse

The world is a dangerous place to live—not because of the people who are evil, but because of the people who don't do anything about it.
—Albert Einstein

CHAPTER 13

A Shot across the Bow

A COUPLE OF YEARS BEFORE DENNIS GOMES HAD TURNED OVER THE Tropicana case to Don North of the FBI, at a time when the case was just starting to fall apart in the hands of the bureaucrats, a man named Allen Glick appeared on the Vegas scene, claiming that he was in the market to buy a casino and looking for financing. So, when it came time for Gomes to select his next investigation, this Vegas newcomer stood out.

On the surface, there was nothing notable about this small-time real-estate investor from California. He was a young, clean-cut, ordinary businessman—a decent entrepreneur, but by no means a Howard Hughes. He was definitely not, in Dennis Gomes's eyes, a likely candidate to buy a casino in August of 1974—especially one as renowned on the Strip as the Stardust.

As Glick's deal moved forward, Gomes knew he would be called in to investigate the source of funds. To most observers, Gomes's interest in this casino would appear to be part and parcel of his job. But Gomes suspected that the Stardust was already a Mob joint, and this sale was just a way to transfer points. Gomes's suspicions were soon confirmed when he learned that a majority of Glick's investment money to make the purchase was to come from the Teamsters' Pension Fund. That fact solidified the Stardust as Gomes's next target—and perhaps his last. The Stardust was do-or-die for Gomes.

The Teamsters' Pension Fund, Gomes and others suspected, was completely controlled by organized crime. Through Glick's purchase money— boom—the Mob would be the real owner of any casino nominally owned by Glick.

Almost immediately after beginning the process to purchase the Stardust, Glick initiated the purchase of three more casinos: the Hacienda, the Fremont, and the Marina. But before any deal could close, Glick had to get licensed. Enter Dennis Gomes, to investigate the collection of massive purchases.

"Listen, we need to make this look like any other source-of-funds investigation," Gomes told Agent Law after the Audit Division headquarters had emptied out one night in August of 1974.

"If they think we're going to find something, who knows what they'll do."

"Preserve the status quo," Law mocked in a deep, authoritarian tone, "by any means necessary—the mission of the Nevada State authority."

Gomes could barely manage a chuckle. "This investigation is going to start tomorrow. I'm not putting any extra manpower on it. I don't want a single person to know what we are really focused on. Dick, I have a bad feeling about this; something tells me that no matter what we find, or don't find, Glick is going to get a license."

———

"Phil, this whole deal is very suspicious," Gomes told Hannifin on the phone the day after kick-starting his investigation into Allen Glick. "It's practically common knowledge that the Teamsters' Pension Fund is totally controlled by the Mob."

"Dennis, you'd see a mobster behind every bush if you had the opportunity," replied the Gaming Control Board chief.

Oblivious to Hannifin's objections, Gomes continued to explain that there was more to this transaction. There was a group of very large and suspicious transactions that took place in Mexico. The funds supposedly came from one of Glick's projects down there, but Gomes didn't believe that. Mexico would be the perfect place for the Mob to launder some money for Glick.

"Dennis—" Hannifin attempted to interrupt.

But Gomes was anxious to lay out his plan, and continued to explain to Hannifin that he intended to hire one of the "Big Eight" US accounting firms to assist them with this, and to help them around the language barrier. And, given the involvement of the Teamsters, Gomes thought this whole transaction was bound to be as dirty as they come. Gomes suspected that Glick was just a front, a straw man. Where did this small-time guy suddenly get enough money to buy four casinos?

Hannifin's voice was measured as he told Gomes that not everyone on planet Earth is in with the Mob. Glick was a war veteran, and an intelligent, well-mannered young man. It was hard to believe that he could be in with the Mob. Hannifin told Gomes to try to relax a little, and that he would be in town in a couple of days. They could meet and talk about this investigation then. Hannifin ended the conversation by telling Gomes that he and Shannon would go to Mexico to check out those transactions.

Gomes pleaded with Hannifin to let him go instead; he had the financial background that would allow him to really investigate those transactions.

"Dennis, you're not going. That's final. We'll talk in a couple of days."

Click . . . and *click.*

The Audit Division was completely dark, except for a single light in Gomes's office.

"Fucking bullshit. I knew I should have lied," Gomes complained to Dick Law. "Maybe, if Hannifin didn't think I was so suspicious of Glick, he would've let me go."

"Glick's been parading around town, making himself part of society. Everyone's just eating it up."

"He's a front. It's so obvious." Gomes sighed. "We need to go to Mexico. I'm going to convince Hannifin to send us when he's in town."

A few days later that summer of 1974, Gomes met Hannifin at the Gaming Control Board chairman's Las Vegas office.

"Listen, Dennis," Hannifin began, sitting down behind his massive desk that looked as though it had never been used for anything other than photo shoots. "There has been way too much tension between your division and the other divisions. It can't go on like this."

Gomes gave him a shrug. "I've been trying to work with them."

"It's more than just that."

"I'll work on it. But for now, I need to go to Mexico. Believe me, if there's a problem with the funds, it's better to find out about it now rather than once the license has been approved."

"Dennis, that's what we need to talk about. We've decided that for departmental accord we are taking your division off the licensing investigations. Your involvement in this process has caused way too much turmoil. From now on, your investigative responsibilities will only extend to existing licensees."

"What? Who decided this?"

"The Board."

"The Investigations Division has no idea what it's doing. They don't even have a basic understanding of financial workings."

Hannifin was intractable. "That's why you are going to transfer a few of your agents to the Investigations Division."

Hannifin explained that there were complaints directed at the Audit Division over the audit cycle, which was the time that went by between audits for each casino. The standard recommended audit cycle was two years; for example, if Circus Circus received a routine audit in 1973, they should expect another in 1975. However, Gomes's actual audit cycle was closer to five years, because of his investigations of hidden interests. Sadly, Gomes knew that the complaint over the lack of audits was simply a way to maneuver the Nevada Legislature to return to the way things used to be, in order to take the heat off the bad guys.

"This is bullshit. You're making a huge mistake," said Gomes.

"Dennis, you are the most talented and aggressive investigator in this agency, but this is not a one-man show."

After a brief pause, Gomes said, "I'll quit."

After an even briefer pause, Hannifin said, "Don't let the door hit you in the ass on the way out."

Gomes stormed out of the office, seething, feeling physically ill and betrayed by the only decent officials he had on his side.

Gomes didn't go back to work that day. He couldn't face his agents.

Dick Law met him later at his house. Barbara was at rehearsal and the kids were at school. Gomes took him into the kitchen, where the two men had a secure, tense, fateful conversation.

It was difficult for Gomes, Law, Iannone, Clark, and all of the Audit agents to keep working toward a goal that no one seemed to want them to reach. Gomes truly did consider quitting. As Gomes and Law sat at the kitchen table, Gomes suggested possibly returning to accounting; Law could become a lawyer again. But Law would have no part of it, and he was not about to let Gomes cop out.

"Dick, don't you fucking get it?" Gomes snapped. "There's nothing we can do. I'm sick of doing all this fucking work only to have to give it to the feds because the State wants to hide everything under the rug and pretend like Nevada gaming authorities are so damned tough—total hypocrisy!"

"So what? It's better to just do nothing?"

"I don't know. Let someone else do it."

Law thought about it for a moment, and then reminded Gomes of when they were just starting out. Gomes, Iannone, and Law used to spend hours talking about how they were making a difference in society. Then Law reminded Gomes what the Mob skim bought: drugs, prostitution, murders. Even if the State was not reacting the way they wanted, they were still making a difference.

But for Gomes, it was hard to remain so idealistic. It was difficult for him to accept the State's decisions and to keep plodding along, particularly their decision to take his division off of the licensing phase. To Gomes, this was like returning the Gaming Control Board back to square one, when every thug that wanted a license was approved.

"Just because you're not part of the licensing investigations anymore," Law ventured, "doesn't mean you can't investigate the casinos for other crimes—skimming and hidden interests, for instance. These imbeciles in the Investigations Division will just provide us with a lot more work because it will be like the old days again. They're going to let everyone in—so, much better for us!"

Gomes stared at his coffee cup, thinking, then said to Law, "You know, if Glick gets licensed, the Mob will have an interest in those casinos."

"Exactly. And no one can stop you from investigating any casino you choose. No one even needs to know what you're doing."

Gomes never admitted to Dick Law how much their kitchen conversation influenced the future of his investigative work. Gomes began running at least twenty-five miles a week as a way of mitigating the physical manifestations of his constant anger. He threw himself into his other investigations and he waited.

As Gomes had predicted, Hannifin and Bybee returned from their Mexican vacation and declared that all of Glick's transactions were clean. Gomes had no choice but to watch as Glick was licensed. He'd known it was bound to happen, but it still stung.

Then, Glick appointed notorious gangsters to run the Stardust. Guys like Frank Rosenthal—a well-known bookie from Chicago, and a close friend and major associate of the top Chicago mob bosses—along with an ex-felon convicted of fixing college basketball games. Rosenthal's good friend and part-time sidekick just happened to be Tony "The Ant" Spilotro. Just the thought of Spilotro sent chills down Gomes's spine.

To make matters worse, Rosenthal, now the CEO of all five of Glick's casinos, then hired George Jay Vandermark, the well-known slot cheat, to be the manager in charge of the five casinos' slot departments. There was only one reason a casino would hire someone like Vandermark to manage their casino, and that was to keep the dirty money flowing.

"I can't do this anymore," Gomes announced to Dick Law on August 7, a hot summer night in 1975. They were enjoying neck bones, an Italian specialty, at the Venetian—a classic little Italian joint a few miles from the Strip.

"I can't believe you can just fucking walk away," said Law.

"Did I fucking say that?" Maybe it was the neck bones, or possibly the beer, but a switch had been flipped. "I will not stop until everyone knows that Glick is nothing but a front—a piece-of-shit puppet whose every move is controlled by the Mob."

"That's the Dennis I know," said Law. "This is exactly what I wanted to hear. We can do this."

"But it's even more important to keep this completely quiet. Not a single person can know about our investigation. I'm not even telling Hannifin. I'm afraid he's gotten caught up in the Glick fan club."

Gomes decided that it was time to start investigating the Argent Corporation—(A)llen (R.) (G)lick (ENT)erprises—the company that owned the Stardust, Hacienda, Marina, and Fremont casinos. He felt that the Mob had had enough time to get their operations up and running. Gomes told Law that they needed to start working on developing snitches. Spilotro had been throwing his weight around at the Stardust, so this would be a good place to start.

Law ventured that Spilotro's presence would probably make it difficult to turn snitches, as people were afraid of him.

"I'm not," Gomes said, sipping his beer. The statement was neither a boast nor an empty threat. It was a simple statement of fact—maybe even a promise.

CHAPTER 14

Trust No One

DENNIS GOMES'S EVERY WAKING THOUGHT REVOLVED AROUND ARGENT
Corporation. The only person who knew where Gomes's mind was (other
than Barbara) was Dick Law.

In the late summer of 1975, Gomes and Law spent almost every
night at one of Argent's casinos. They soon discovered that the Stardust
was the center of everything, so they began spending most of their time
there. Gomes would sit at the bar for hours, absorbing everything and yet
hearing none of the background laughter, no jangle of slot machines, no
din of drunken chatter. He only heard data, information, intel. He could
no longer smell the cheap perfume of the casino floor, or the smoke and
the booze. He was at once detached and obsessed.

While Gomes and Law began to develop a network of snitches
within Argent Corporation, they had Frank Rosenthal, Allen Glick, and
Tony Spilotro under the microscope.

One potential informant of interest was Tony Albanese. During surveillance, Gomes had seen Albanese and Spilotro together on numerous
occasions. Albanese was known around town as being associated with the
Crazy Horse Saloon and Strip Club—a Mob joint.

Ultimately, there wasn't much more intelligence on Tony Albanese.
All Gomes could discover was that Albanese hailed from Long Beach,
California, and was in the strip-club business. However, during surveil-
lance, there was something about Albanese that stood out to Gomes.

Although he was middle-aged, of average height and build, and not
tough enough to cross the street to avoid, something told Gomes that
Albanese knew things, and, more importantly, that he was the type of guy

who did not possess a moral code (either good or bad), which meant that he would not be restricted by a sense of loyalty to anyone. Guys like this were pretty easy to turn; Gomes just needed to figure out the right angle.

In the meantime, Gomes concentrated on the concrete. It takes a leap of faith to act on instinct, but facts are facts. Gomes knew that Frank Rosenthal was tied in to the Chicago crime family. And the fact that Tony Spilotro was spending a great deal of time at the Stardust made it clear just how strong these ties were.

Thanks to the LEIU, Gomes had a good relationship with the Chicago Police Department's organized-crime task force. He decided to take the two-and-a-half-hour flight to the Windy City in order to gain a better perspective.

On September 19, 1975, there were no pit stops. Gomes went straight to the Chicago PD's organized-crime unit, housed in a Loop police station.

The Chicago Police Department is the second-largest urban force in the country, and, dating back to 1837, it is also one of the oldest departments. The chaos of the station did not surprise Gomes; he was used to it. Most police stations—at least the ones he had been to—were nondescript government buildings abuzz with activity. This station was no different . . . until he spoke to the woman at the welcome desk.

"Well, hi there. What can I do for you?" she asked.

"My name is Dennis Gomes, and I'm from the Las Vegas GCB." He handed her his credentials. "I'm here to see the station commander"

"Okay. I'll take you up there." She wore a fuzzy black sweater which matched her short frizzy black hair.

Her warm greeting startled Gomes. He wasn't used to Midwestern hospitality, especially in the chaos of a police station.

The woman hopped down from her perch and motioned for Gomes to follow her. She had no trouble getting through the throngs of officers, criminals, and residents. Everyone seemed to sense that she was coming and moved out of her way. They took an elevator to the top floor.

"Dennis, it's great to finally meet you," the station supervisor said as he stood to greet Gomes in the cluttered outer office.

The supervisor was by far the biggest guy Gomes had ever seen. Adding to the impact of his massive size was his uniform—dark blue, formal, like a throwback to the 1800s. It was adorned with pins and ribbons that framed his badge. Shiny gold buttons completed the regal look.

Gomes shook the station commander's massive hand. He had never felt so small.

"Thanks for meeting with me," Gomes said.

"I just have to say, I pictured you to be a lot bigger and a whole heck of a lot older," the commander said with a room-shaking chuckle.

"I get that a lot." Gomes couldn't think of anything else to say.

"Follow me."

They walked into a small conference room, which held a desk and two chairs. There were no windows and only one door, and everything in the room was white except for a pile of files on the desk. The top one read ANTHONY SPILOTRO.

"Look, Dennis, I know you're here to get some information on Frank Rosenthal and Tony Spilotro, but I'm afraid I can't let you see the Spilotro file. It's an active investigation, and we can't risk any information getting out." He winked at Gomes. "But you can use this room, and I'll be back in a couple of hours to answer any questions you may have."

The station supervisor left the room and closed the door behind him.

Pure Chicago.

—⌣—

Volumes on Tony "The Ant" Spilotro were laid out on the table for Gomes "not" to read. This was the most detailed intelligence file Gomes had ever examined. Spilotro had recently escaped a murder conviction in the death of Leo Foreman, a juice loan collector for Mad Sam DeStefano. Gomes remembered being told about this murder at the LEIU convention in April 1971.

Mad Sam had earned his nickname because of the pleasure he took in sadism, torture, and murder, not to mention his bizarre nonviolent behavior. Mad Sam was Tony Spilotro's first mentor, and had taught him everything he knew. Spilotro was an ace student who enjoyed torturing his victims as much as Mad Sam did. The Leo Foreman murder must have been a big party for the pair; in fact, according to the testimony of Chuckie Crimaldi—a participant in this murder party that later flipped—Mad Sam and Spilotro savored every minute.

Gomes read Crimaldi's testimony. Then he came across a picture of Mad Sam DeStefano's April 14, 1973, murder scene. Allegedly, the Chicago Outfit and Tony Spilotro did not want the attention that Mad Sam's crazy courtroom antics were attracting during the Leo Foreman murder trial, so Spilotro shot his mentor twice with a shotgun, in his own garage. Gomes saw the picture of Mad Sam lying in a slick pool of black blood. One arm appeared to be completely severed from his body. It was a haunting sight—not so much because of Mad Sam, but because the person on the other side of the trigger was now very much a part of Gomes's investigation.

Gomes heard the doorknob start to turn and closed up the file.

"Do you have any questions?" the station commander asked.

"I knew Spilotro was bad, but now I think he may be pure evil. Is torture his MO?"

"I think if he has an opportunity, he definitely enjoys torturing his victims. But if he doesn't have time to indulge himself, he uses a twenty-two."

"What can you tell me about Rosenthal?"

"He's been arrested a few times. Did some time for fixing a basketball game. He's an oddsmaker for the Outfit. We don't think he's a triggerman, but he's good buddies with Spilotro, who worked his way up from a button man in Chicago."

A button man is a hit man for the mob, a soldier.

"So, are they running things for the Outfit in Las Vegas?"

The big copper smiled.

Gomes had his answer.

⚊ ⚊

Back in Vegas, Gomes tightened the vise on Argent.

Gomes, Law, and Iannone began spending more time than ever at the four Argent casinos. The focus was to get ground-floor informants—regular frontline employees who could provide Gomes and his small team with any information concerning unusual discrepancies or strange happenings at the casinos.

After coming up dry for several weeks, Gomes found an informant who was willing to give him exactly what he was looking for. The guy was around Gomes's age, married, with two young kids. He had been living in Las Vegas for about five years, coming from San Diego in search of better opportunities. The man had found a job as a slot and warehouse attendant at the Hacienda; no college degree, but supporting his family, and content where he was. He had no problem talking to Gomes, and agreed to meet him in his office as long as no one found out—a very typical concern.

"There was something strange," the informant said on October 6, 1975, standing with his back to Gomes, staring out an office window at the desert sky. "We collected about, oh, somewhere between a hundred and ten to a hundred and fifty slot machines from the casino floor during construction, just after Glick took over sometime during 1974. We brought the slots to the warehouse, stored them there for a while, and then sold them to someone named Mr. Arrington. Then when the receipt came back, it only recorded the sale of fifty to sixty slot machines."

Gomes made a note. "You're sure that they were all sold to Arrington?"

"Yeah, I started to do a count. I got to eighty-five, and then I was told by Vandermark that I didn't need to finish the count, so I stopped, but they were all there."

"And they weren't put back on the floor?"

"No, definitely not."

"So they left with Arrington but weren't recorded?"

"Exactly."

"Thank you. Keep me posted. Let me know if anything turns up, or if anything else strange happens. You can call me anytime." Gomes gave the informant his office and home numbers, thanked him at least ten more times, and sent him on his way, in keeping with his practice of making informants of this sort feel appreciated and important.

Gomes headed straight to the Stardust with Law and Iannone after getting the tip about the Hacienda slot machines. They found Jay Vandermark in his office, hunched behind a desk. He was middle-aged, but had the posture of a ninety-year-old man. Every time Gomes saw him, he couldn't help but marvel at his uncanny resemblance to a weasel. *Maybe God does have a sense of humor,* he thought.

"What can I do for you, gentlemen?"

Gomes leveled his gaze at the man. "We're investigating some lost or stolen slot machines out of the Hacienda's warehouse. They were part of a group that was sold to Mr. Arrington. What can you tell us about those?"

"Not much, really," Vandermark said. "Frank asked me to—"

"Frank Rosenthal?" Rich asked.

"Yeah, Frank Rosenthal asked me to take an inventory of the Hacienda's warehouse, and I did what he asked. There were, oh, I can't remember exactly, but about fifty to sixty machines that we prepared and sold to some antiques dealer. I think his name was Roy Arrington."

"There were about a hundred and fifty slot machines brought to the warehouse," Gomes corrected Vandermark. "Then at some point, close to a hundred of those machines just disappeared."

"I don't know about that. When I took inventory there were only about sixty machines in the warehouse. It's funny that you brought this up, because I was in Frank's office, and we came across a newspaper article about fifty slot machines from the Hacienda that were confiscated in LA by California police. We laughed about it, because we figured they were stolen before Glick took over and we came in."

"I don't remember seeing any article like that," Gomes said.

"Me neither," Iannone chimed in.

"I haven't heard anything like that," Law said. "What paper were you reading?"

"I can't remember; one of the local papers," Vandermark said.

"Well, we'll look into this for you," Gomes said.

"I appreciate that."

"How are things going with your license application?" Gomes asked, just to ruffle Vandermark's feathers. Gomes had heard that he was having trouble, thanks in part to his own work.

"Fine, as far as I can tell," Vandermark replied.

＊

Gomes knew Vandermark was lying; he suspected that Frank Rosenthal had sold those machines "off the books." But Gomes didn't care about the missing one-armed bandits. They were old, and could not have been worth more than $10,000 to $15,000. The situation did, however, give Gomes a reason to question various officers of Argent Corporation.

As expected, each interview played out similarly; nobody knew anything about the sale of any slot machines: *It happened before I started here . . . Maybe you should ask somebody else . . . It's a total mystery . . . This is a strange place, and sometimes things just go missing in the desert.*

＊

Realizing that he needed more manpower, Gomes brought on Bowen Call, whom he'd hired as an audit agent about a year earlier. Call was a tall, dark-haired Mormon kid, whose religion provided him with a strong moral foundation. However, he still managed to remain open-minded, and was not a fanatic. Best of all, Call would do anything Gomes asked, and do it well.

Around this time, in October 1975, Gomes also began working closely with a Gaming Control Board enforcement agent named Ron Tanner, whom he referred to as Mr. Cool. He was the epitome of style and good looks, more movie star than law enforcement agent. He had perfect hair, a neatly groomed mustache, and an eye for the ladies—and they certainly noticed him. The handsome Tanner was also a solid, focused agent who had a knack for developing informants.

After completing his investigation, Gomes put together a thorough report that detailed what had happened to the hundred or so slot machines that had disappeared under the watch of Jay Vandermark and Frank Rosenthal. This investigation both impressed and concerned Phil Hannifin, but Gomes didn't really care how Hannifin and the Board were going to act on this matter; it was more of a distraction tactic than anything else.

Still, he was definitely not prepared for what was about to happen when, one day, shortly after the report was filed, Tanner walked into Gomes's office.

"I need to talk to you, Dennis. I'm not . . . I . . . I'm not sure what to think."

"Just tell me."

"Hannifin called me today and had me hand-deliver an envelope to Allen Glick," said Tanner. "It was sealed. He didn't tell me what was in it."

"It was probably some licensing paperwork that needed signatures."

"That's what I thought, at first. But why wouldn't he have just told me to wait for his signatures? Anyway, something just didn't feel right. So I opened it, and it was your confidential investigation of the missing slot machines."

"What?"

"It was your investigation of the missing slot machines," Tanner repeated. "It was addressed to the Board members, from you, and it was marked confidential."

Gomes was stunned. "Holy shit."

"I'm sorry. I just thought you should know," Tanner said.

"Thanks."

"You don't think Hannifin is on the take or dirty, do you?"

"No. Hannifin's a really good person," Gomes said. "He would never do anything he thought was wrong—or against the letter of the law."

"Then why would he want to give Glick a copy of your investigation?"

"Because he thinks he's helping him," Gomes said. "If Hannifin likes you, he'll do anything for you. Hannifin's convinced that Glick's a good guy, a good businessman."

Tanner rolled his eyes. "Yeah, right. I never understood what all this hoopla over Glick was all about."

"He's a front—an empty suit. But he's got everyone eating out of the palm of his hand. He knows exactly what he's doing."

"Sorry to be the bearer of bad news. But, on a better note, I've got a guy I think you should talk to. He works at the Stardust. I'll bring him by tomorrow."

Gomes shook Tanner's hand. "Thanks. I really appreciate your help."

"No problem, Gomes. See you tomorrow."

Next came surprise raids on the count rooms in every casino in Nevada. Gomes initiated a program by which his agents would raid at least five casinos a week. Phil Hannifin thought that this was a good idea, a nice precaution to add into the law enforcement mix.

But the morning after speaking to Hannifin about the planned raids, Gomes gave separate instructions to his closed-door team in a private meeting.

"When you're in the count room," Gomes announced to his operatives in the privacy of his office, "I want you to make sure that you check the scales. Double-check and triple-check the scales. I think they're skimming out of the slot wins, but I'm not sure how."

"Dennis, get this," Law excitedly piped up. "I had an informant tell me that she saw Glick and Rosenthal get into a fight on the casino floor, and Rosenthal slapped Glick across the face."

"You're kidding. Can you bring this informant in?"

"She's actually on her way. I knew you'd want to talk to her."

"What owner gets slapped by his employee?" Iannone asked.

"Exactly. I just can't believe Rosenthal was stupid enough to act like that in public," Law marveled. "We need to try to find out what the chink in the armor is."

"Who's this informant?" Gomes asked.

"She knows you. She wanted to talk to you, so I told her to come in," Law said. "She's Glick's girlfriend."

"You mean mistress," Iannone corrected him. "How the hell did you get to Glick's side dish?"

"It was dumb luck, really," Law admitted. "I noticed her hanging out one night and approached her. She was having a drink. She looked upset, so I figured she'd just gotten into a fight. We started talking. She was really pissed off at Glick. I had a gut feeling, so I told her that I was a gaming agent. She asked me if I worked with Dennis Gomes, then told me she needed to talk to you. She called me first thing this morning and I told her to come in."

As if on cue, there was a knock on the door. One of his agents poked his head in to tell Gomes that Rose* was here to see him. The agent promptly showed her in.

---

* Pseudonym

Gomes immediately recognized her. Rose had been a purchasing agent at the Dunes when Gomes's dad had worked on a big construction job there. Iannone offered her his chair and leaned against a wall.

Beautiful was not the word to describe Rose. She was sexy, a knockout with a killer body, slender but curvy. Her blonde hair cascaded in soft waves to her slim shoulders. She wore a tight pencil skirt that accentuated her long legs and perfect calves. A tight cardigan sweater fit her so well that little was left to the imagination.

"Hi, Denny—it's so good to see you. Thanks for meeting with me. How's your dad?"

"He's great," Gomes replied with a warm smile. "So, what did you want to talk to me about?"

Rose confessed that she had been having an affair with Allen Glick, and two nights earlier, she'd been at the Stardust. She had witnessed Rosenthal and Glick getting into an argument on the casino floor. She'd seen Rosenthal slap Glick across the face and then storm off.

"Do you know what the fight was over?"

"Yeah—Tamara Rand. She invested money in the Stardust because of Allen."

"So what was the problem?"

"She wanted to get her money out, along with the interest, according to the agreement she had. Allen wanted to give her the money, but Frank just flat out said no."

Rose told the agents in the room that Glick wanted to give Tamara Rand the money because she knew things about this deal that could get Glick in trouble; mainly, that Glick was in with the Mob. Gomes made sure that Rose knew not to tell a single person that she had made a visit to the Audit Division.

"One more thing: How do you know all of this?" Gomes asked.

"I guess Allen thought I would be impressed that he was in with the Mob. But as we became more serious, all he wanted to do when we were . . . you know, *intimate* . . . was whine and complain. So, I heard a lot."

"Mrs. Rand, my name is Dennis Gomes," he said into the phone minutes after Rose walked out. "I am with the Gaming Control Board in Nevada. I recently became aware of the issues you are having with Allen Glick, and I would like to help you get your fair share."

There was the briefest pause on the other end of the line. "Really? Well, I would appreciate that. What did you say your name was again?"

"Dennis Gomes. I am the chief of the Audit Division for the Gaming Control Board."

"What do you need from me?"

"Information." There was static on the line, but Gomes could faintly hear Tamara's shallow breaths, so he just waited.

"All right . . ." Mrs. Rand sighed finally. "I'm tired of Allen's games; this is not what I invested in. I have a lot to say. I'll be in Las Vegas in a week. We can talk then."

Gomes never got the chance to have that talk. A few days after their phone call, on November 9, 1975, Mrs. Rand was murdered in her San Diego home. The cause of death was a fatal gunshot wound from a .22 caliber gun—Spilotro's weapon of choice. Tamara Rand's lifeless body was found slumped over in her own kitchen with five bullet holes in her.

Don North called Gomes and told him about the murder early one morning, just days before Gomes was set to talk with her. Nothing like a hard slap in the face to get your day going. But before Gomes even had a chance to let the news sink in, his phone rang again.

The voice on the other end said, "Hey, Gomes . . . Man, I just heard about Tamara Rand." There was controlled anger in Ron Tanner's voice. "This has gone too far."

"I know. I . . . I can't believe they killed her."

"It's terrible that the poor woman is dead because she trusted Allen Glick. But I've got some better news for you. Frank Rosenthal and Jay Vandermark are getting denied their gaming licenses."

"They'll probably find some way around it."

"True, but at least it makes things a little harder for them."

"I guess."

"Will you be in your office in about an hour? I was going to drop off someone I think you should talk to. He's a shift boss in the slot department at the Stardust."

"Yeah, bring him in through the back."

———

About an hour later, Gomes had assembled Law, Iannone, Call, and the newly admitted Bill Clifford in his office. Clifford was a tall, nerdy mathematical genius with an intense sense of loyalty to Gomes.

"Ron Tanner is bringing someone from the Stardust for us to talk to," Gomes told his men minutes before the snitch arrived. "But before he gets here, I want an update on the count-room raids."

"Everything checked out," Call assured Gomes.

"Same for me," Law said.

"Yeah, same," Iannone said.

"Did you check the scales?" Gomes asked.

"Five times. They were perfect," Iannone said.

"At least five times," Law said. Iannone just shook his head in agreement.

"You missed something. There's something illegitimate going on in that count room," Gomes grumbled.

"Then it's hidden really well," Iannone said.

There was a knock on the door and Ron Tanner poked his head in.

"Hey, Ron, come in."

"It's crowded in here," Tanner said.

"Rich and Bowen, you two stand and let Ron and his guy sit," Gomes said.

"One of you can keep your seat," Tanner said with a dismissive wave. "I'm headed out. I just wanted to drop Dale Clark off. Call me when you're done and I'll pick him back up."

Gomes raised a hand. "Wait a second. Ron, do you think there is someone leaking information in either Investigations or Enforcement?"

"As a matter of fact, I meant to mention this to you." Tanner closed the door. "I heard that that fucking asshole Bob has been getting gifts from Frank Rosenthal. In fact, he just got his entire apartment furnished by Rosenthal."

This rumor about the Enforcement Division agent did not surprise Gomes.

Gomes nodded, and Tanner opened the door and motioned Dale Clark into the office. Clark was of average height and had a hefty build. He had sandy brown hair, small eyes, and a prominent nose that was held up by a bushy mustache.

Gomes stood up and shook his hand. "I'm Dennis Gomes, chief of the Audit Division. Go ahead and sit down. The big guy behind you is Rich Iannone." Iannone shook his hand. "This is Dick Law, Bowen Call, and Bill Clifford."

"No one will find out that I was here, right?" Clark asked.

"Definitely not."

"It's not that I've been threatened or anything. I just don't want people at work thinking I'm some sort of rat or something."

"We completely understand. You don't need to worry. So, what can you tell us?"

Clark explained that he had never seen anything illegal. He had never seen anyone flat-out steal. However, he'd noticed some strange things recently. For example, the Stardust was buying $30,000 in coin from the Marina every Wednesday, in mostly nickels. Clark couldn't figure out any reason for this practice. Also, there was a strange bank on the casino floor. The employees had nicknamed it the "phantom bank." Every day it was stocked with coin, and throughout the day, when the change booths ran out of coin or change, they would give their cash to the shift bosses to buy the coin out of the auxiliary bank.

"Can you explain that process in detail?" Gomes asked.

According to Clark, the special bank was basically a cabinet with two locked compartments, both a top and a bottom. The bottom compartment was stocked with the coin that the shift bosses purchased throughout the day. The top one had a slot where the shift bosses would place envelopes containing cash in exchange for the coin they took out. The shift bosses were the only casino-floor employees with keys to this bank.

"Do the shift bosses have a key to the top cash section?" Gomes asked.

"No. The only person with that key is Jay Vandermark. He collects the cash, and I'm not sure what happens after that," said Clark.

Alarms were going off in Gomes's brain. This was it. He knew this "special bank" held the key to his investigation. There was nothing illegal about the use of a special or auxiliary bank. In fact, the Las Vegas Hilton was known to have used this method. However, all casinos were required to submit their operations in the form of a control manual to the Gaming Control Board. Neither the Stardust's control manual nor any of Argent's control manuals acknowledged the use of a "special" or "auxiliary" bank. This was the clue Gomes had been looking for.

If, as Gomes supposed, Vandermark was helping Argent skim money from the slots, it would be in the form of coin, which would have to get converted to paper in order to be smuggled out. Coin was far too heavy and cumbersome to smuggle out of a casino without attracting attention. The "special bank" was the perfect way to convert the skimmed coin to cash. This was clearly how they were laundering the coin.

But, more precisely, how were they skimming?

Gomes needed more information. He knew Rosenthal was getting tipped off before their raids, so he would need to figure out a way around that. He needed to talk to Tony Albanese. If Spilotro was running the Chicago Outfit's interests in Vegas, like the feds suspected, then there was a chance Albanese knew what was going on.

Early one brisk December morning in 1975, Gomes slipped a piece of paper with his name, title, and phone number into Tony Albanese's daily newspaper.

Then the waiting began.

CHAPTER 15

Loophole

A SHARP PAIN SEARED THROUGH GOMES'S LEFT TEMPLE . . . *ANOTHER migraine coming on*, he thought. The bright glare of the early-morning winter sun off the desert floor made his eyes water. He looked at the clock in his State-issued unmarked Ford Galaxie. Then he heard a noise, looked up, and saw in the distance the faintest disruption of dust.

A car was making its way toward him, the grill of the Lincoln Town Car unmistakable. The vehicle pulled up opposite Gomes's Ford, so that the driver's-side windows were facing each other. Gomes waited for the dirt to settle, and rolled down the window.

"You got the money?" Tony Albanese asked. Gomes marveled at this rat of a guy who could sell out for $1,000 of the GCB's intelligence fund. His dark eyes looked almost black, completely empty.

"Yeah, as long as you have some good information."

"So, whaddya want to know?"

"How Spilotro's running things."

"Tony ain't runnin' nothin'. He's just a soldier, an enforcer."

"I have good information that he's the one running things in Vegas. This makes me think that you may be trying to feed me bad information."

Albanese began cackling. "The Outfit ain't fuckin' stupid. Tony's too unhinged. Besides, he ain't got the brains to run things."

"Still, how do I know you're not lying?"

"Okay, Frank kicked Tony out of the Stardust the other night. He was so bent outta shape. He came right to my club and started fuckin' whinin' about it. Do you think if Spilotro was runnin' things, Frank woulda kicked him out?"

"Do you know why Frank kicked him out?"

"Yeah. Frank thought he was drawin' bad attention. Tony was so fuckin' pissed. I thought he was gonna burst a fuckin' vein in his head."

Gomes tossed the envelope full of twenties through Albanese's open window. "What families hold an interest in Argent?"

"From what I hear, it's Chicago and Kansas City, but Chicago controls it."

"How are they skimming the money?"

"I ain't too clear on the details. They got some fuckin' technical wiz that did somethin', and they're skimmin' coin somehow. I don't know, but it's a lot of fuckin' money."

"Are Frank Rosenthal and Tony Spilotro close?"

"Yeah. Been in my club together a bunch of times. Frank's runnin' things. He's a smart guy. Tony . . . Tony does his fuckin' dirty work. Ah, but yeah, they're close. Real good friends from the way I see it."

"Thanks for this information. The offer stays on the table. Call me if you have any information you think will be useful, and we'll set up another meeting."

Gomes rolled up his window and drove back toward the city. He couldn't wait to get out of the desert. His skin was crawling.

———

The stabbing pain of his migraine sliced across the bridge of Gomes's nose as he drove back to his office. He felt like he had been running into the same wall over and over again. Gomes knew coin was getting skimmed, but his raids on the count rooms were proving to be worthless. No one was working with him. The year 1975 was coming to an end, and Gomes wasn't any closer to proving that Argent was a mob operation.

An innocent woman, Tamara Rand, was killed by the Mob, and no one seems to care.

Each thought sent another throb of pain from his frontal lobe to the base of his neck.

"Gomes, you don't look so hot," Iannone said when he saw Gomes skulking in.

"Got a headache . . . no big deal." Gomes made it to his office, shut the door, left the lights off, lay on the floor, and closed his eyes.

There was a quiet knock on his door about a half-hour later.

"One second," Gomes croaked, still half asleep. When he opened his eyes the daggers were no longer slashing his brain. The pain had relaxed to a steady throb—something he could handle. He opened the door.

"Robert Murillo, the coin wrapper, is on his way up. Here's some aspirin." Iannone handed over the bottle. Gomes gladly accepted, turned on his office lights. The sudden brightness was only mildly painful.

"Which guys are in?"

"Just Law. Call and Clifford are out on a raid."

"Grab Dick, then bring the coin wrapper into my office." Gomes sat behind his desk rubbing his throbbing temples and looked up to see Iannone leading Robert Murillo into the office, with Law trailing a few paces behind.

Murillo looked to be in his early twenties, a clean-cut kid. He had an olive complexion and dark hair. He could have been Italian, but Gomes guessed he was Hispanic. Gomes stood up to shake his hand.

"Thanks for coming in."

"No one will know I was here, right?" Murillo asked. "I don't want to lose my job."

Always the same question from every one of these guys. "No, definitely not. No one will know you spoke to us." And always the same answer. "As a coin wrapper, you're in the count room; you must be familiar with the count process, right?"

"Oh, yeah—very familiar."

"Does Jay Vandermark always oversee the count?"

"In the beginning he did. Then he hired one of his buddies, Lee Northey. So either Jay or Lee would do the count. But Jay just transferred positions, so now Lee oversees every count."

"He works seven days a week?" Law asked.

"Yeah."

"Where did Jay Vandermark transfer to?"

Murillo explained that Jay Vandermark had had trouble getting a gaming license, so he had transferred positions, becoming Frank

199

Mooney's assistant. However, before he transferred, Vandermark completely changed the count procedures. Prior to Vandermark's tenure, the accounting representative would monitor the weighing and counting of the coin and then re-count it after it was rolled. Vandermark changed this so that the accounting representative would leave the count room as soon as the coin was weighed.

"Who's the accounting representative?"

"Usually, it's Vicki Lee." Gomes looked at Law to make sure he wrote that name down.

It would become a critical piece of the evolving puzzle.

The intense pain that had first begun in the desert that morning had dulled to more of a constant tension in the base of his neck. It was bearable by afternoon, but every once in a while a surge of pain would remind Gomes that it was still there. Nonetheless, he still managed to focus his investigation with laser-like intensity on Jay Vandermark and Lee Northey.

Vandermark was a self-proclaimed crossroader. Born in Yakima, Washington, in 1923, he had been arrested four times—on three occasions for drunk driving, and once for disturbing the peace. From approximately 1950 to 1960, Vandermark was a member of a slot-cheating ring that operated out of Reno. In 1956 he operated his own slot-cheating school. In 1960, Vandermark was hired as a slot manager at the Pioneer Club, and spent the next decade and a half working in a multitude of casinos. In 1969 he was placed in the "Griffin Book"—aka the Black Book—as a known casino cheat.

Leland (Lee) Northey, like Vandermark, was also born in Yakima, Washington, but thirteen years later, on November 30, 1936. He was five-foot-eleven, 155 pounds, with brown hair and blue eyes. His identifying mark was an eight-ball tattoo on his left arm. Vandermark and Northey, who did not have a criminal record, were longtime family friends. Northey had arrived in Las Vegas in 1973 to work at the Aladdin with Vandermark, then went to the Stardust in 1974—six days after Vandermark was hired there.

Gomes and his crew had a good handle on where the majority of the skim was taking place, and who the principal players were. Gomes just needed to figure out how the money was getting skimmed. He wanted to raid the Argent count rooms again, but he needed the Gaming Control Board's authorization before he could raid any casino, and that raised the same old concern—Argent would get tipped off. Gomes needed a way around the rules. He had to find a loophole.

At the French Café with Dick Law, Gomes started the search. The French Café had come to be a place where Gomes felt safe. Don North and Gomes had made a deal that they would not tell any of the agents they worked with about this restaurant. It was a secret he had kept from everyone else—up until now.

"So what's the occasion?" Law asked.

"I have a project for you. You're going to need to draw on everything you learned in law school."

"Okay. What's it all about?"

"There has to be some sort of loophole that will allow me to order a raid without authorization; you need to find it."

"What if there isn't one?"

"There has to be."

———

While Gomes was waiting for his legal sleuth to find a loophole, he decided to take another trip to the desert to check in with Tony Albanese. He made sure to bring his sunglasses this time.

It had rained briefly that morning, and now it was a beautiful spring day, the precipitation leaving the sweet perfume of sagebrush in the air. Gomes rolled down the windows and took in the intoxicating scent. He didn't have to wait long for Albanese to arrive.

The car rolled up to Gomes's window. "Hey, Dennis, how goes it?"

"Good, Tony. You?"

"I'm good. Gettin' ready to open up another club."

"Can you tell me anything about Glick and Tamara Rand?"

"Yeah, that's shameful. That shoulda never happened. She was fightin' with Glick. She wanted more money out. They didn't wanna give it to her.

She got in the way, and I guess that was the easiest way to get her outta the way. Tony was always complainin' about that broad. Said that dumb bitch was tryin' to play in a man's game."

"Did Spilotro kill her?"

"I honestly don't know. But he wasn't with me that night. You ask me, he did it."

"How is the skimming going?"

"Tony's always braggin' about how much fuckin' money they're gettin'. He's been playin' in these big poker games at the Dunes."

⌓

Gomes was home sleeping when the call came. It was the first time that week when he hadn't been woken up by a recurring nightmare in which he was fighting the massive school bully but his body wouldn't work.

"Dennis, I found it," said the voice on the phone.

"Dick? What time is it?"

"Quarter to three. I found a loophole," Law said.

"What?"

"A loophole. I know how we can raid the count room without authorization." Then Dick Law proceeded to tell Gomes how to rig the system in his favor.

⌓

Gomes didn't go back to sleep. He needed to figure out if the proposed course of action was practical. He quietly got out of bed, doing his best to avoid waking Barbara, who was recovering from an injury she'd suffered during a recent performance. Her *pas de deux* partner had dropped her from an overhead lift and caught her rib cage with his knee. The result was a couple of broken ribs, and so much pain that it had been difficult for her to sleep.

Gomes's mind was racing as he snuck down to the kitchen.

I can't call them at night, because I would definitely be able to get ahold of one of the Board members. And, I need documentation. I need to call them while they are in some sort of hearing or meeting. Something that can't be disrupted. But what?

He pulled out his calendar.

That's it. Perfect. What's the date today? April 27th.

In three weeks the Board members would be in Carson City for a series of public hearings with the governor. There would be no interrupting them then.

Gomes now had a time frame—a countdown. But how to fill the time till then?

The next night, Gomes decided to while away some hours with an unscheduled surveillance of the Dunes. Fake palm trees, marble, gold, and neon made this desert oasis visible from miles away to the thirsty gamblers lost on the Strip. It was a fancy crowd, and even in their best surveillance duds, Dennis Gomes and Larry Clark stood out. But it didn't bother Gomes. He was done trying to blend in.

Gomes and Clark made their way through the crowded casino and walked straight to the large poker room. Sitting at a high-limit private game, Tony "The Ant" Spilotro held court. He was playing with Major Riddle, part owner of the Dunes, and future poker world champions Chip Reese and Stu Ungar. Tony Albanese was hanging around with a few other questionable-looking characters.

The playing stopped and every set of eyes at the table looked Gomes's way, but he just crossed his arms, puffed up his chest, put his head back, and stared directly at Spilotro. The agents' presence obviously bothered the thug because he didn't play much longer, and left the Dunes in a huff. Gomes and Clark tailed Spilotro to the Crazy Horse, where he dropped off Tony Albanese, and then to his house where he remained for the rest of the night.

Did Gomes accomplish anything on that night? He didn't obtain any useful intelligence or uncover any crimes, but he did interrupt Spilotro's night, and he felt like he was doing something other than waiting around.

Finally, Gomes had made it to the day of the planned Argent raid: May 18, 1976. So many things had to line up perfectly in order for this to work. And, if it didn't work, there was a good chance that Gomes would no longer be chief of the Audit Division. He was well aware of what was on the line.

Gomes made it in to his office around 9:30—his normal time—and needed only one look at his men to tell that Dick Law, Bowen Call, and Bill Clifford were as anxious as he was. Rich Iannone just looked angry. The four men kept to themselves for most of the day, sitting at their desks and blankly looking at whatever reports were in front of them.

By lunch, Gomes's adrenaline had kicked in just enough so that he was able to force himself to eat a turkey sandwich, which tasted like cardboard. As he choked down each bite he let his mind drift off into the "what if's": *What if they see us coming? What if we don't find anything? What if the special bank is legitimate? What if we actually find skimmed money?*

When he closed his eyes, he could see the Stardust; he could practically feel the asphalt beneath his feet. He could even hear the crunching as he walked through the parking lot. He could see Law, Call, Iannone, and Clifford lining up. They were ready to bust through the front entrance. As soon as he walked through the door there was an assault on his senses. He heard slot machines ringing, the loud clanging of coins pouring out, and sirens. There were bright flashes of lights preventing him from seeing. He wasn't sure which direction to go first. Then he panicked and opened his eyes. His pulse was racing. He could feel sweat building under his collar.

Gomes took a deep breath and closed his eyes. He was back in the Stardust again. He knew what he had to do . . .

Gomes checked his watch. It was 3:30 p.m. He picked up his phone and called Roger Toundry's office. (Shannon Bybee had recently resigned from his Gaming Control Board position, and Roger Toundry had replaced him.)

The secretary answered. "No, Dennis, I'm afraid he can't be reached right now. You will just have to wait. I'll get a message to him to call you as soon as he can."

Next, Gomes called Jack Stratton's office. "No, Mr. Gomes, he is not available, and will not be available until tomorrow."

Lastly, Gomes called Phil Hannifin's office. "I'm sorry, but Phil is in a public meeting with the governor, so I won't be able to reach him, or even get a message to him until probably tomorrow, or possibly late tonight if he checks in with me."

That was it. Gomes had tried to reach all three Board members, and his attempts were now documented. This was the loophole in gaming regulations that allowed Gomes to conduct a raid without approval from a Board member. As long as Gomes was documented attempting to reach each Board member, he was free to order a surprise raid on his own authority.

———

At approximately 4:00 p.m. Iannone and Call left the office first. Gomes, Law, and Clifford followed. They drove across town and met up in the Stardust parking lot. The four Audit Division agents and their chief approached the casino entrance and crossed the threshold. Without a word, Call and Clifford broke left at a hurried pace to secure the count room. Gomes, Iannone, and Law headed straight to the center of the casino floor. The noise of the slot machines, the smoke, the people—it all blended into the background.

It was a matter of seconds before Gomes found a casino shift boss—his target. Maybe it was instinctual, or maybe he recognized the man from hours and hours of surveillance, but at this moment all Gomes knew was that this short, pudgy, bald, middle-aged man was exactly who he was looking for.

"Are you the shift boss?" Gomes asked.

"Yes; how can I help you?"

"We are agents with the Audit Division." In a swift, almost imperceptible flow of motion, Gomes, Iannone, and Law flashed their credentials. "We are conducting a raid of this casino, and we need you to take us to the special bank."

"I don't know what you're talking about."

"The special bank on the casino floor, where coin is converted to cash."

"I'm sorry, I don't know what you're talking about." The shift boss let out an odd chortle that sounded like a cross between the Mad Hatter and a girlish giggle.

"I'm not sure what you find funny," Iannone said, glowering, "because we're not joking."

"No, no . . . I . . . I'm sorry, it's a nervous habit."

"Just take us to the special bank," Gomes urged.

"Look, we don't have anything called a special bank. I'm sorry. I wish I could help you."

"I don't give a fuck what you call it," Gomes told him. "There is an auxiliary bank on the casino floor. Take us to that."

"Ahh," the man said, shaking his head from left to right. "I really don't know what you're talking about."

"If you don't fucking drop the dumb act right now, we will arrest you and charge you with obstruction of justice for interfering with a criminal investigation," said Gomes.

"Tim," Iannone spoke up, addressing the man by the name on his ID tag. "That's a criminal offense. We know for a fact that there is a bank that holds coin in a bottom cabinet, and there is a slot for the deposit of cash in the top portion. Shift bosses, like yourself, are issued keys to the coin section. Are you following me?"

Tim nodded his head in agreement while beads of sweat poured down his forehead.

"When someone needs coin, you take their cash," Gomes interjected. "You place it in an envelope and deposit it into this 'special' bank. You then unlock the bottom section and take the corresponding amount out in coin."

Gomes narrowed the already-tight gap between himself and the man named Tim, then leaned in and lowered his voice. "Where is that bank?"

Tim blanched. "Oh, okay, now I know what you're talking about. Sorry, sorry . . . we just don't have a name for it." Tim let out another bout of his nervous cackling as he turned and led the investigators deeper into the casino.

They quickly walked past the table-games pit and to the back of a coin booth, where an inconspicuous-looking locked cabinet easily went unnoticed. It was made out of painted metal and designed to blend in with the surrounding decor.

"Open it," Gomes demanded.

"What?"

"Open it."

"I can't. I have to get authorization. Would you like to come to my office while I make a few phone calls?"

"No. We're staying here until this bank is opened. Use that house phone right there."

Tim picked up a house phone just out of earshot from Gomes. It was a quick call.

"The casino manager is on his way down here. But I can open up the coin section of the bank."

Tim pulled out a key that was attached to a lanyard. His hands were shaking so badly that he needed to use both of them just to get the key into the aperture. It took everything Gomes had not to grab the key and open the bank himself. The metal door finally creaked open to reveal stacks and stacks of rolled quarters.

"We need to count, secure, and bag this coin. And I need to get into the top of this cabinet."

Law and Iannone were already counting and logging the coin, then sealing it into large, clear evidence bags.

Tim nervously chuckled. "Just wondering what you're going to do with that coin. I don't mean to interrupt your work, but, but . . . umm . . . we're going to need it."

"We are just securing the coin until it is accounted for," Gomes replied. "As soon as the coin has been verified in the cage records, we will release it."

An older-looking man joined the group. He was overweight and had thinning white hair. Up close, his face appeared young and plump. He was either a late middle-aged guy that looked terribly bad for his age, or an elderly guy that had retained some youthfulness.

"Oh," Tim spoke up. "Don, this is Dennis Gomes. He's with the Gaming Control Board."

"Hi, Dennis, I'm Don Tomblin, the slot boss. I'm here to help you in any way possible. But no one has a key to get into the top portion of this bank. Jay Vandermark has the only key, and he's away on vacation."

"Listen. I don't give a fuck who has the key," Gomes snapped. "I am going to get into this cabinet, so call Maintenance and have them bring a drill."

"Umm . . . well . . ." Beads of sweat were quickly forming on Don's large forehead. "I'm going to go make a phone call and see what I can do."

At this point, Don Tomblin disappeared while Gomes, Iannone, and Law worked on counting and securing the coin. Later, during the course of the investigation, under sworn testimony, Don Tomblin would tell Gomes about the following phone call that occurred during this frenzied counting period:

Jim Powers, the casino manager, phoned the residence of Stardust executive Bobby Stella Sr. Then, Powers passed the phone to Tomblin.

"Don, Jay [Vandermark] wants to talk to you," Stella said.

"Okay," Don replied. Don then heard Stella yell off the phone, "Lee [Northey], tell Jay I have Don on the phone for him."

Vandermark picked up the phone. "What's going on over there?" he asked.

"Dennis Gomes from the GCB is here, and he's demanding to get into the auxiliary bank. He said he's going to drill it open if someone doesn't bring a key."

"Let 'em drill it," Vandermark said, and hung up the phone.

They had the cabinet opened with two quick drills. The interior was exactly how Gomes had pictured it. The bottom was littered with a day's worth of glossy, sealed envelopes, which, Gomes suspected, contained the cash that had been used to buy the skimmed coin—in other words, the laundered cash. Each envelope was signed by the shift boss and labeled with the amount of money inside.

Gomes and his team quickly counted the money, then re-counted it twice, and then secured it in sealed evidence bags. The total found in the auxiliary bank for May 18, 1976, was $10,750 in both coin and cash.

Now, Gomes needed to check the cage records and the casino log to make sure that the money from the auxiliary bank was not accounted for. Skimmed money was never accounted for in the casino's logs that were routinely checked by the Gaming Control Board.

Following the opening of the auxiliary bank, things happened very quickly that night. It was organized chaos. Gomes immediately sent Dick Law to the cage where he, Bill Clifford, and Bowen Call would try to identify any record that acknowledged that the money in the special bank was accounted for. Gomes and Iannone remained on the casino floor more or less to keep an eye on Don Tomblin and the cabinet.

"Dennis, can I talk to you?" Call quietly and calmly asked. They walked over to a noisy row of nearby slot machines.

"Did you find anything?" Gomes asked.

"We each went through the cage and the count records. That bank and the money in it is not listed anywhere. We are one hundred percent sure."

"I knew it. Listen: I need you to guard the stairway to the executive offices. Do not let anyone in. I am going to call in Frank Mooney. Send him to me, here. Do not let him or anyone else into those offices. No one."

They parted ways, and Gomes rejoined the group gathered around the special bank.

"Don, I need you to get Frank Mooney on the phone, now."

Don had Frank Mooney, the CFO for Argent, on the phone within a minute.

"Dennis, hi," Mooney greeted the investigator. "What can I do for you?"

"We have a problem here. We cannot find any record of the money located in the auxiliary bank attached to coin booth two."

"Well, it must be recorded somewhere."

"I need to see where."

"Can you come by my office tomorrow? We'll straighten all of this out then."

"No. I'm at the Stardust. I need you to come over and figure this out now."

"I'm an old man. It's not easy for me to just rush out. I was just about to sit down with my family for dinner. In fact, I was just leading my family in grace when you interrupted."

"Okay. Either you're here in twenty minutes, or I will go into your office and go through your records on my own. It's completely up to you."

"I'll be right over."

Precisely twenty minutes later, an angry old man with thin gray hair trundled up to Gomes. Mooney was slightly on the tall side, not too heavy but definitely not thin, just all-around soft and pudgy-looking. He was still wearing his suit, but he'd clearly taken off his tie and unbuttoned his collar and redressed in a hurry. Everything was crooked and wrinkled.

"I don't appreciate your goon refusing to let me into my office," said Mooney.

"That's my fault," Gomes said. "I just wanted to make sure that you spoke to me before you went there."

"I'm here. I'll go up to my office to locate any information that you need, then bring the ledger down here to you."

"That's all right. I'll just go up to your office with you and we can find it together."

"You know, I don't appreciate being treated like this. I prefer to work on my own. I will get to you when I'm ready."

"That's not going to work. I'm going to your office with you, now." Gomes motioned with his hand for Mooney to lead the way.

Mooney walked slowly—a little too slowly. Gomes saw Bowen Call faithfully guarding the entrance to the stairwell. Mooney grunted in disapproval as he walked by. They finally made it to his office, where Mooney perched behind his grand wooden desk. Gomes was too wired to take in the full comfort of the plush leather chairs. He sat down and waited. Mooney slowly pulled out the ledger.

"So, Dennis, what do you need me to confirm?"

"Where is the money that was placed in the special bank, attached to coin booth two?"

"It must be part of booth two's contents. Why'd you drag me up here?"

"It's not. We checked everything on the casino floor. It's nowhere."

"Well, then it must be in here. What amount are we looking for?"

"Ten thousand, seven hundred and fifty dollars."

"Okay. Well, this is . . . Sorry, no, that's not it. Mmm . . ."

Mooney slowly tortured Gomes, page by page. He went through the entire ledger three times, as if the money might magically appear.

"It's not here. I don't know what else to tell you."

"So, if the money is not here, and it's not in the casino cage or any of the count records, then it's not accounted for. What do you think that means?"

"I guess it's not accounted for."

"So, this is skimmed money."

"Uhh . . . I . . . I guess so. You're going to have to ask Jay Vandermark about that."

"Okay, bring him in."

"He's on vacation."

"Show me his vacation slip."

"He didn't fill one out."

"Isn't that a company policy?"

"Yeah, but we're pretty lax about it."

"When did he tell you he was going on vacation?"

"He just gave his notice yesterday."

"That's fucking bullshit. I'm confiscating the general ledger, and we're going to the count room."

From Mooney's office, Gomes hightailed it to the count room. By that time, Iannone and Call had secured the skimmed coin and cash from the special bank and had locked it away. When Gomes reached the count room, the only thing left to do was find out how coin was getting skimmed from the drop. This was the key to the entire investigation. If Gomes and his crew could identify a way that money was getting skimmed on a daily basis, their investigation would be solid, undeniable.

Gomes secured Frank Mooney and Don Tomblin in the cage supervisor's office and went to work on the count room.

Count rooms are always bare: a plain table, two chairs, a few basic shelves, no drawers, nowhere to hide anything, and the scale. The Stardust used the Toledo 8130 model. The scale took up a large portion of the room. It was roughly six feet long, four feet tall, and four feet wide. It had a metal basket where the coin was placed in bags to get weighed—counted.

"Did you check this scale?" Gomes asked.

"At least five times. It's accurate," Bill Clifford said.

"Did you check it with quarters?"

"Yeah. It was perfect."

"Rich, count out a hundred dollars in quarters. I want to check." Everyone quietly watched as Iannone counted exactly $100 in quarters, placed it in a coin bag, and handed it to Gomes. He put it in the basket—$100.

"Fuck! I know there's something else."

"Maybe they just took out a certain amount before it was weighed," Iannone suggested.

"No, no, no—someone would've seen something." Gomes began frantically feeling around the scale. Nothing.

"There's nothing there," Clifford said. "We've been in here for hours."

"No," Gomes insisted from the floor, where he was feeling around under the scale. "There is something here."

"Dennis, give it up," Iannone pleaded. "We found skimmed money. Isn't that enough?"

"No. That's not fucking enough! Don't you understand? If we don't prove that this is something they do on a regular basis, we'll be screwed. They'll find some way to say the money was not skimmed. Rich, help me slide this scale out."

Iannone obliged, and they slid the scale out a few inches.

That's when Gomes saw it: a small metal switch. It was very inconspicuous, but once you noticed it, the miniature silver lever seemed completely out of place.

Gomes pulled it. The lights on the scale momentarily flashed, then went back to normal. Gomes put the bag with $100 in quarters back in the basket. This time it registered $72—a 30 percent difference. Gomes weighed $25 in quarters: $17.50. He weighed $50 in quarters: $35. It was precise. Every weigh registered 30 percent less.

There was a knock on the door, and a Stardust employee peeked in.

"Excuse me, Mr. Gomes?"

"Yeah?" Gomes was too busy taking pictures and documenting the skim switch on the Toledo scale to look at the nervous employee.

"There's a Mr. Hannifin on the phone. He said it's urgent. I will transfer the call in here, okay?"

"Yeah, okay," Gomes replied, and the nervous employee quickly fled the scene.

The phone began ringing.

"This is Dennis Gomes," Gomes said into the receiver, a certain defiance in his voice.

"Would you like to tell me what in the shit is going on over there? My phone has been ringing off the hook, and a lot of people are really pissed off." The anger in Phil Hannifin's voice was unmistakable. "I have received a million frantic calls from Argent's people."

"Phil, we have them by the balls. We seized thousands of dollars in skimmed money from just today. And I just found a switch on their count-room scale that under-weighs coin."

"Holy shit. Are you kidding me?"

"I'm completely serious. We have hard proof of their massive skimming operation. But I need to wrap this up and get some sleep. I haven't slept in at least thirty-six hours. I'll tell you more tomorrow."

Gomes hung up the phone, read the Argent employees their rights, and made sure he and his agents had gathered everything they would need to tie the noose as tightly as they could. Then he went home and collapsed into his bed.

The raid was a major success. Gomes and his team discovered that the count-room scale was under-counting the coin by 30 percent. They also confirmed that this skimmed coin was placed in the auxiliary bank and sold back to the casino for cash. This amounted to Gomes not only discovering the crime, but also the weapon.

There was only one question that lingered in his mind as he drifted off: Where in the hell was Jay Vandermark?

CHAPTER 16

Cat and Mouse

THE WEEKS FOLLOWING THE MAY 18, 1976, RAID WERE FRANTIC. GOMES and his agents put together all the evidence for what he believed would be a slam-dunk case. But during this time, Gomes began to notice a change in the way Nevada's politicians behaved toward him. It was almost as if Gomes carried a plague: one touch from the man and your political career would be over. The exception to it all was Phil Hannifin, who was in complete support of Gomes's investigation.

Having gathered hard proof, Gomes took the next official step and presented his case to the district attorney in order to get indictments. Not only was the DA afraid of the possible political fallout that could come from helping Gomes, but he also did not appreciate all of the additional work Gomes had created for him. However, the DA had no choice but to present the case to the Clark County grand jury under the burden-of-proof rule. Though the efforts of the deputy DA of Clark County were halfhearted, he managed to come away with two indictments. One was for Jay Vandermark, and the other for Lee Northey—both of whom were now missing.

This was a situation Gomes had not wanted, but it was a step in the right direction. Still, Gomes wasn't satisfied as long as there were bigger fish to fry . . . and he knew exactly where to go fishing.

———————

Toward the end of May, Gomes and Law were sitting in a city hall boardroom next to Gaming Control Board member Jeff Silver. As Silver faced down Argent Corporation treasurer Frank Mooney, who sat opposite

Gomes, this "sworn-in" interrogation seemed to Gomes like an endless root-canal procedure.

"On May 21, 1976," Gomes said flatly to Mooney, "you received advanced notice that Audit Division agents were going to the Stardust to examine documents from Jay Vandermark's office. Why did you instruct Louise to place his documents in her car?"

Mooney shook his head. "No. I had no idea that any agents were coming to look at Jay's documents. Jay's girl, Diane, or whatever her name is, was already cleaning out his office because the maintenance department was going to change it over to a [hotel] room, and I sent Louise down to help her, my secretary."

"Did you instruct Louise to put the documents in her car?" Silver asked.

"The box, yes."

"Why?" Silver asked.

"To keep them safe until we got a chance to go through them."

"Wasn't there another place other than someone's secretary's car to store things?"

"Not in our offices. Not where they'd be safe. Vandermark has keys to all those offices."

"Mr. Mooney, wasn't this just part of the situation whereby you were aware that Vandermark was still active in the slots department after his gaming-license denial? I'm assuming, rather than have us find out that he was still active, you had these documents removed?"

"No. The answer to that is negative. Absolutely negative."

"Then why remove them from the building?" Gomes asked.

"I told you what the reason was. To keep Vandermark or his people from getting them."

"Why were we not advised that there were other documents that we hadn't seen?"

"I don't know."

"You have no reasonable explanation of why you did not inform Agent Gomes of the fact that those documents were in the car?" Silver asked.

"No reason. No. No."

"But, you do admit that you instructed Diane Kohn to remove documents pertaining to the slot department from Vandermark's files?"

"No, I don't admit that," Mooney replied.

"What did you tell her to do?" Gomes asked.

"I told her to clean out Vandermark's office and move the stuff upstairs, which she did."

"Well, at any rate, that's contrary to their testimony," Gomes commented, again tightening the noose for the record. "They stated that your specific instructions—and we questioned all these people independently— your instructions were to remove anything pertaining to the slot department out of his files . . ."

"And bring that up to your office," Law added.

"And also you specifically told Louise to take it out to her car and store it in her car," Gomes said.

"If there's anything in his stuff related to the slot department, Dennis, that came to light to me, I would have turned it over to you."

"But they stated that all that stuff related directly to the slot department, and that's why they took it out. In other words—"

"Anything related to the slot department had to be in the cabinet, because in the box, when they went through the box, they said it was just junk mail, and they showed me some of it."

"No, they said they took the stuff out of the cabinet, specifically for that reason, that it related to the slot department."

"That had to be somebody else's instruction," Mooney maintained.

"So you deny that . . . ?" Law asked.

"I deny it emphatically."

After interviewing and interrogating more than one hundred individuals who were involved with the Argent Corporation, Gomes concluded that Frank Mooney, the company's CFO, was a liar. Mooney contradicted his own testimony numerous times. But, in the end, nothing Frank Mooney admitted to or lied about brought Gomes any closer to pinning this skim on Allen Glick, Frank Rosenthal, and the Chicago Outfit. Gomes had plenty of testimony verifying that Vandermark had met with Rosenthal on a daily basis and would often take the paper-money envelopes from the auxiliary bank straight to Rosenthal's office. But if Gomes was going to get charges brought against Argent, he needed more.

— ⁓ —

June 1976: This was the first time that Tony Albanese arrived early to one of the desert meetings—already waiting when Gomes arrived.

The two cars, facing opposite directions, sidled up to each other.

"Dennis, you are not gonna believe what I found out. This is gonna knock your fuckin' socks off! After I found this I couldn't wait to tell you."

"Let's hear it." Gomes tossed the envelope filled with the money over to Tony Albanese.

"Spilotro comes into my club real pissed off. I mean, fuckin' angry."

"So? He's always pissed off about something."

"This was different. He wanted to kill someone."

"Who?"

"After your bust with the papers and all, word gets around about how much money had been skimmed."

"I still don't see where this is going."

"Not all of the fuckin' money that was skimmed made it to Chicago."

"Oh."

Gomes's mental cogs began to turn: Was Vandermark peeling off a taste for himself? Vandermark was the key, the one person who could tie Allen Glick, Frank Rosenthal, and the Chicago Outfit to the Argent skim. If Gomes could get Vandermark to flip, the best political game-making wouldn't be able to cover this up. Gomes needed to find this guy.

Badly.

— ⁓ —

Vandermark had a twenty-seven-year-old son who lived in Las Vegas. He had a few drug arrests on his record, which Gomes used to locate him.

Jeff Vandermark lived in a run-down apartment building on the border of Vegas's Naked City neighborhood, which was situated just north of the Strip, and served as a link to downtown. The Naked City supposedly earned its name from all the showgirls who would sunbathe at their affordable apartments, close to their work. By the late 1970s this area had become home to dilapidated housing for drug addicts, or anyone who was down and out.

Gomes brought Larry Clark with him to talk to the younger Vandermark. Together they drove the short distance to the apartment complex. When Gomes knocked on the apartment door, pieces of paint flaked off the battered wood. No answer. Gomes knocked again. No answer, but he could hear movement inside, so he clenched his fist and pounded as loudly as he could.

"Goddammit. What?" Jeff yelled.

"This is an urgent situation," Gomes boomed through the door. "We need to talk to you about your dad."

"He's not fucking here!"

"We know. He is in serious danger. We need to talk to you."

The young Vandermark yanked open the door. His bright red hair was wild, sticking out in every direction. He was built like his father, tall, skinny, and gangly.

"Come in. I don't want people to see me talking to you."

"Thanks."

The instant he stepped inside, Gomes determined that this was the single most disgusting home he had ever been in. The cramped space reeked of garbage, stale beer, vomit, and rotten food.

"I haven't talked to my dad in years. I don't know where the fuck he is. Now, leave me the fuck alone."

"I just want to lay out the situation for you. Your dad skimmed a lot of money, over seven million dollars. But somewhere along the line, three million of it went missing. Now your dad's life is in serious danger. There's a team of hit men after him as we speak. I can protect your dad. I'm willing to give him immunity. He'll do a couple years' time at most, and he'll stay alive. But I need you to help me find him."

"If I knew where he was I'd help you, but I don't."

"Look, I know you know where your dad is. We need you to help us." Gomes stared at the young man. A flash of red filled his face. A vein in his forehead bulged.

"I fucking told you: I don't talk to my fucking dad. I don't know where the fuck he is. Now, get the fuck out of my house and never come back!"

— ◦ —

That night Gomes did something he had never done before as a crime fighter: He broke the law. Gomes knew that Vandermark's son was the key to saving Jay Vandermark's life, but he needed to find some sort of evidence that proved Jeff knew his dad's whereabouts. He wasn't going to use this evidence in any official manner; he just needed it to coax Jeff into cooperating.

In the parking lot that night, outside the Audit Division, Gomes laid it out for his boldest agent. "Larry, go back to the kid's apartment tonight. Wait for him to leave. Then go in and look for any information that could help us."

"You want me to break in?" Larry Clark asked, his brow furrowed.

"Yeah."

"I don't know . . ."

"Look, this kid can save his father's life. He's just too stupid or stubborn or scared to understand that. We need to coax him into doing the right thing, something he's probably not all that familiar with."

"Isn't this illegal?"

"Technically, yes. But, we're not going to use anything against him. We're not even going to tell anyone that we ever spoke to this kid. We just need him to get a message to his dad."

— ◦ —

The following day, Gomes and Clark returned to the younger Vandermark's apartment. This time he opened the door after the first knock.

"I told you, I don't know where my fucking dad is. Stop fucking bothering me!"

"Look, I'm not trying to bother you," Gomes said, in the most calming tone he could muster. "We'd like to come in and talk to you."

"About what? I don't know where he is."

"This is only going to take a minute. Then you have my word that we'll never bother you again."

Jeff begrudgingly opened his door just wide enough to let Gomes and Clark in. Jeff did little to hide his irritation at their presence. Gomes didn't care; he needed to get Jeff to bring a message to his dad, and he was going to make sure it happened this time.

The conversation went the same as it had the previous day. Gomes asked Jeff to help Gomes find Jay; Jeff swore he had no idea where his dad was.

Gomes pulled out a picture of Jay Vandermark sitting on a park bench with a Mexican girl, in front of a Mexican sign. The picture was time-stamped with a recent date.

"Now tell me that you don't know where your dad is."

"Where'd you get that?" Jeff asked.

It didn't matter how Gomes found that picture; the fact was that if Gomes was able to find it, a hit man was likely to find it too. This scared Jeff, and he finally agreed to help Gomes.

"Tell your dad that if he agrees to testify against Glick, Rosenthal, and any members of the Chicago Mob that he can link to the skim, we will give him immunity from prosecution, and State protection."

After an agonizing pause, Jeff said, "Okay. I'll tell him. I'm going down to Mexico in a couple of days."

"Listen carefully: Tell your dad that the Mob is after him, and they will kill him if he doesn't get protection soon. So, you need to be careful going into Mexico. Don't tell anyone."

"I won't. I'll call you in a couple weeks, as soon as I get back."

—◆—

Vandermark's son called Gomes two weeks later, almost to the minute.

"Hey, Dennis. I spoke to my dad, and he wants to take you up on your offer. I have more to tell you, but I don't want to talk over the phone."

"Are you free today?"

"I just got back. I mean, like, just walked in my door. I'm tired, and I have a lot to do tomorrow. Can you come by my place on Thursday?"

"Sure. Thursday's fine."

Gomes hung up the phone. Jumped up and down in his office. Waved his hands in the air. Dick Law walked in and caught a little of Gomes's uncharacteristic dancing.

"Umm, is there something you need to tell me? You're not planning on joining the ballet with Barbara, are you?"

"Ah, no. You weren't supposed to see that."

—◦—

That same day, a couple of hours later, Gomes received a call from Las Vegas Metro advising him that he had better come down to "your prime suspect's son's apartment." Gomes grabbed Clark and they made their way over to the apartment.

—◦—

When Gomes first walked into the squalid apartment, he was startled by a loud slurping sound. He looked to the left to see a detective loudly sucking down a milk shake. There were more cops and detectives inside; most of them had burgers in their hands.

The smell alone was enough to make Gomes gag. The rotting garbage odor that had previously filled the apartment now carried a heavy metallic scent with it. Something inside Gomes recognized that smell. He couldn't directly place it, but it was familiar enough to fill every fiber of his being with panic. The detective slurping down the milk shake motioned for Gomes to go into Jeff's bedroom.

A double juicy, rare cheeseburger was the first thing Gomes saw when he walked into the bedroom. A cop in the doorway was messily devouring his lunch. He pointed to the bed.

It took Gomes a few moments to register what he saw there. Vandermark's son was lying on the bed with his head completely crushed, almost flattened. One of his eyeballs was hanging from the socket by one fraying fiber, possibly the optic nerve. The other eye was gone altogether. The kid's head must have exploded, because there was blood and brain matter everywhere. The wall behind the bed looked like it had been painted red and covered in chunks of raw meat.

Gomes felt the blood drain from his face. He had to look away just to keep from passing out.

He focused on the cops and detectives enjoying their lunch—just another day at the office. It took Gomes everything he had not to puke that very second as he watched a plump officer tear into his burger and then wash it down with the final loud slurp of his soda. Gomes looked back at the lifeless pulp on the bed. His head was spinning.

"Hey, Gomes," one of the detectives spoke up. "Feel free to look around. See if you can find anything that will help your case."

"I've already spoken to this kid," Gomes said. "He doesn't even talk to his dad. There's nothing here."

Gomes knew this cop—knew that he had a "dirty" reputation. Gomes was not about to let on too much.

"Any idea who did this?" Gomes asked.

"Yeah. It was a drug buy that went bad. See that?" The detective pointed out a small bag of cocaine.

"That can't be worth more than fifty bucks. You think that's what got him killed?"

"Yep."

"You don't think this is the Mob's payback for the crimes of his father?" Gomes asked.

"Nah. There's absolutely nothing here that points to the Mob."

"Thanks for keeping us informed," Gomes said, and left as fast as he could.

—◆—

Gomes had a pounding headache by the time he got back to his office. Whenever he closed his eyes he saw the brutal death scene at Jeff Vandermark's apartment.

He called Hannifin.

"Phil, I have to go to Mexico. I need to find Vandermark."

"No way. We have no jurisdiction in Mexico. You're not going."

"I have to."

"If you set one foot on the other side of the border, I will fire you before you're even back."

"No you won't."

"Yes I will. I will not have your life on my conscience. I will fire you and drop this case."

Gomes hung up the phone, knowing Hannifin would, in fact, fire him if he went to Mexico, and then so much hard work and sacrifice would be lost. Gomes pounded his fist on his desk out of frustration. He had no choice but to wait and hope that Jay Vandermark would make it back to Las Vegas.

Going through Vandermark's files in his office, compulsively looking for something he may have missed, Gomes received an unexpected and uninvited visitor.

"Hey, Dennis," Tony Albanese said with a nod as he brushed past Gomes's secretary and barged into the room. "Wait till you hear what I have to tell you."

"What the fuck are you doing here, Tony?"

"I got somethin' real good to tell you, and I need some money."

"How many Metro officers did you see walking in? They will tell your friends you were here."

"Ah, you worry too much. I know these guys. They ain't gonna do nothin' to me. I'm friends with 'em. They trust me."

"Get out of my office. I will not be responsible for your stupidity."

"Dennis, relax."

Something in Gomes snapped. He looked at Tony Albanese and saw flashes of the younger Vandermark's death scene. He knew Albanese had nothing to do with it. Albanese wasn't a killer; he owned a couple strip clubs and hung around with some made guys, but murder wasn't in his repertoire. However, if any of the made guys he hung around found out that he was talking to Gomes, they would put a bullet in him without a second thought. Gomes didn't want Albanese's blood on his conscience, and he just couldn't stand to be around him for one more second. He jumped out of his chair, grabbed Albanese by his collar and belt, used his head to open the door, and threw him out.

It was the last time Gomes had any dealings with Tony Albanese. The man's careless assessment of his associates eventually got him killed. His decapitated head was found in June 1981 near a desert highway in Needles, California.

Gomes had to get to Vandermark before the goombahs did. Out of desperation, he called his good friend, Al Delugach, a reporter for the *L.A. Times*. He won a Pulitzer Prize for his investigative reporting in 1969 and wasn't afraid of anything.

"Al, I need your help. I need to get Jay Vandermark out of Mexico, but I'll get fired if I go."

The voice on the other end was unequivocal. "I'm on my way."

Gomes gave Delugach the address of Vandermark's last known location—a campground in Mexico just south of Rosarito. Delugach bought a bus ticket and was there in a day, but he just missed Vandermark.

Camp neighbors told Delugach that the man he was looking for "had just left, and in fact, there was another group of men that had just missed him."

CHAPTER 17

Into Thin Air

"DENNIS, I'VE GOT THIS KID IN THE INTERROGATION ROOM," RICH Iannone announced on September 8, 1976, peering into Gomes's office. "He worked in the coin-count room at the Stardust, and he knows things. With a little coaxing, I think you may be able to get him to testify."

A good interrogation sounded to Gomes like the perfect medicine for much of what was ailing him. Following Iannone into the interrogation room, Gomes saw a nervous, fat kid at the table, fidgeting uncontrollably. The young man, named John,* had a sandy blond mop of hair. Sweat rained down his ashen face.

"John, this is Dennis Gomes, the chief of the Audit Division. He uncovered the skim, and he'd like to talk to you a little."

"You worked in the hard-count room at the Stardust?" Gomes asked.

"Yeah. I was basically Lee's assistant."

"Lee Northey?"

"Yeah . . . Yes, sir."

"Then you must know about the skimming."

"Well, ahh . . . umm . . . I don't really know that much."

"Look, John, don't waste my fucking time. You're here because you know something—so tell me what you fucking know."

Iannone could tell that Gomes was starting this interrogation too angry, and tried to calm him down.

John started crying quietly. He admitted to knowing that Vandermark and Northey were skimming, but he didn't want to get in trouble, so he'd kept his mouth shut and looked the other way.

———
* Pseudonym

Gomes felt the blood rush to his face. Something about this kid made him want to explode. Gomes pummeled John with a flurry of curses, and told him that people had been murdered in cold blood because of this skim. He was now three inches from John's face.

"Dennis. Calm down." Iannone tried to get in between the two men.

John and his crying had gotten under Gomes's skin, and Gomes let him know it.

The kid sniffed. "Okay, okay . . . I'm sorry. I didn't know anyone was going to die. I . . . I just did what I was told."

"What were you told to do?" Gomes asked.

"I made sure that thirty percent of whatever coins were weighed were separated out so that Lee could put it in the special bank. But I didn't know who was getting the money. I . . . I'm sorry. I didn't know anyone would die."

"Who knew that the skimming was taking place?" Gomes asked.

"When I first started working with Lee and figured it out, I mentioned to Bobby that something strange was happening . . ." Iannone handed John a tissue and the kid continued. "Bobby Stella. He told me not to mention it to anyone else and just do whatever Lee or Jay told me to."

"Who else knows?"

John explained that Bobby Stella was the only person that had ever directly mentioned the skim to him, but he knew that Frank Mooney, Allen Glick, and Frank Rosenthal had all talked to Jay Vandermark about it many times.

Gomes released John, who grabbed a handful of tissues and practically ran out of the room.

"Dennis, what the hell got into you?" Iannone asked after John had cleared out of the room. "You almost destroyed that kid. I was worried you were going to try to strangle him."

"I don't know. His whining and crying just . . . I don't know . . . it pissed me off." Gomes took a deep breath and struggled to collect himself. "Too many people have already gotten hurt—or worse. Too many lives have been ruined to tolerate that sort of bullshit."

The following day, Gomes received a phone call informing him that he "had better come over to Sunrise Hospital." Not a good sign.

Gomes's stomach roiled as he rushed across town to the medical center. A skinny kid met Gomes at the entrance to a hospital room.

"Hi, Mr. Gomes, my name's Eric.* I'm friends with John." The kid was so nervous and shaky that he made Gomes a little uneasy. "We work together at the Stardust, where I'm a bellman. Last night we were at a bar on the west side, and these four men came in."

"What did they look like?"

"They were real professional-looking, all wearing nice suits, but they were real big guys, scary-looking guys. Two stayed inside and the other two told John they needed to talk outside."

Gomes gently nodded in an effort to keep the young man's nerves in check.

"Then, they took . . ." He paused for a moment, and Gomes feared the guy was about to lose it. Then he took a deep breath and continued. "They took a baseball bat to him."

"Did you get any of their names?"

"No, sir. But I heard them threaten to kill John if he ever talked to you again."

Gomes got Eric's contact info, thanked him for coming forward, then walked into the room. He was immediately reminded of how much he hated the constant beep of monitors, and that overpowering antiseptic smell. He would have never recognized John if he hadn't known that it was in fact him lying in the bed. Virtually every bone in John's body had been broken, including his jaw.

A nearby nurse instructed Gomes that John would not be talking for a while; the best thing for him right now was rest. Gomes sighed, patted the kid's arm guiltily, and left.

It was hard for Gomes to watch his Argent investigation crumble. He was certain that Vandermark wasn't coming back. There were a few reports

* Pseudonym

that he had made it to Arizona, but nothing was confirmed. The DA had dug his feet in and refused to move beyond the indictment of the missing man. It was all pure agony for Gomes.

However, some recent changes in Nevada's political landscape signaled potential movement on the case.

A new governor had been elected—Robert List, former attorney general for Nevada—and he had appointed a new Gaming Commission chairman, Harry Reid, a prominent attorney and aspiring politician. George Swarts, another member of the Gaming Commission, reached out to Gomes confidentially a week after the beating incident.

Swarts called Gomes at home, late in the evening. "Dennis, you can't tell anyone that I suggested this, but you should ask the new governor to appoint a special grand jury to try the Stardust case, bypassing Clark County altogether." Swarts was a CPA and an all-around good person—someone who worked hard and always tried to do what was right.

"I didn't know that was possible," Gomes finally marveled, gripping the phone tightly.

"Yeah. I think List may be more likely to push the Argent case because this could look good for his political career. I mean, I'm not sure, but it stands to reason. He could possibly gain political points by making a public example of this major skimming case."

"I agree. I'm going to put in the request tomorrow."

"Just don't tell anyone that I suggested this."

The following morning Gomes submitted a formal request to Governor List, and was assured that he would receive an answer from the governor in about a week.

To help pass the time, Gomes checked in with some of his informants. One of them, a man named Mike,* was in his early twenties, a self-proclaimed ladies' man never short on the hair gel or cologne. Mike worked in VIP services at the Stardust, knew everything that was going on, and loved the sound of his own voice.

Gomes met him at a small coffee shop on Rancho and Charleston just before Mike's swing shift.

---

* Pseudonym

"Anything unusual happening?" Gomes asked.

"Nah—everyone's been laying low."

"Any questionable individuals check in?"

"Are you kidding? I've barely seen Frank Rosenthal there. Supposedly he's been in his office, but I haven't seen him around the casino. Everyone's still shaken up by all this skimming business."

"How has business been?"

"Well, my friend who works in Accounting told me that the Stardust had been losing money ever since Glick took over. But apparently, over the past couple of months, you know, since your raid, the Stardust has had record profits."

Gomes sighed. "Based on our audit of Argent and our statistical analysis, the probability of Argent performing as badly as it has in the past is a 1 in 3.87 times 10 to the 51st power chance."

"What?"

"There is a 1 in 387 followed by 51 zeros chance of a company performing so badly."

Mike still looked confused.

Gomes explained: "Okay, to put it simply, there are no words in the English language to express a probability this small."

"Numbers just go right over my head."

Gomes rolled his eyes. He was hoping that Mike would spread the word that Argent's "poor" performance, as reported by Accounting prior to the raid, was very near statistically impossible, but Mike clearly was not following the conversation. Gomes decided to just let it go.

"So, can you believe Bob List was elected governor?" Mike marveled. "He's been comped so many times at the Stardust he's considered a regular. He always had girls sent to his room; in fact, he was usually given the 'girl room.'"

Gomes was shocked; he'd never heard any of these tales about Bob List before. Mike mistook Gomes's expression for confusion.

"The 'girl room'—you know, the room that's kept out of circulation for, ah, *special* occasions. All the executives know about it."

"I get it."

Governor List's alleged Stardust business—and that's all it was, an allegation—was the last thing that Gomes wanted to "get." He never confirmed the informant's claim; there wasn't any documentation of this sort of thing. But it didn't come as a surprise when the governor turned down his request to convene a special grand jury to try the Argent case.

At this point, Gomes was out of options. He couldn't keep waiting for his pocket ace, Jay Vandermark, to show up. Gomes had to do what he always did in these situations: In the summer of 1977 he called his friend Don North and handed his investigation over to the feds.

Nobody could've known—not for a few decades, really—that this was a turning point.

Gomes would be pulled off the Stardust case in the coming weeks, and other investigations would keep him up at night. But he had a strange feeling in his gut about the Stardust that would not go away for a very long time.

In the months after the Stardust debacle, Phil Hannifin would eventually resign as Gaming Control Board chairman, and Gomes would stare into the abyss. Gomes's resignation—the culmination of an amazing stint, the legacy of the youngest man ever to head up the GCB's Audit Division—would follow closely on the heels of Hannifin's exit. On September 27, 1977, Gomes said good-bye to his job. His resignation hit the press just two months after Hannifin left the Gaming Control Board.

Gomes would find that his circuitous journey—part of which would hit the big screens in the form of the film *Casino*—would bring him back to Argent and Stardust in a completely surprising fashion in a Chicago courtroom, close to a quarter century later.

EPILOGUE
No More Secrets

Carve your name on hearts, not tombstones.

—SHANNON L. ADLER

THE DECADES SINCE THE GOLDEN AGE OF CORRUPTION IN THE GLITTER Gulch had rolled by. Dennis Gomes had left law enforcement for a successful career in gaming, and had managed fourteen major casinos—from Indiana to Atlantic City—during a twenty-eight-year span.

In 1995, Martin Scorsese made the movie *Casino*, with Robert De Niro playing a thinly veiled version of Gomes's old nemesis, Frank Rosenthal. But years after that, on a sweltering July day in 2007, Dennis Gomes sat in a hushed pressure cooker of a federal courtroom, ready to plunge the detonator down on what would come to be known as the "Family Secrets" trial—the largest organized-crime prosecution in the history of the United States.

Silence crashed down on the room as Gomes drew in a breath in preparation to field the first question from Mitch Mars, the lead prosecutor. Gomes was about to exhume those long-buried events that had occurred in Las Vegas, when men wore wide ties and wider sideburns, and no respectable politician or casino could get by without bedding down with the Mob.

The light from the high ceiling fixtures spaced throughout that burnished, dark, musty courtroom glared in Gomes's face. But there was also the glare of the press, eagerly awaiting the bombshells about to be dropped by this "rock star" of an expert witness. There was the glare of Judge Zagel, watching over the sensational proceedings from behind his high bench, eyeing Gomes with a patient stare. And there was the collective glare of the men at the defense table—those heavy-lidded, dead eyes of killers.

The lead prosecutor, Mars, was one of the most intelligent individuals Gomes had ever met. The Family Secrets trial was not just attempting to solve and prosecute Jay Vandermark's murder from Gomes's case, but it was also attempting to prosecute fourteen defendants in a Racketeer Influenced and Corrupt Organizations Act (RICO) case spanning four decades, which included charges for eighteen Mob murders. Mars had an innate handle on every aspect of this case, and an incredible ability to seamlessly link and convey the whole dark picture of the murderous Chicago Outfit to the jury.

"Sir," Mars greeted Gomes with a slight smile, "I'm going to ask you to state your name for the record, please, and spell your last name for the court reporter."

"Dennis Gomes, G-O-M-E-S."

"Excuse me," Rick Halprin, representation for Joey Lombardo, interrupted. "Could the witness please speak closer to the microphone?"

"Mr. Gomes," Mars continued, "are you currently employed?"

"I've got my own gaming company. I was in the casino business before that, running casinos, and now I manage casinos for others, investors that don't have casino experience."

"And when you say casinos, are you talking about casinos, for example, in Las Vegas and New Jersey?"

"Yes."

"Mr. Gomes, have you ever been in the law enforcement side of casino regulation?"

"Yes, I have. That's where I started my casino career."

Gomes then told his story, led by Mars and encouraged by the jury that hung on every word out of his mouth. When Gomes got to the part of the story that involved the murder of Jay Vandermark's son, there were audible gasps from many of the jurors.

Gomes realized precisely at this moment that justice was being served. He was telling his side of the story, and that's all that mattered. Gomes looked over at his beautiful wife, Barbara, who had supported him through all of this, and he silently thanked God for her. Barbara gave Gomes one of her subtle smiles that conveyed all the strength in the world. Then Gomes took in his daughters, both beaming with pure admiration. Danielle gave her dad two thumbs up, and Gabrielle gave the Outfit defendants a quick flash of the evil eye. No one messes with her dad.

This was all Dennis needed.

The nearly thirty years of trying to cover the void of injustice had been instantly cauterized by simply speaking the facts aloud into the public record. From this flowed the realization that regardless of the situation, Gomes had always done the right thing, which at times was the most difficult path to take.

And now, his family beamed with pride. For Dennis Gomes, in the end, this is all that mattered—*family*.

The Family Secrets Trial, led by Mitchell Mars, was successful on all counts. The five defendants were convicted on a list of conspiracy charges that span decades and included eighteen murders. Frank Calabrese Sr., Joseph Lombardo, and James Marcello all received a sentence of life in prison. Nick Calabrese received a twelve-year sentence in exchange for his cooperation in the trial. And Anthony Doyle and Paul Shiro each received twelve-year sentences because they were not convicted of murder charges.

Several days after the Gomes family returned to their home in Margate, a sailboat operated by a man dressed in a suit anchored a mere twenty feet off of their dock in the bay directly behind their house. The sailboat remained there for about two weeks, taunting the family. Was it someone watching the family, or were they merely on edge from the trial?

Afterword
A Daughter's Thoughts

I never intended to write this last section. Frankly, it breaks my heart to do so. I co-wrote this book with Dennis Gomes, my father, a desk away. He passed away suddenly while I was writing the epilogue of this book—his story.

I hope by now that you've learned what an exciting life he lived, especially during the 1970s in Las Vegas. However, his story would be incomplete if I didn't also write about what an incredible father, husband, brother, friend, and mentor he was. My sisters, Mary and Gabrielle, and my brother, Aaron, have joined me in writing this last section.

Quite simply, Dennis Gomes is our hero. He managed to accomplish the impossible. I'm not sure how, but the man must have been able to be in more than one place at a time. Our dad never missed a dance recital, soccer game, or distraught phone call, and he did all of this while chasing down the Mob, revolutionizing the gaming industry, and convincing people that it was a good idea to play tic-tac-toe with a chicken. (Customers in his casinos played this game with a live chicken, with the chance to win $10,000.) Even better, he had the uncanny ability to make each of his kids feel like he or she took center stage.

And it wasn't just his five kids who felt like he put them in the spotlight. Anyone lucky enough to have known Dennis Gomes, whether it was for an hour or a lifetime, felt like the sole recipient of his attention.

While he was always impossibly attentive to the needs of those around him, and deeply committed to the pursuit of his career goals, he never once sought personal betterment at the cost of other people's livelihoods. My brother Aaron followed in my father's footsteps and entered the gaming industry right out of college, taking a position in table-games marketing at the Mirage Casino in Las Vegas. Upon his hiring, several high-level executives warned Aaron that it was difficult to gain acceptance in the table-games department, comprised as it was of a tight-knit group that valued age and experience. These were "the good ol' boys." When Aaron was instantly welcomed into this department, everyone was shocked—Aaron most of all!

It was so notoriously unusual that Aaron asked the casino manager why he had been so heartily welcomed into the table-games department. This was the manager's answer:

Word got out that you were Dennis's boy. You know, your dad's a hero among the casino-floor staff in Vegas.

When your pop was the president of the Aladdin Casino, they had an Arab sheik that would come in and lose millions of dollars almost every weekend. On one trip the sheik lost every hand in the first shoe. He called up your old man and said, "I want that dealer fired." Your dad told him he'd take care of it. You know, he had to make sure that the dealer wasn't cheating or anything, and in the meantime, he just moved the dealer to a far section in the casino.

The following day, the sheik was back, and he bumped into that dealer. He immediately called your dad, yelling, "I thought you fired him!" Your dad apologized and assured him that it must have slipped through the cracks, and he would take care of it. The sheik left and your dad examined the video footage, talked to the pit boss, and concluded that the dealer did absolutely nothing wrong. So your dad assigned this dealer to a section of the casino the sheik never gambled in.

On the sheik's next trip, of course he saw this dealer, and once again became so irate that he called the Aladdin's owner, a Japanese billionaire. Your dad was called into the owner's office that same day and was told that he had to fire this dealer. Your dad responded that he'd watched the footage and determined that the dealer had done nothing wrong. The sheik was just unlucky.

The owner was a complete nut. He had this little poodle that barked and sniped at everyone. He always wore bathrobes and had a handgun on him—a real weirdo. He told your dad, "If you don't fire him, I will fire you." So your dad walked away from the Aladdin that day. Then, at your dad's next stop, the Dunes, the first guy he hired was that dealer.

Dennis Gomes never sacrificed another person's well-being for his own gain. He did this because he lived his life according to one simple principle: Love is the most powerful force in the universe. The five Gomes kids have heard that mantra no less than ten times a day, every day of our lives. *Love is the most powerful force in the universe.* Our dad taught us that when you pursue life from this foundation, you will fundamentally be unable to do anything that would harm another human being.

Following the passing of our dad, we received an e-mail from our cousin, Jon, containing sentiments our father had expressed to him. Reading this e-mail felt like listening to our dad speaking directly to us, as if he needed to make sure that we had a clear blueprint to follow for the rest of our lives. These are Dennis Gomes's words, and what he believed to be the secrets to his success:

1. *Always care about the people that work for you and those that work with you. Every decision that you make affects others, and should be made from a position of love.*

2. *Never do anything to wrongfully hurt another human being, but if someone attempts to seriously hurt you or your family, then respond fairly but with thunder and lightning.*

3. *Never follow the crowd. Think outside the box, don't accept the status quo, and dare to be different. Don't do things a certain way just because they have always been done that way, and don't allow yourself to be set into some type of corporate mold.*

4. *Never forget what is most important in your life. Family, both your immediate and your extended family, is first and paramount.*

Next is self. After that in importance are your friends, and last is business and material things.

5. *Always make time during the day for exercise. It will keep you stress-free.*

6. *Do something spiritual every day. It does not necessarily have to be religious. One of the best things you can do is set aside about fifteen to twenty minutes every day to meditate and to feel the connection with the life energy that exists all around you.*

7. *Trust that God's (life force) energy will guide you through life, and that whatever happens is part of God's plan. By doing this you can let go and not worry about what is coming next, because you know that it is the right thing for you and your family.*

8. *Work hard, be proactive, seize opportunities, and don't wait as long as I did to become your own boss.*

9. *Remember that you do not obtain true happiness from other people, materialism, religion, or other external things. It comes from within you, and therefore, you are responsible for your own happiness.*

Those are my secrets, and they work. Sometimes we lose track of them and fall off the wagon, but when we realize that we have fallen off, we should not hesitate, but should jump right back on and continue with the plan.

With love,
Uncle Dennis

That is how our dad lived each and every day of his life. We will forever cherish and abide by the principles he instilled in us.

Dennis Gomes ensured that everyone around him appreciated every moment of life, and that they grew with each obstacle they encountered. So in this moment, take a second to look up and smile . . . smile as big as you can. Smile for our dad, our hero. Smile for the man that accomplished the impossible. Smile for a world full of opportunities to do the right thing. Smile for Dennis Gomes, because he is smiling down on us.

—Danielle Gomes
Atlantic City, 2013

NOTES

Hit Me! is by definition a nonfiction narrative. However, it could arguably also be considered an autobiography because of the role Dennis Gomes played in the writing of this book. Gomes spent hours upon hours being interviewed, and when each chapter (with the exception of the epilogue) was completed, he went through the pages with a fine-tooth comb. Due to the level of involvement and the accessibility of Dennis Gomes, we were able to re-create each event in the book with great detail, including conversations.

Gomes also had the foresight to save reports from each investigation that he conducted. We were able to interview many of the individuals that played a role in this story. And finally, we accessed many news articles from the era, along with court transcripts from the 2007 "Family Secrets" trial.

The following sections will specify the sources used for each chapter. For the most part, names were left unchanged, with the exception of the names of those government informants or law enforcement personnel that Gomes had promised never to reveal.

Prologue: Don't Look Away

ix. In late 2004 . . . Interview with Dennis Gomes (2010–11) (hereafter, "Gomes interview").

(Note: Much of the information from the prologue came from interviews with Dennis Gomes and Barbara Gomes. Information pertaining to the "Family Secrets" trial was obtained through interviews, court transcripts, and the indictment. As a side note, I, co-author Danielle Gomes, sat in with Dennis Gomes for part of his initial meeting with the prosecutors for the "Family Secrets" trial, which included Mitchell Mars and the FBI agent. In fact, Mr. Mars told me that my dad's role in this trial had the potential to be "a great ending for your book"—a book that at the time was still not much more than an idea.)

x. "Mr. Gomes . . ." Gomes interview.

(Note: The FBI agent that initiated contact with Dennis Gomes is still an active agent and as such, works hard to maintain a low profile. His name was concealed for professional reasons as well as safety issues.)

xviii. "Mr. Gomes?" the voice of the bailiff came from across . . . *United States of America vs. Frank Calabrese, Sr., James Marcello, Joseph Lombardo, Paul Schiro, Anthony Doyle* court transcript, July 30, 2007.

Chapter 1: Double-Down

Dennis Gomes felt very strongly about including the events from his childhood that bred in him his innate sense of justice. These are the events Gomes credited with driving his desire to become a law enforcement agent. As his daughter, these are the stories I grew up with. It's important for me to note that in my thirty-one years of listening to my dad's stories, they never changed. He had the uncanny ability to remember scenes from his life in vivid detail.

12. "That's the guy," Steve Gomes replied. . . . Gomes interview.

13. "to clean out organized crime . . ." Ibid.

16. "Hey, kid. What do you want?" Ibid.

Chapter 2: Gunsmoke

Shortly after Gomes left law enforcement, he and Dick Law wrote a detailed historical record of their experience in the Audit Division. This unpublished manuscript was titled *The Ostrich Conspiracy*. This text contained the original information Gomes had compiled while first researching Nevada's gaming history.

21. "It's not as bad as it looks, Dennis" . . . Gomes interview; Law, Dick, with Dennis C. Gomes, *The Ostrich Conspiracy* (1983) (hereafter, "Law, 1983"). (Note: Gomes remembered the interactions with Gary Reese so vividly because it was his first taste of bureaucratic politics, before he even knew what *bureaucracy* was.)

22. "Don't let them kid you . . ." Law, 1983.

24. "Are you comfortable carrying . . ." Gomes interview.

26. "Dennis, what's wrong with being a CPA?" Ibid.

28. "Raise your weapons! Ready!" Ibid; Law, 1983.

Chapter 3: Whispers

31. "Screw that asshole . . ." Gomes interview.

33. "Gomes, take out your pad . . ." Ibid; Law, 1983.

34. "So, Frank . . ." Gomes interview.
(Note: "Frank" is a pseudonym for this informant from Circus Circus. Certain informants risked their own well-being to do the right thing, and Gomes refused to reveal their true identity. Frank is one of these individuals.)

35. "Have you ever dealt with a tramp?" Ibid.

36. "Hey, sweetie," she purred. . . . Ibid; Law, 1983.

38. (Note: "Mack" is a pseudonym. Gomes never investigated this officer for corruption, and as such, did not feel comfortable using his real name. However, in the late 1970s, Mack was fired and eventually arrested on corruption charges.)

39. "Dennis, I can't believe that Hannifin . . ." Gomes interview.

Chapter 4: The Cookie Jar

43. "Don't worry, we'll get the job done" . . . Gomes interview.

45. "What's wrong with you?" Ibid.

47. "Larry, you look tired" . . . Ibid; Interview with Larry Clark (2012).

49. "Did anyone notice anything unusual . . ." Gomes interview; Law, 1983.

52. "Please identify yourself and your position . . ." Law, 1983.

54. "We conducted undercover surveillance . . ." Ibid.

Chapter 5: Hard Lessons

57. "Where are the kids?" Gomes interview; Interview with Mary Gomes-Swain (2011); Interview with Larry Clark (2012).

59. (Note: "Rob" is a pseudonym for the count-room clerk that Gomes went after as an informant. Gomes gave Rob his word that he would never reveal his identity. As such, there is no documentation of Gomes's investigative work with Rob. In instances when Gomes relied on informants and used the information they provided to further his investigation, he would identify them as a "reliable source." Gomes used Rob as a jumping-off point; Rob would provide Gomes with tips that Gomes in turn would investigate.)

60. "Rob, I'm going to be completely straight . . ." Gomes interview; Law, 1983.

62. "Dennis, you have been doing . . ." Law, 1983.

63. (Note: "Will" is a pseudonym for this Enforcement Division agent. Gomes never investigated this agent, and was not comfortable using his real name.)

64. "Just stand there and observe" . . . Gomes interview; Interview with Richard Iannone (2012).

65. "Gomes, they know! They know!" Gomes interview; Law, 1983.

Chapter 6: The Girl with the Legs

71. "Are you ready?" Gomes asked Sam . . . Gomes interview; Law, 1983.
(Note: The background investigation of Michael Wichinsky and Bally Sales commenced on April 2, 1971, and was conducted in Las Vegas, Los Angeles, Chicago, New Jersey, and New York. The investigation involved personal contact with officers of the following agencies: Las Vegas—Federal Bureau of Investigation, Internal Revenue Service Intelligence Division, Clark County Sheriff's Office Intelligence Unit; Chicago—Federal Strike Force [Chicago], Internal Revenue Service Intelligence Division, Chicago Police Department Intelligence Division; New York—New York City Police Department Intelligence Division, New York District Attorney's Office [Manhattan], New York State Income Tax Special Investigation

Unit, Federal Strike Force [Brooklyn]; Miami—Florida Bureau of Law Enforcement, Miami Police Department, and the Internal Revenue Service Intelligence Division. In addition to the above, telephonic and written contact only was made with officers of the agencies listed below: The Gaming Board for Great Britain, Division of Administrative Intelligence; Florida Department of Law Enforcement; New York State Police, Commission of Investigation; State of New Jersey; Ontario Police Commission; US Attorney's Office, New York City; and the US Securities and Exchange Commission, Washington, DC.)

73. "Have I got a girl for *you*" . . . Gomes interview.

75. "Mr. Itkin, I'm Dennis Gomes . . ." Ibid; and Gomes, D. C., *Confidential Introduction to Investigative Findings in the Matter of Michael Wichinsky—Gaming Licensee* (1972).

(Note: The interview with Herbert Itkin was re-created based on the findings in the Wichinsky/Bally Sales investigation, direct quotes by Itkin contained in the Wichinsky investigation, and extensive interviews with Dennis Gomes.)

77. "Hey, Gomes. How goes it?" Gomes interview.

78. "I was getting worried" . . . Ibid; Interview with Barbara Gomes (2011).

Chapter 7: Rules of the Game

83. "I know the Mob is involved . . ." Gomes interview; Law, 1983.

83. "Everyone, listen up" . . . Law, 1983.

85. "This is Sorkis," came the voice . . . Ibid.

86. "Dennis, I just want to go over . . ." Ibid.

87. "Is it okay to make copies . . ." Ibid.

88. "You want to know about Charles Goldfarb?" Gomes, D. C., *Confidential Report of Investigation Relating to Possible Organized Crime Involvement in the Aladdin Hotel* (1974); Gomes interview.

91. "You look beautiful." Gomes interview; Interview with Barbara Gomes (2011).

92. "What are you talking about?" Gomes interview; Interview with Barbara Gomes (2011).

93. "So it's better to have the Mob . . ." Gomes, D. C., Aladdin (1974); Gomes interview; Law, 1983.

Chapter 8: Unholy Pact

96. "Well, this is what concerns me . . ." Gomes, D. C., Aladdin (1974).

98. "Denny, Linda is dropping Doug . . ." Gomes interview.

98. "We're going to investigate the Aladdin" . . . Ibid; Law, 1983.

100. "Oh man, you look like a grit" . . . Gomes interview.

101. "Hey, Dennis," said Rosenberg. . . . Ibid; Law, 1983; Gomes, D. C., Aladdin (1974).

101. "Could I speak to Dennis Gomes?" Gomes interview.

102. "Hey, Dennis, can I come in?" Law, 1983; Gomes interview.

103. "So, what's the plan?" Gomes interview; Interview with Geoff Gomes (2011).

106. "Dennis. Dennis!" Gomes interview.

107. "Barbara—congratulations!" Ibid; Interview with Barbara Gomes (2011).

Chapter 9: Sledgehammer

109. "Will you marry me?" Gomes interview; Interview with Barbara Gomes (2011).

110. "Dad, are we going to meet our new mommy?" Gomes interview; Interview with Barbara Gomes (2011); Interview with Douglas Gomes (2011); Interview with Mary Gomes-Swain (2011).

112. "Shit. Fuckin' shit. Dammit!" Gomes interview.

112. "This is Hannifin," came the voice. . . . Ibid.

115. "We're with the Gaming Control Board" . . . Ibid; Law, 1983; Gomes, D. C., Aladdin (1974).

118. "Dennis, Jack Joseph is here to see you." Gomes, D. C., Aladdin (1974); Law, 1983; Interview with Richard Iannone (2012); Gomes interview.

122. "This is Gomes." Law, 1983; Gomes interview.

122. "Jesus Christ, Dennis." Gomes interview.

125. "Are they going to revoke the Aladdin's license?" Ibid.

Chapter 10: Crash Course

127. "My name is Don North" . . . Gomes interview.
(Note: Don North passed away in 2005. Following his stint in Las Vegas, he eventually ended up in New York City, where he attacked the ranks of the major Mafia families throughout New York and New Jersey. His investigative work helped lead to the conviction of John Gotti in 1992.)

129. "This is Dennis Gomes" . . . Gomes interview; Law, 1983.

129. "We need to get our next major . . ." Gomes interview; Interview with Richard Iannone (2012); Law, 1983.

130. "Where are you going?" Gomes interview; Interview with Barbara Gomes (2011).

130. "Okay, Duane, sit down." Gomes interview; Law, 1983.

131. "Gaming control, right?" asked the cage clerk . . . Gomes interview; Gomes, D. C., *Confidential Memorandum re: Regulation 8.130* (1975) (hereafter, "Memo re: Regulation 8.130 [1975]").

132. In the 1970s the sons and nephews . . . Burnstein, Scott M., *Motor City Mafia* (2006).

135. "*Send him in!*" boomed a voice . . . Gomes interview; Law, 1983.

136. "This needs to be sent to Robert List . . ." Law, 1983.

Chapter 11: In the Red

139. "How did it get that low?" Gomes interview; Memo re: Regulation 8.130 (1975).

140. Gomes learned that the loan . . . Memo re: Regulation 8.130 (1975).

141. "Thanks for meeting me today" . . . Gomes interview; Memo re: Regulation 8.130 (1975).

144. The link was not difficult to establish. . . . Gomes, D. C., Hearing: Edward LaForte (1975); Memo re: Edward LaForte (1975).

147. "I'm so glad that you're in" . . . Gomes interview; Law, 1983.

148. (Note: "Jane" is a pseudonym for a valued informant that never went on the record.)

149. As luck would have it . . . Memo re: Regulation 8.130 (1975); Law, 1983; Gomes interview.

150. "Where were you? Did you forget?" Gomes interview; Interview with Barbara Gomes (2011).

Chapter 12: The Gamer's Wife

153. "I want you to examine every single . . ." Gomes interview; Law, 1983.

153. "Hi, Dennis, it's Jane" . . . Law, 1983.

154. The very next day . . . Ibid; Gomes, D. C., Confidential Report, Tropicana (1976).

155. "Smells good. I'm starving" . . . Gomes interview; Interview with Barbara Gomes (2011).

155. "Guess what?" she said . . . Interview with Barbara Gomes (2011).

156. "As far as I'm concerned . . ." Law, 1983.

156. Turning "inside snitches"—those informants . . . Skolnick, Jerome H., *House of Cards* (1978).

157. (Note: "Tom" is a pseudonym for an informant Gomes worked with; Gomes agreed to protect his identity.)

157. "Dennis—for God's sake!" Law, 1983; Gomes interview; Gomes, D. C., Confidential Memo to Tom Carrigan (1974).

158. "Hey, Dennis," the man said . . . Gomes interview; Law, 1983.

159. "Guess what happened at work tonight?" Interview with Barbara Gomes (2011); Gomes interview.

161. "Joe, I wanted to talk to you . . ." Gomes, D. C., Confidential Report, Tropicana (1976); Gomes interview; Law, 1983.

162. "Dennis, if you come in right now . . ." Law, 1983.

164. "Joe, what the hell made you . . ." Gomes interview. (Note: Gomes never told anyone that Agosto had been an informant for him—partially to protect Agosto, and partially because Gomes did not trust the information that Agosto provided.)

166. "Yeah, there's been friction buildin' . . ." Law, 1983; Gomes interview.

166. "Joe, tell me about Carl Thomas. . . ." Gomes interview.

167. Gomes made the simple connections first . . . Gomes, D. C., Confidential Report, Tropicana (1976).

168. "Dennis," Hannifin whispered . . . Gomes interview; Law, 1983.

169. "Dennis, you ain't gonna believe this. . . ." Gomes, D. C., Confidential Report, Tropicana (1976); Gomes interview; Law, 1983.

169. "Dennis, Bob List said that we . . ." Law, 1983; Gomes interview.

170. "Dennis, you scared me. What are you doing?" Gomes interview; Interview with Barbara Gomes (2011).

Chapter 13: A Shot across the Bow

175. "A man named Allan Glick appeared . . ." Law, 1983; Gomes interview; Gomes, D. C., Embezzlement (1977).

176. "Listen, we need to make this look like . . ." Ibid.

176. "Phil, this whole deal is very . . ." Gomes interview.

177. "Fucking bullshit. I knew I should have lied" . . . Ibid.

177. "Listen, Dennis," Hannifin began . . . Ibid; Law, 1983.

179. "Dick, don't you fucking get it?" Law, 1983.

180. Guys like Frank Rosenthal—a well-known bookie . . . Gomes, D. C., Results of Embezzlement (1977).

180. "I can't do this anymore" . . . Gomes interview.

Chapter 14: Trust No One

185. "Dennis, it's great to finally meet you" . . . Gomes interview.

185. Volumes on Tony "The Ant" Spilotro . . . Law, 1983; Gomes interview.

186. "Do you have any questions?" Gomes interview.

187. "There was something strange" . . . Gomes, D. C., Confidential Report, Possible slot machine defalcation (1976); Gomes interview.

188. "What can I do for you, gentlemen?" Ibid.

190. "I need to talk to you, Dennis. . . ." Ibid.
(Note: Gomes was hesitant to include this in the book because he did not want to show Hannifin in a bad light. Gomes knew that Hannifin believed Glick was an innocent individual who was getting taken advantage of, and as such, wanted to help him.)

191. "When you're in the count room" . . . Gomes interview; Gomes, D. C., Embezzlement (1977).

191. (Note: Rose is a pseudonym used to protect this witness's identity.)

193. "Mrs. Rand, my name is Dennis Gomes" . . . Gomes interview.

193. "Hey, Gomes . . . Man, I just heard . . ." Ibid.

194. "Ron Tanner is bringing someone . . ." Gomes, D. C., Embezzlement (1977); Gomes interview; Interview with Rich Iannone (2012).

Chapter 15: Loophole

197. "You got the money?" Gomes interview.

198. "Gomes, you don't look so hot" . . . Ibid.

199. "Robert Murillo, the coin wrapper . . ." Gomes, D. C., Embezzlement (1977); Gomes interview.

200. Vandermark was a self-proclaimed crossroader. . . . Gomes, D. C., Embezzlement (1977).

200. Leland (Lee) Northey, like Vandermark . . . Ibid.

201. "So what's the occasion?" Gomes interview.

201. "Hey, Dennis, how goes it?" Ibid.

202. "Dennis, I found it," said the voice . . . Ibid.

204. "No, Dennis, I'm afraid he can't . . ." Ibid.

205–13. Beginning with "Are you the shift boss . . ." and ending with "I'm completely serious. . . ." Gomes, D. C., Embezzlement (1977); Gomes interview.
(Note: The Stardust raid and witness testimony are highly detailed in the Argent embezzlement investigation.)

Chapter 16: Cat and Mouse

216. "On May 21, 1976," Gomes said flatly . . . Gomes, D. C., Embezzlement (1977).
(Note: Frank Mooney was under oath for this testimony.)

218. "Dennis, you are not gonna believe . . ." Gomes interview.

218. Jeff Vandermark lived in a run-down apartment . . . Gomes interview; *United States of America vs. Frank Calabrese et al.* (2007) (hereafter, "*USA vs. Calabrese*"); Law, 1983.

220. "Larry, go back to the kid's apartment . . ." Gomes interview; *USA vs. Calabrese*; Interview with Larry Clark (2012).

221. Vandermark's son called Gomes . . . Gomes interview; *USA vs. Calabrese*.

223. "Hey, Gomes," one of the detectives spoke up. . . . Gomes interview.

223. "Phil, I have to go to Mexico. . . ." Ibid.

224. "Hey, Dennis," Tony Albanese said . . . Ibid.

225. "Al, I need your help. . . ." Ibid.

Chapter 17: Into Thin Air

227. "Dennis, I've got this kid . . ." Gomes interview; Gomes, D. C., "Results of Stardust Embezzlement Investigation" (1977).
(Note: Dennis Gomes was always slightly haunted by this interrogation, because he noticed a distinct change in himself, in particular when the kid started crying and he found that he couldn't have cared less.)

229. "Hi, Mr. Gomes, my name's Eric." Gomes interview.

230. "Dennis, you can't tell anyone that I suggested this . . ." Ibid.

231. "Anything unusual happening?" Ibid.
(Note: "Mike" was a frontline employee who provided Gomes with information that he used as a starting point in his investigation. In the book *House of Cards: Legalization and Control of Casino Gambling*, on pages 280 and 281, author Jerome Skolnick discusses the types of informants Gomes used, and how he used them to begin investigations or audits. Skolnick was a sociologist and law professor studying gaming control, and spent a great deal of time with Gomes over a three-year period. Mike was the type of "disgruntled employee" that easily confided in an "auditor" as opposed to an officer with the demeanor of a "conventional policeman" because they were less threatening. Gomes further stated that most employees at one point or another would feel "disgruntled," and could often offer up valuable information. Furthermore, Skolnick stated that the Audit Division chief "maintained contact with more informants than anyone else in the agency.")

Epilogue: No More Secrets

234. (Note: All dialogue in the epilogue was taken directly from the official courtroom transcripts for the Northern District of Illinois Eastern Division: *United States of America vs. Frank Calabrese, Sr., James Marcello, Joseph Lombardo, Paul Schiro, Anthony Doyle* on July 30, 2007, at 10:35 a.m.)

Sources

Books

Burnstein, Scott M. *Motor City Mafia: A Century of Organized Crime in Detroit.* Charleston, SC; Chicago, IL; Portsmouth, NH; San Francisco, CA: Arcadia Publishing, 2006.

Calabrese, Frank, Jr., Keith Zimmerman, Kent Zimmerman, and Paul Pompian. *Operation Family Secrets: How a Mobster's Son and the FBI Brought Down Chicago's Murderous Crime Family.* New York: Random, 2011.

Kling, Dwayne. *The Rise of the Biggest Little City: An Encyclopedic History of Reno Gaming, 1931–1981.* Reno: University of Nevada Press, 2000.

Law, Dick, with Dennis C. Gomes. *The Ostrich Conspiracy.* Unpublished manuscript/journal not submitted for publication, 1983.

Pearl, Ralph. *Las Vegas Is My Beat.* Secaucus, NJ: Lyle Stuart, Inc., 1973.

Reid, Ed, and Ovid Demaris. *The Green Felt Jungle.* New York: Trident Press, 1963.

Skolnick, Jerome H. *House of Cards: Legalization and Control of Casino Gambling.* Boston, Toronto: Little, Brown and Company, 1978.

Newspapers and Magazines

"Agosto had personal rivalry with Doumanis." (1979, June 22). *Las Vegas Review Journal.*

Associated Press. (1979, July 10). "Four Aladdin czars get prison terms." *Trailblazer,* 73(89).

"Casino boss Thomas tells Mob 'how to skim': FBI recorded conversation between Carl Thomas, Joe Agosto, and Nick Civella." (1979, June 18). *The Valley Times,* p. A9.

Dahlberg, T. (1979, June 21). "FBI tapes expand LV casino audits." *Las Vegas Review Journal,* pp. 1A–2A.

Day, N. (1979, May 23). "Trop skim probe widens." *The Valley Times.*

———. (1979, June 18). "Mob bid to control Vegas sheriff, DA." *The Valley Times,* pp. A1, A9.

———. (1979, June 26). "New fed tapes zing Reid." *The Valley Times*, pp. A1–2, A11.

———. (1979, June 27). "Rosenthal-Glick conflict: FBI tapes tell of feud, mistrust." *The Valley Times*, pp. A1, A11.

———. (1979, July 3). "Why mob bosses want Glick out: FBI affidavit alleges Glick was stealing." *The Valley Times*, p. A1.

———. (1979, July 12). "State seeks to slap Argent with 12 million in fines." *The Valley Times*, pp. A1, A11.

———. (1979, July 19). "Agosto suing gamers over 'Nazi' tactics." *The Valley Times*.

———. (1979, August 24). "Glick's deal with state: Gets 16 months to sell." *The Valley* Times, pp. A1–2.

———. (1979, August 24). "How politics rules state gaming control." *The Valley Times*.

———. (1979, September 12). "Reid blasts gaming staff over 'leaks.'" *The Valley Times*, pp. A1, A11.

Delugach, A. (1976, July 1). "$7 Million skimming at 4 Nevada casinos probed: Case involving slot-machine funds may be the biggest scandal in State's history, officials say." *Los Angeles Times*, p. B3.

———. (1977, September 28). "Nevada's top gaming prober quits: Friction may have sparked move." *Los Angeles Times*, p. F13.

———. (1978, August 3). "Casino, four men indicted by U.S. grand jury: Accused of conspiracy to permit secret control of gambling operations." *Los Angeles Times*, pp. B3, B20.

Drinkhall, J. (1979, September 10). "Nevada jackpot: State gaming officials say millions vanished from Argent's slots." *Wall Street Journal*.

"FBI: Vegan briefed Mob on skimming: FBI recorded conversation between Joe Agosto, Carl Thomas, Nick Civella, and Carl DeLuna." (1979, June 18). *Las Vegas Sun*.

"Federal investigations." (1980). *Rouge et Noir News*, 3(3), pp. 8–23.

"The feds and casino gaming." (1978). *Rouge et Noir News*, 10(12), pp. 1–3.

"Feds: Mob told Glick to get out of Argent." (1979, June 18). *Las Vegas Sun*, pp. 1, 4.

"Folies Bergere dancer denies Agosto charges." (1977, October 29). *Las Vegas Review Journal*, p. 11A.

"Gamers detail what's hurting control effort." (1979, August 28). *The Valley Times*, p. A6.

"Gamer's wife fires back: Got job on talent, not juice." (1977, October 29). *The Valley Times*, p. A1.

Hevener, P. (1979, February 3). "Gaming Board reviews Argent's slot theft." *Las Vegas Sun*, p. 2A.

——. (1979, June 6). "Gamers may strip Thomas' licenses." *Las Vegas Sun*.

——. (1979, September 12). "Gaming gambit." *Las Vegas Sun*.

"How the K.C. Mob ripped into Rosenthal: FBI recorded conversation between Frank Rosenthal and Nick Civella." (1979, June 19). *The Valley Times*, pp. A6–7.

"How state's largest slot skim was pulled off." (1979, September 12). *The Valley Times*, pp. A1, A11.

Kelley, D. (1979, June 23). "FBI affidavit confirms Reid is 'Mr. Clean.'" *Reno Evening Gazette*, p. A1.

——. (1979, June 24). "State suspected mob ties in '74: Linked Trop's Agosto to crime figures but …" *Nevada State Journal / Reno Evening Gazette*, pp. A1, A3.

Lalli, S. (1986, January 26). "The saga of the Stardust skim." *Las Vegas Review Journal*, pp. 1A, 4A, 11A–12, 13A–14.

Lancaster, H. (1979, August 13). "Nevada's links to mob persist." *The Valley Times*.

Laurer, K. (1979, September 14). "Reid criticizes state's investigation of Argent." *Las Vegas Review Journal*, p. 3A.

McFarren, J. (1979, September 14). "Gaming chief says state 'botched' Argent probe." *Reno Evening Gazette*, pp. A1, A5.

McFarren, J. (1979, September 15). "Argent skimming complaint defended." *Nevada State Journal*, pp. 1, 7.

Morrison, J. A. (1979, May 23). "Attorney files affidavit appeal: Affidavit asserts mob got skim money from Agosto." *Las Vegas Review Journal*, p. A3.

——. (1985, July 22). "New regulations on junkets requested." *Las Vegas Review Journal*, pp. 1B, 3B.

Odessky, D. (1979, June 22). "A new ballgame for LV casinos." *The Valley Times*, p. A2.

———. (1979, July 18). "Reactions vary to fines proposed against Argent." *The Valley Times*, p. A6.

"Publisher challenges List to take lie test." (1979, June 22). *The Valley Times*, pp. A1, A6.

Richards, B. (1978, November 24). "Serious leaks of intelligence material to underworld laid to national police unit." *Los Angeles Times*, p. D8.

Riley, B. (1979, September 13). "Gaming Board orders agents to shut up." *The Valley Times*, p. A3.

Riordan, P. (1978, October 27). "It's hard for the regulators to stay ahead of mobsters." *The Miami Herald*.

"Rosenthal lashes gamers at meet: FBI recorded conversation between Joe Agosto and Nick Civella." (1979, June 19). *The Valley Times*, pp. A6–7.

Stelzer, C. D. (2008). "No hall of fame for them: Al Delugach and Denny Walsh won the Pulitzer Prize in 1969, their reward, one-way tickets out of town." *St. Louis Journalism Review*, vol. 38, issue 306.

"Trop license issue nears Gaming Board." (1979, June 18). *Las Vegas Review Journal*.

Reports

Audit Division of the Nevada Gaming Control Board. (1977). *Results of Stardust, Hacienda, Marina, and Freemont embezzlement investigation conducted by the Audit Division during the period May 18, 1976, through May 9, 1977*. Unpublished.

Gomes, Dennis C. Chief of the Audit Division of the Nevada Gaming Control Board. (1972). *Confidential introduction to investigative findings in the matter of Michael Wichinsky—Gaming Licensee*. Unpublished.

———. Chief of the Audit Division of the Nevada Gaming Control Board. (1973). *Confidential memorandum to the Board Members regarding Aladdin Hotel—Sorkis Webbe*. Unpublished.

———. Chief of the Audit Division of the Nevada Gaming Control Board, at the request of Shannon Bybee, Board member. (1974).

Confidential report of investigation relating to possible organized crime involvement in the Aladdin Hotel. Unpublished.

——. Chief of the Audit Division of the Nevada Gaming Control Board. (1974). *Confidential memorandum to Tom Carrigan, Chief of the Investigations Division of the Nevada Gaming Control Board, regarding: Intelligence dispersal.* Unpublished.

——. (Chair). Hearing: Edward LaForte. (1975). Offices of the Gaming Control Board—Las Vegas. Present: Dennis C. Gomes (Chief, Audit Division), Richard Iannone (Senior Agent, Audit Division), Lee Bennett (Agent, Audit Division), and Edward LaForte. Official transcripts from the proceeding, unpublished.

——. Chief of the Audit Division of the Nevada Gaming Control Board. (1975). *Confidential addendum to June 13, 1975, Memorandum Re: Edward LaForte.* Unpublished.

——. Chief of the Audit Division of the Nevada Gaming Control Board. (1975). *Confidential memorandum regarding: Regulation 8.130—Tropicana Hotel and Country Club.* Unpublished.

——. Chief of the Audit Division of the Nevada Gaming Control Board. (1976). *Confidential report of investigation relating to possible organized crime involvement at the Tropicana Hotel and Country Club.* Unpublished.

——. Chief of the Audit Division of the Nevada Gaming Control Board. (1976). *Confidential memorandum: Possible defalcation of slot machines from the Hacienda Hotel and Casino.* Unpublished.

——. Chief of the Audit Division of the Nevada Gaming Control Board. (1977). *Confidential memorandum to Phillip Hannifin, Chairman of the Nevada Gaming Control Board regarding: Summary of the types of investigations engaged in by Audit Division Agents.* Unpublished.

——. Chief of the Audit Division of the Nevada Gaming Control Board. (1977). *Results of Stardust, Hacienda, Marina, and Freemont embezzlement investigations.* Unpublished.

——. Chief of the Special Investigations Bureau of the New Jersey Division of Gaming Enforcement. (1978). *Memorandum to SIB files: Interview with Dino Vincent Cellini.* Unpublished.

United States of America vs. Frank Calabrese, Sr., James Marcello, Joseph Lombardo, Paul Schiro, Anthony Doyle. No. 02 cr 01050. July 30, 2007.

Interviews

Clark, Larry. (2012, June 15). Personal interview by D. N. Gomes. Close friend of D. C. Gomes and Nevada Audit Division agent.

Gomes, Barbara. (2011, October 10). Personal interview by D. N. Gomes. Wife of Dennis C. Gomes, 1973–2012.

Gomes, Dennis C. (2002, July 17). Interview by D. Kling [audiotape transcription]. Dennis Gomes. University of Nevada Oral History Program, Gaming Regulators.

——. (2010, October–2011, December). Personal interview by D. N. Gomes. *Hit Me!* interview series.

Gomes, Douglas S. (2011, September 15). Personal interview by D. N. Gomes. Son of Dennis C. Gomes / Barbara Gomes and Linda Layman.

Gomes, Geoff. (2011, May 15). Personal interview by D. N. Gomes. Younger brother of Dennis C. Gomes—Spilotro surveillance.

Gomes-Swain, Mary. (2011, December 22). Personal interview by D. N. Gomes. Daughter of Dennis C. Gomes / Barbara Gomes and Linda Layman.

Iannone, Richard. (2012, November 1). Personal interview by D. N. Gomes. Nevada Audit Division agent.

Index

About the Authors

Danielle Gomes, daughter of the late Dennis Gomes, who owned and operated Resorts Casino Hotel in Atlantic City, is a freelance writer and filmmaker. She co-wrote and narrated a documentary short on America's homeless that won a Telly Award and a Videographer Award of Excellence. A member of the Association of Writers and Writing Programs, she lives in Margate, New Jersey.

Jay Bonansinga is the author of *Pinkerton's War* (Lyons Press), *The Sinking of the Eastland,* a Chicago Reader Critic's Choice Book, and more than ten novels. He is also the author of the novelization of the television series *The Walking Dead,* a book titled *The Walking Dead: Rise of the Governor.* He lives in Evanston, Illinois.